inclusive
education

inclusive
education

Supporting diversity in the classroom
Second edition

Tim Loreman, Joanne Deppeler,
and David Harvey

Routledge
Taylor & Francis Group

LONDON AND NEW YORK

First published in Australia by Allen & Unwin

This first edition published 2010 in the UK by Routledge
2 Park Square, Milton Park, Abingdon, Oxon, OX14 4RN

Simultaneously published in the USA and Canada by Routledge
270 Madison Avenue, New York, NY 10016

Routledge is an imprint of the Taylor & Francis Group, an informa business

© 2010 Tim Loreman, Joanne Deppeler and David Harvey

Typeset in Birka 10.5/15pt by Post Pre-press Group Australia
Printed by South Wind Productions, Singapore

British Library Cataloguing in Publication Data
A catalogue record for this book is available from the British Library

Library of Congress Cataloging-in-Publication Data
A catalog record has been requested for this book

ISBN13: 978-0-415-60147-4 (hbk)
ISBN13: 978-0-415-60148-1 (pbk)

Foreword

Michael Peterson

What is the purpose of school? The question draws many answers. And the answer to that question creates different types of practices in the school and classroom.

I've been thinking about that question for many years. In countries that consider themselves political democracies, most schools have mission statements that include statements like—'becoming a citizen in a democracy', 'lifelong learner', 'developing skills to be a valuable member of the community'. Yet, too many schools continue to structure their operations to assure another message—that democracy and community are only for some. The ongoing, systematic segregation of students by ability, race, and class sends a powerful and well-learned message.

Throughout the world, many people are developing a different vision of their communities and the schools in them. They see communities where all are valued, all are included. These same people see that inclusive community building must start in schools. Unless we teach children in school how to live and work together, not only tolerating but valuing differences in culture, ethnicity, language, background, and, yes, even dramatically different cognitive, social-emotional, and sensory-physical abilities, we almost always are teaching the opposite—systematic forms of segregation, oppression, and elitism.

The champions of this view of schooling realise that having children with substantial differences learning together in an inclusive classroom is not about being 'nice' to 'those' people. Rather it's a fundamental condition for a good school, one that pays attention to both excellence and equity. But can you have both equity and excellence together? Loreman, Deppeler, and Harvey clearly state that we can. The message comes through clear—that excellence cannot exist without equity.

Inclusive Education: Supporting diversity in the classroom is an important book because it adds a clear voice that helps teachers, administrators, and parents visualise in concrete form truly inclusive instruction. The approach the authors have taken is helpful from many perspectives in giving readers strategies and tools. I'd like to point out a few of these.

First is the issue of who we are discussing—children with 'diverse educational needs'. While the authors focus clearly on students who have disabilities and are considered gifted, in this second edition they have expanded the focus to all categories and types of difference found in a school. They recognise well that creating an effective inclusive classroom requires that the range of intellectual and behavioural functioning be accommodated. This is a very important perspective.

Second, they use very honest and plain language in addressing what are frequently seen as uncomfortable topics, such as personal responses to disability and other differences. They discuss in clear terms the reactions that people sometimes have to substantive differences and suggest ways of dealing with such reactions in a proactive way.

Third, they combine practical, clear strategies with concrete stories that illustrate how to make such approaches real. These strategies are based on sound research, which the authors share. However, their focus is on practical strategies rather than acting as a review of the literature. This approach will be appreciated by teachers who need answers to questions like: 'What do I do on Monday?'

Fourth, the authors are clear about their viewpoint. This is not a text that reviews the 'options' in the way schools deal with children in a pseudo-objective manner. Rather, they state clearly their view of a good school—one that includes all children in learning well together. Yet, they also recognise the absolute importance of beliefs, values, and attitudes, and provide opportunities to explore the cognitive and emotional dimensions of this important foundation.

Finally, the authors describe strategies from the perspective of a practising general education teacher regarding how to develop individualised programs for students and then design inclusive instruction so that these programs can be implemented as part of the general education curriculum. They discuss the practicalities of collaboration as a form of teacher support, organising the classroom, and, most importantly dealing with the social-emotional needs of students by promoting positive behaviour and social competence. They communicate well to teachers who will live this world of diversity in their practice.

The first edition of this book provided valuable information and resources. However, the authors have provided substantial revisions in this second edition to keep up with a fast-changing field and look forward to more effective practices for the future.

In 1997, I joined with a small group of people to create a new vision of schools. We identified Eight Principles of what we now call Whole Schooling—empowering citizens for democracy, including all, authentic-multilevel instruction, building community, supporting learning, and partnering with parents and the community (see www.wholeschooling.net). We created the Whole Schooling Consortium involving teachers, schools, parents, administrators, and university faculty, now an international network.

From this perspective, we are happy to see useful documents and tools that help educators and parents move towards schools based on these principles. *Inclusive Education: Supporting diversity in the classroom* provides a powerful, value- and research-based, practical set of tools, ideas, and strategies to equip those on the journey towards schools that truly *do* link equity and excellence, schools we call 'Whole Schools'. May you enjoy and appreciate this text as I have.

Michael Peterson, Ph.D.
Professor and Coordinator
Wayne State University
Whole Schooling Consortium

Contents

Foreword   *v*
Figures   *xiii*
Preface to the second edition   *xvii*

1 The case for inclusion   **1**
What is inclusion?   1
Teacher concerns about inclusive education   6
The benefits of inclusion   12
Case study: Outlining the process approach   14
Key terms   20
For discussion and reflection   21
Further reading   21

2 Who are our students with diverse learning needs?   **22**
Defining diversity   23
Using medical definitions: Special education model   25
Using socio-political definitions: Inclusive education model   25
Discrimination   26
To label or not to label?   28
Labels and teaching the full spectrum of diverse needs   32
How do I talk about students from diverse backgrounds?   35
Key terms   36
For discussion and reflection   36
Further reading   36

3 Attitudes and inclusion   **37**
Is history repeating itself?   37
Attitudes   39
Values   40
Ideologies   42
Facing disability   43

Plan realistically	46
Key terms	47
For discussion and reflection	47
Further reading	47

4　Psychological and teacher-based assessment　48

Intelligence tests: What are they and what are they good for?	51
The normal curve	54
Percentile ranks	56
The pieces of intelligence	56
Qualitative assessment	61
Classroom-based assessment	63
Assessment for learning (AFL)	64
Key assessment for learning practices	66
Curriculum-based assessment	71
Specific assessment tools and strategies	77
Key terms	86
For discussion and reflection	86
Further reading	86

5　Collaboration　87

Professional learning community	88
Collaborative inquiry	91
Teacher reflection and collaborative discussion	95
Collaboration with the wider school community	101
Collaboration within the inclusive classroom	102
Collaboration with families	105
Collaboration with students	107
Key terms	112
For discussion and reflection	112
Further reading	112

6　How to develop and manage an individualised program　115

The individual program plan	116
Role of the Program Support Group in individual program planning	118
Compiling an individual program plan	118
Vision statement	120
Assessment results summary	121

Long-term goals   125
Specific objectives   129
Indicators of achievement   132
Inclusive strategies and materials   133
Review and monitoring schedule and strategies   134
Key terms   135
For discussion and reflection   135
Further reading   136

7 Inclusive instructional design   137
Defining curriculum   138
Universal design for learning or curriculum adaptations?   139
Universal curriculum design for learning   140
Differentiated instruction and universal design   141
The educational environment   143
Curriculum adaptations and modifications   152
Identifying links between individual objectives and the classroom
      curriculum   152
Unit planning   153
Individual lesson plans   155
Key terms   160
For discussion and reflection   160
Further reading   160

8 Collaborative student learning   161
Collaborative learning arrangements   162
Cooperative learning   164
Enhancing the effectiveness of cooperative learning groups   176
Peer support   179
Key terms   183
For discussion and reflection   184
Further reading   184

9 Organising the inclusive classroom   186
Physical layout of the inclusive classroom   187
Seating plans   190
Traditional expository teaching seating plan   190
Ability groups   192
Heterogeneous grouping   193
Individual learning spaces   194

Using a combination of approaches   195
Classroom procedures   196
Plans for substitute teachers   198
Meeting students' personal care needs   199
Medication in the classroom   202
Key terms   204
For discussion and reflection   205
Further reading   205

10 Inclusive classroom management   206
What is challenging behaviour?   207
Understanding the reasons for the challenging behaviour
   of individuals   208
Developing an action plan for individual students   212
Violence and touching   213
Building a classroom community   214
Class meetings   217
Classroom management tips that work   221
Key terms   222
For discussion and reflection   222
Further reading   223

11 Social and emotional learning   224
What is social and emotional learning?   225
Benefits of social and emotional learning   226
What supports social and emotional learning?   228
Social and emotional learning and the school curriculum   228
Social and emotional learning programs   229
Teachers and social and emotional competence   236
Key terms   238
For discussion and reflection   238
Further reading   238

12 Reflection: The key to lasting change   240
Mentally coping with diversity   241
The importance of practice   245
Deliberate practice   245
Reflecting on practice   246
Tools for teacher reflection   248
The effects of reflective practice on teaching   252

Key terms   254
For discussion and reflection   254
Further reading   254

Useful forms   255
Bibliography   275
Index   300

Figures

1.1	The inclusive education process	20
2.1	Practical example of the process approach	34
4.1	The normal (or bell-shaped) curve	54
4.2	Single-figure IQ scores	55
4.3	Triangulation of assessment data	74
4.4	Martin's spelling test results	77
5.1	Collaborative inquiry: Working together in repeated cycles of research, reflection and change	92
5.2	Adam Fletcher's cycle of meaningful student involvement	110
6.1	Program Support Group agenda	119
6.2	Individualised program development process	120
6.3	Individual program plan	122
6.4	Long-term goals	127
7.1	Unit planner	156
7.2	Unit planner—Infusing individual targets	157
7.3	Individual lesson planning form	159
8.1	Observation wheel	169
8.2	Five-point listening scale	174
9.1	Traditional expository teaching seating plan	191
9.2	Ability groups seating plan	193
9.3	Heterogeneous groups seating plan	194
9.4	Individual learning spaces plan	195

Differences hold great opportunities for learning. Differences offer a free and abundant renewable resource. I would like to see the compulsion for eliminating differences replaced by an equally compelling focus on making use of these to improve schools. What is important about people and about schools is what is different, not what is the same.

(Barth, 1990, pp. 514–515)

For Lizz, Holly, Tom, Mum and Dad.

—T.L.

For John and Marge for their support and positive examples of lifelong learning.

—J.D.

For Bronwyn, our children and grandchildren, in the hope that the educational experiences of the latter group reflect the aims we had in mind when writing out our ideas in this book.

—D.H.

Preface to the second edition

Inclusion means the full involvement of all students in all aspects of schooling, regardless of the presence of individual differences. It implies the elimination of segregated school settings such as special schools and classrooms for those who do not fit the conventional view of what is 'normal'. Under an inclusive model, all students learn together in conventional schools, classrooms and other contexts, and these adapt and change in a responsive and proactive way in order to meet the needs of all. This book is based on research on inclusion, and on the way in which information from that research can be used to influence inclusive practices in classrooms in a positive way. It is written for pre-service teachers or working classroom teachers who want some research-informed tips and strategies on how to better include students with diverse learning needs across the wide variety of regular classroom activities. It is written with a range of age groups in mind, and should be relevant to students from the first through to the final year of school. The practices and strategies suggested are as universal as possible, and we believe they are relevant internationally across a wide variety of school systems and contexts.

In the first edition of this text we recognised that teachers are busy people and so went to considerable effort to make the book accessible. We tried to avoid large slabs of text in favour of a more user-friendly approach, including text boxes, examples, and blank forms that could be copied and used (you can also find these now for download on the website for this edition: <http//:www.allenandunwin.com/inclusiveeducation/>). Those wanting a more in-depth treatment of a particular subject were encouraged to seek out materials listed in the further reading sections at the end of each chapter. In this edition, we have tried to retain and improve these features, and have added the additional feature of discussion questions for reflection at the end of each chapter.

Another feature of the first edition was our emphasis on the process of inclusion. In this text, we have deliberately not provided chapters on how to work with students with specific diagnoses (such as autism, English as a second language (ESL) or learning disabilities) or in specific curriculum areas. This is a feature common to many other texts in this area; however, we believe this approach is far less helpful than outlining a process for inclusion that applies broadly to all students. When it comes down to it, inclusion is about implementing a process, and we believe that the label a child has been given is largely irrelevant to the educational process and also often unhelpful. With respect to specific curriculum areas, we assume that teachers already generally have a high degree of expertise in their subject areas and wish to respect this. In this text, we examine the process of assessing, planning, implementing and evaluating inclusive curriculum and learning.

While the second edition has hopefully retained the strongest aspects of the first edition, there are of course some changes and additions that we believe strengthen the work considerably. We have, for example, examined with greater clarity areas like differentiated instruction, collaboration, assessment for learning and more social constructivist instructional approaches. Importantly, while the first edition was framed by students' abilities, we have broadened our perspectives to reflect those who may be marginalised in the context of social inclusion due to their culture, religion, gender, and/or sexual orientation. This does not imply that student's abilities are any less important, but rather that a wider lens takes us a step further in addressing barriers to education, exclusion and the disparities faced by students. Whereas in the first edition we referred to 'children with diverse abilities', our terminology has shifted to focus on those with different learning needs. Further to the topic of terminology, whereas in the first edition we spoke of 'children', we now speak of 'students'. We believe this to be more appropriate—especially for those in secondary school settings. In the United Kingdom, of course, the term 'pupils' is more widely used; however, we believe that, internationally, 'students' is more commonplace so have made the decision to work with that term.

There is no formula that can be applied for successful inclusive education. Readers looking for easy solutions and prescriptions are likely to be disappointed by any thoughtful text on this subject. What this text offers instead are possibilities for inclusive education processes. It brings together the results of the available literature regarding approaches that have been used extensively and that are practically relevant for schools—approaches that support the capacity of students to access quality teaching and realise enhanced learning outcomes. Teachers will enact the processes of inclusive education in different ways, responding to the issues that are important for them and their particular context. We hope that this book will support teachers and school leaders who are making serious efforts to work towards equality and equity to build upon their successful practices in order to enable an effective and caring education for all.

– Tim Loreman, Joanne Deppeler and David Harvey

1
The case for inclusion

Key ideas in this chapter

- Defining inclusion
- Concerns about inclusion:
  - teacher training
  - curriculum
  - resources
  - school organisation
- Benefits of inclusion
- One school works towards inclusion: a case study
- Outlining the process approach

This chapter sets out to provide readers with enough background information on the theory and practice of inclusion to be able to use the rest of the book in an informed way. It by no means serves as a comprehensive review of the theoretical underpinnings to the current movement towards greater inclusion, but rather is intended to provide a broad portrait of what inclusion is and why it is important, and to examine some of the main issues with which teachers and schools are dealing today.

What is inclusion?

As university researchers and teacher educators with a background and interest in the education of students with diverse learning needs, we are often in a position to speak with groups of other educators about inclusion. We sometimes find that these educators are misinformed and confused about inclusion. What exactly is inclusion and why is it important? We believe that, by its very nature, inclusion cannot exist in environments where some students are educated separately or substantively differently to their peers, and this view is consistent with the vast majority of definitions of inclusion. Sometimes, however, it is easier to describe what inclusion *is not* rather than what it *is*. To clarify; educating students part time in special schools and part time in regular schools is not inclusion. Educating students in special, mostly segregated environments in regular schools is not inclusion. Educating students in regular classes, but requiring them to follow substantially different courses of study from their peers in terms of content and learning environment, is also not inclusion (unless all students in a class follow individual programs) (Loreman & Deppeler, 2001). It is not uncommon to hear educators speak of these examples as 'inclusion', furthering the confusion, but the fact is that there has been some degree of broad agreement on what constitutes inclusion for some time (see, for example, Sailor & Skrtic, 1995; Uditsky, 1993).

At its best, inclusion involves the full participation of all students in all aspects of schooling. It involves regular schools and classrooms being responsive, willing to genuinely adapt and change to meet the needs of all students, as well as celebrating and valuing difference. Differences can be based on gender, culture, ability, sexual orientation, socio-economic context, religion, or any other area in which learning and/or development are impacted. This definition of inclusion does not imply that students with differing learning needs will not receive specialised assistance or teaching outside of the classroom when required, but rather that this is just one of many options available to, and in fact required of, all students (Loreman & Deppeler, 2001). Extra help in the course of a school day should be the norm for all.

'Integration' and 'inclusion' are two terms that have in the past often been used interchangeably by teachers and schools, as if they were synonymous. The idea of integration preceded that of inclusion, and there are important differences between the two terms about which educators are now becoming increasingly aware. One simple distinction between the terms is that integration occurs from the outside (Loreman, 1999). Integration programs were initially aimed primarily at students with disabilities, and attempted to place them into the existing classes and structures within a school. They endeavoured to 'normalise', to help a student fit into a pre-existing model of schooling. Inclusion differs in that it now goes beyond disability to include all forms of diversity, and assumes that all students are a part of the regular school system from the very beginning of school. This difference is more than one of mere semantics. Under the integration model, the student was expected to adapt to meet the requirements of the school; under inclusion, the school adapts to meet the needs of all students. Schools, after all, primarily exist to meet the educational needs of students, not the other way around. Meeting those needs, then, is fundamental to the work done by schools. With inclusion, schools assume that a variety of students with unique needs will attend, and they welcome them, responding to individual differences in their pedagogy, school activities, and curriculum. Difference is acknowledged and respected. Becoming inclusive has proven to involve not only a change in the way schools are structured and work, but also a change in the attitudes of many special and regular education teachers, who might previously have viewed their job as being to educate a certain 'type' of child (Loreman, 1999). Indeed, positive attitudes are critical to the success of inclusion. Without the presence of positive attitudes from school staff, any attempt to include will almost certainly fail. All teachers need to be enthusiastic about meeting the needs of all children, and this enthusiasm needs to be fostered in teacher preparation programs and, perhaps just as importantly, in school systems and individual schools.

Box 1.1: Elements of inclusion

Sailor and Skrtic (1995, p. 423) list the following elements in their early definition of inclusion:

- inclusion of all children with diverse abilities in schools they would attend if they had no disability
- representation of children with diverse abilities in schools and classrooms in natural proportion to their incidence in the district at large
- zero rejection and heterogeneous grouping
- age- and grade-appropriate placements of children with diverse abilities
- site-based coordination and management of instruction and resources
- 'effective schools'-style decentralised instructional models

Any teacher who has had experience with students with a variety of learning needs in regular classrooms will tell you that catering to this diversity can be a difficult and complex matter. Teachers need to be highly skilled and motivated to be successful. This is not, however, an argument against inclusion. It is because inclusion demands such high levels of teaching competence and organisational changes aimed at promoting effective learning that it is so important for schools to engage in it. Improving learning through the development of outstanding educational practice should be a primary aim of every teacher and school (Loreman & Deppeler, 2001).

Initially, many of the educators we support through consultation and professional development want two things of us. First, they tend to want to know whether inclusion *really works* in schools. Second, they want to know *how* to make inclusion work in their schools. The answers to both questions are complex, and often disappoint those looking for quick, straightforward answers. Inclusion is context dependent, and because of this a 'recipe book' on how to include every student in every situation can never exist. Your attitude, skills as a teacher and ability to solve problems, along with support from your colleagues and school, will ultimately contribute to your success as a responsive, inclusive teacher.

Having said that, not every attempt at inclusion is successful, and there are those who would have us abandon the practice for all but children with the most minor needs on that basis (see, for example, Kauffman & Hallahan, 2005; Mock & Kauffman, 2005). This view, however, represents flawed logic. Not every attempt at teaching mathematics is successful, but that doesn't mean that we throw up our hands and stop teaching it! Teaching mathematics is, of course, important and necessary. Good teachers try to find new ways to teach and use fresh approaches until they meet with success. The same can be said for good inclusive teachers. Inclusion is seen as important and necessary, so such teachers persist with new ideas and approaches until (hopefully!) they meet with success. There is sufficient evidence to suggest that inclusion—even of students with the most evident and significant differences—can work if teachers take a lead role and if schools have a culture of shared values and are genuinely committed to improving their practice (see Downing & Peckham-Hardin, 2007; Fox et al., 2004; Loreman, 2001). Individual teachers are not always in the position to promote a culture of shared values in their schools, but they can improve their own classroom practice to promote better inclusion, and in doing so act as an example of what is possible for others. We hope this book will help you to do that.

Box 1.2: Reasons why school inclusion may not work

- **Rationale.** The benefits of inclusion have not been communicated to those involved in the process.
- **Scope.** The changes necessary for inclusion to work are either too ambitious to begin with, or too limited.

- **Pace.** Required changes are either implemented too quickly or too slowly, allowing enthusiasm for the change to drop off.
- **Resources.** Adequate resources are either not provided to ensure inclusion can work, or resources are not allocated in a way that is helpful.
- **Commitment.** Long-term commitment to inclusion is not fostered. It is seen as a 'fad'.
- **Key staff.** Staff members who are crucial to the success of inclusion may either not be committed, or could be taking on too much of the workload. This might alienate other staff members.
- **Parents.** Parents are not included in the school as collaborators.
- **Leadership.** School leaders are either too controlling, too ineffectual or do not encourage staff to progress to higher goals.
- **Relationship to other initiatives.** Inclusion is dealt with in isolation from other school initiatives.

Source: Hargreaves (1997).

The second question from educators, 'How can I make inclusion work at my school?', also cannot be answered easily or simply. Inclusion is context dependent, and as such there is no formula or prescription for how to successfully include all students that can be applied to all contexts. Inclusion works best with teachers who understand and demonstrate effective teaching and learning practices within a framework of collaboration and support from the school and local community. Even without that support from the school and local community, however, there is a lot you can do as an individual teacher to make your classroom more inclusive while continuing to reach out to your colleagues and wider school community.

In order to make inclusion successful, you must become good at problem solving. Of course, the problem is not the individual student. Rather, it rests with the school community and the individuals who comprise it. How are you going to meet the needs of all students? Coming up with creative solutions to problems as they arise, based on sound pedagogical platforms, shared values and positive leadership, represents the best way for schools and classrooms to become more inclusive. Solving problems often comes naturally to good teachers, who are called on to solve any number of problems in their interactions with students and other adults every day.

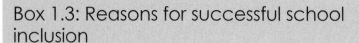

Box 1.3: Reasons for successful school inclusion

- **Rationale.** All school staff have been involved in the development of the rationale for inclusion, and the benefits of inclusion for all students are clearly communicated.
- **Scope.** The school has started off small (one or two students) and has been careful to learn from its mistakes and successes before moving incrementally forward to including other students.
- **Pace.** The pace of implementation for inclusion will vary from setting to setting. Frequent collaboration with all involved parties and regular reviews of the pace of change will help to ensure success.
- **Resources.** Where extra resources are available, they are accessed. Schools also must be creative about the best way to use resources to support inclusion. The provision of adequate resources will help to ensure commitment from those implementing inclusion.
- **Commitment.** Collaboration between all parties involved in inclusion will help to ensure long-term commitment. When team members are involved in an initiative, they take more ownership of it, and have more of a vested interest in its success.
- **Key staff.** Key staff members are viewed as leaders and motivators whose job it is to ensure equal collaboration between all members of the school community. They are not seen as being any more responsible for the success of inclusion than any other staff member.
- **Parents.** Parents are welcomed in the school as collaborators, and supported so that their views, knowledge and skills are used and valued by school staff.
- **Leadership.** School leaders facilitate collaborative school teams working towards inclusion, support individual team members, and ensure that ideas are acted upon.
- **Relationship to other initiatives.** Inclusion is viewed as an integral part of general school improvement, and relationships to other initiatives are clearly outlined.

Sources: Hargreaves (1997); McGregor & Vogelsberg (1998).

Teacher concerns about inclusive education

Many teachers are highly positive about inclusion, especially those who have had the opportunity to practise it and see the benefits. However, the idea of catering to the needs of all students in a classroom is daunting to some, and is by no means without its controversies. Teachers are commonly concerned about four main areas with respect to inclusive education:

- training for inclusion
- appropriate curriculum for all students
- available resources
- school and classroom structures that inhibit inclusion.

Teacher training

Teachers and researchers often express concerns about training when discussing the capacity for teachers to cater to the different learning needs in inclusive classrooms. A common theme in the literature and in our discussions with educators is that regular classroom teachers feel they do not have the prerequisite skills and knowledge to enable them to effectively include students with significantly diverse learning needs (MacPherson-Court et al., 2003). It is clear that being a competent teacher in an inclusive context requires the acquisition of a specific set of skills, knowledge and attributes. Some teachers may believe that this specific set, which has traditionally been viewed as the domain of those specially trained in special education, requires the use of extraordinarily different teaching strategies to those generally seen in the regular classroom, and those taught in teacher preparation programs. However, it has been argued that this set does not differ significantly from the skills an effective teacher would need to possess in order to teach in a non-inclusive context (Lewis & Norwich, 2005). Loreman (in press) conducted an analysis of the literature in order to ascertain the sorts of skills, knowledge and attributes teachers entering the profession would need in order to enable them to effectively teach in an inclusive environment. The results were grouped into seven domains: an understanding of inclusion and respect for diversity; collaboration with stakeholders (including parents and professionals); fostering a positive social climate; instructing in ways conducive to inclusion; engaging in inclusive instructional planning; engaging in meaningful assessment; and engaging in lifelong learning. It might be argued that any effective teacher, regardless of context, requires competence in these areas. It boils down to sound pedagogy that works for all students, and the willingness to respond to challenges and learn new techniques as the need arises (Lewis & Norwich, 2005).

There are two main contexts in which teachers can develop the skills, knowledge and attributes they need in order to be effective inclusive teachers. The first of these contexts is in their initial teacher preparation. The second is through professional development as a practising teacher. Both are important.

It is unreasonable to expect that teachers will have advanced expertise in matters relating to inclusive education upon leaving their teacher preparation programs. Rather, beginning teachers should have a firm grounding in the fundamentals in order to enable them to function effectively as they enter the profession, and to provide a basis for ongoing professional learning (Ford, Pugach & Otis-Wilborn, 2001). It is this ongoing professional growth and reflection as a practising teacher that is critical to continued success in an inclusive classroom. Barber and Turner (2007) found that new teachers who engaged in professional learning opportunities through an induction program during their first year of teaching experienced an increase in confidence in working with students with special needs, and also felt that they had developed more skills in the area. Anderson, Klassen & Georgiou (2007) conducted a study of 162 teachers in inclusive classrooms in Australia and found that 84 per cent of these teachers felt confident in including students with disabilities, and that this confidence was highly correlated with the amount of special education training a teacher had. In other words, those with more special education training felt better prepared to include. Anderson et al. (2007) demonstrated that training is effective in assisting teachers in inclusive contexts. A significant concern from the literature that should also be highlighted, and which might be addressed through training, is teacher attitudes towards students who have different learning needs. Positive attitudes towards these students are essential to the success of inclusion programs; these attitudes, however, can and need to be fostered through training and positive experiences with students who have differing learning needs (Avramidis & Norwich, 2002). Practising teachers have a professional obligation to seek out opportunities for learning in this and other areas.

Further, while we encourage teachers to undertake extra training when they can, we also believe that, due to the uniqueness of every teaching situation, teachers have much to learn from each other in a collaborative and supportive school atmosphere. Collaboration with colleagues as a way to better cater to all students in a school is discussed throughout this book.

Curriculum

Issues surrounding the provision of curriculum suitable for all students in inclusive settings are central to successful inclusion (Dymond, Renzaglia, Gilson & Slagor, 2007; Giangreco, 2007). The idea that students with exceptional needs should be provided with individualised programming has been incorporated into the legislation or policy of almost every Western country for some years now (OECD, 1994a), and individualised education programs, while they are not without their detractors, are more or less widely accepted as an appropriate tool for aiding in the education of students with significantly diverse needs. Nevertheless, the efficacy and morality of individualised plans are increasingly under scrutiny.

Supporters of individualised education argue that ensuring a student's specific educational goals are targeted and met can be done through the effective use of an individualised educational program (Jung, 2007). The careful and systematic structuring of appropriate educational goals for a student with different learning needs through the adaptation and modification of the regular curriculum, when done under the right conditions, is viewed by many as an excellent method of providing an appropriate education while also allowing for inclusion in a regular class (Tennant, 2007; Wilczynski, Menousek, Hunter & Mudgal, 2007).

While modification of curriculum to suit the individual student with differing needs is a widely accepted practice, it does have its critics. Teachers are generally expected to provide instruction in well-defined learning problems related to the specific needs of students with differing learning needs, while also ensuring that they are included in the regular program as much as possible (Soukup, Wehmeyer, Bashinski & Bovaird, 2007). Under this system, students with different needs may be viewed as being fundamentally different from their peers in how they learn and what they need to know. Indeed, the very act of implementing individualised plans in the context of a curriculum that is not generally written to include all students can be viewed as exclusionary (Lloyd, 2008). The idea of modification of the regular curriculum is based on a number of negative assumptions about students with diverse needs—for example, that students requiring such modification might learn at slower rates, are unable to perform certain required assessment tasks, and often require more practice and repetition to consolidate learning (see Lewis & Norwich, 2005). While each of these may be true for some individuals, such assumptions should never be applied prior to a thorough investigation of the nature of individual needs.

The increasing popularity of differentiated instruction, discussed further later in this text, raises a challenge to the need for individualised programs. Broderick, Mehta-Parekh & Reid (2005) recommend planning responsive lessons that differentiate instruction for all students from the outset, instead of modifying them for students with diverse learning needs. Further, for a number of years critics have viewed the process of individualised instruction as a means of singling out as 'other' and marginalising people with diverse abilities in order to exercise control over them through special programs (Corbett, 1993; Danforth, 1997; Evans & Vincent, 1997). Hehir (2007) refers to this kind of thinking as ableism; the assumption is made that it is preferable for a child to learn skills representative of the majority (for example, walking rather than using a wheelchair), under conditions and assumptions dictated by the majority, even if a modified program is required in order to attain such learning. This type of thinking, Thomas argues, maximises the impact of disability and minimises the opportunities for students with disabilities (or, in our terms, any form of difference) to participate in schooling and the community.

Such a curriculum is also criticised for presenting students engaged in it with a form of learning that is too prescriptive. Such a tightly constructed plan of learning is seen by critics as leaving little opportunity for students to direct their own learning; as a result, the instruction becomes teacher-centred and moves away from social constructivist pedagogy (Loreman, 2009). We have known for some time that individualised goals frequently focus on specific skills rather than cognitive aspects of learning (Collet-Klingenberg & Chadsey-Rusch, 1991); Goodman & Bond, 1993; Weisenfeld, 1987). Often these skills are applicable only to a limited number of situations. There is some evidence to suggest that such narrow skill development is not a thing of the past, and continues to be the overriding focus of the curriculum for students with different learning needs. As one example, Wilczynski et al. (2007) outline a very specific and limiting range of such objectives for individualised programs, including such mundane tasks as matching objects and pictures, or waiting in line. These objectives, they suggest, are appropriate for students with Autism Spectrum Disorder. Not only does this view assume that students with autism all have similar needs (they may not), but also that addressing those needs requires a narrow, prescriptive approach.

Slee (2008) suggests that deploying strategies and resources intended to enable inclusion to work (such as the sorts of assessments that lead to individualised programs) can in itself be disabling, and is a process that problematises disability (makes it a problem that must be addressed). To some degree, this supports the continued marginalisation and exclusion of students who are different. Slee advocates change in school systems, away from traditional special education and from using inclusion to remediate deficits in individuals. He argues that creative, irregular models of schooling should be considered as a means of moving away from this sort of thinking. Essentially, the view is that schools are institutions which no longer work well for students, and radical changes should be considered in order to produce a system that is more accommodating of all.

Whatever one's thoughts on the direction inclusive schooling should take in the future, it is clear that the present classroom reality of having to modify and adapt curriculum, and/or to teach in ways consistent with differentiated instruction and what is known as universal design, is something with which teachers must become conversant. We believe that whatever the failings of our current techniques may be (and we acknowledge that there are many), it is possible to provide instruction targeted towards the strengths and needs of the individual student, while at the same time remaining inclusive in terms of the daily curriculum and activities conducted in a classroom. This book is based on that premise.

School resources

The need for additional funds to be provided to schools for the purposes of educating students with unique needs and strengths has long been, and continues to be, recognised by researchers (O'Shea & O'Shea, 1998; Wu & Komesaroff, 2007). Well over two decades ago Gow, Ward, Balla & Snow (1988) identified 'expensive and often wasteful systems of service delivery' (1988, p. 15) as being one of the barriers to effective integration in Australia. Idol (1997) admits that inclusion programs are expensive, but outlines ways in which schools can achieve more effective cost accommodations. These include utilising support staff to work with a number of students in a classroom, reconsidering how funds are spent and making changes where possible, using funding from other special programs within the school that already support students with diverse learning needs, and site-based decision-making. Each of these is consistent with what has come to be seen as best practice in the field today.

Yet there seems to be a perception amongst some educators that the extra funding often provided to support students with differing learning needs in Western schools is inadequate, and that an increase in that funding would assist in solving any number of problems they are currently experiencing (Loreman, 2001). Is this necessarily the case? Does extra funding improve the quality of the school experience for all children? There is some evidence to suggest that extra funding does produce inclusive programs that deliver more adequate instruction to students with differing learning needs that are more closely aligned to that received by students who do not demonstrate the need for extra funding (Skårbrevik, 2005). However, while a certain level of extra funding is important, it may not be as critical to the success of inclusion as one might think. Some have suggested that it is staff attitudes, the quality of school organisation and the capacity to think creatively that have a greater impact on the success or otherwise of inclusion (Ainscow & Sebba, 1996; Vislie & Langfeldt, 1996). Indeed, the additional resources and services provided by extra funding can sometimes work against inclusion by singling some students out in a classroom. We believe that while it is true that financial resources are often required to improve inclusion and assist in the daily care and well-being of some students, extra funds alone are not sufficient to ensure successful inclusion. We hope to provide strategies for inclusion that do not necessarily require large amounts of additional funds for implementation.

Organisational structures

The ways in which many schools and classrooms are organised and structured are often not conducive to effective learning for many of the students they serve. This is especially apparent in secondary schools (Kennedy & Fisher, 2001; McGhie-Richmond, Barber, Lupart & Loreman, 2008). Teachers are often faced with inflexible timetables that schedule them with students for brief periods of time during which little can be achieved, especially with those students who might require longer to complete tasks or to organise themselves to begin learning after transition. Teachers can be constrained by the oppression of inadequate time in the day, and professional pressures to work through prescribed amounts of curriculum within a given time (Hilton, 2006). In becoming more inclusive, schools—and indeed school systems—will need to examine the ways in which they work. How should students be grouped to enable them to learn most effectively? How can teachers' workloads be managed in order to allow them to address individual needs? Ultimately, it is probable that structural and organisational changes made to allow schools to become more inclusive will benefit all students, not just those with evident different needs (Jorgensen, 1998; Kennedy & Fisher, 2001).

While there is often little an individual teacher can do about the way a school is structured and organised, what occurs in the classroom is influenced to a large degree by the teacher. This book will discuss ways in which schools can be organised better for inclusion while maintaining a strong focus on the individual classroom.

The benefits of inclusion

When inclusion is done well, everyone wins. The sorts of practices in which inclusive teachers engage have been shown to improve learning for all students, regardless of significant individual differences (or a lack of them). Importantly, there is scant empirical research evidence supporting segregated forms of education. Overall, it can be argued that research is currently slightly in favour of the superiority of inclusion as a practice (Lindsay, 2007), and while more research is needed to categorically claim that an inclusive approach is defensible in all situations, the recent trends evident in research are clearly supportive of inclusion. It must be remembered that the concept of inclusion is relatively new, both as a practice and a field of research, so time must be allowed for the development of a substantial body of research on the topic.

The alternative—segregation—has existed for centuries, yet supporters of this approach still cannot advance a strong case either philosophically or in empirical research for its continuation (Connor & Ferri, 2007; Lindsay, 2007). There are, however, some long-held and generally unsupported beliefs that students with differing learning needs will disrupt classes and impair the learning of others in a class; that teachers will be unable to cope with the extra tasks expected of them, and that students with differences will ultimately receive an inferior education and possibly come through the process with damaged self-esteem. A growing body of research seems to indicate that many of these beliefs are founded more on myth, preconceived notions or anecdotal support than on any solid empirical evidence. Some of the main positive outcomes of inclusion that have been identified through a selective (but certainly not exhaustive) examination of the research literature are outlined below.

- Students with individual differences realise greater academic benefits such as higher levels of academic attainment than do their counterparts in non-inclusive settings, and are more likely to engage in the same courses of study as their peers (such as maths, science, language arts, and so on) when they are in inclusive settings (Fisher, Roach & Frey, 2002; Frederickson, Dunsmuir, Lang & Monsen, 2004; Newman & Institute of Education Sciences, 2006).
- The academic achievement of students without significantly diverse learning needs is not impacted by the presence of those who do have those needs. Indeed, there is evidence to suggest that their learning is actually improved by the presence of such students, possibly because teachers use different strategies and instructional technologies, and resources such as teacher assistants are available to help all students to learn (Cole, Waldron & Majd, 2004; Demeris, Childs & Jordan, 2008; Gallagher & Lambert, 2006; Hines, 2001; Kalambouka, Farrell, Dyson & Kaplan, 2007).
- Students with diverse learning needs benefit from the enhanced development of communication, social skills and other forms of adaptive behaviour in inclusive settings (Fisher et al., 2002; McDonnell, Thorson, Disher, Mathot-Buckner, Mendel & Ray, 2003). Indeed, the social benefits of inclusion are well illustrated in the research literature (Frederickson et al., 2004).
- Inclusion is more cost effective than segregated models of education in the long term, and we have known this for some time (Halvorsen, Neary, Hunt & Cesca, 1996; McLaughlin & Warren, 1994; Roahrig, 1993; Salisbury & Chambers, 1994).
- Students who are involved in helping others in their classroom through peer tutoring and other similar opportunities for interaction (common

in inclusive classrooms) reap the benefits of improved self-esteem, understanding of and empathy for difference, and friendships (Jones, 2007; Naraian, 2008).

- Teachers benefit from inclusive education. It can act as a catalyst for enhanced skill development in professional learning communities (Carrington & Robinson, 2004; van Kraayenoord, 2007).
- Inclusion seems to have a positive impact on post-school outcomes for students with special learning needs in areas such as gaining employment, the amount earned, and associated costs for support in the community when compared with non-inclusive educational environments (Alper & Ryndak, 1992; White & Weiner, 2004).

The arguments supporting inclusion are compelling. The opposing argument that students with differing learning needs receive an inferior standard of education in an inclusive setting, or that others are somehow disadvantaged, is difficult to sustain. The following case study, presented as a snapshot of a school trying to adopt an inclusive approach to education, illustrates this. While the school under examination had by no means perfected the art and science of inclusion, it is outlined as a real example of inclusion being realised at the school level. It is also an example of the need for schools and teachers to continuously be revising and adjusting how they work in order to maintain an inclusive environment.

Case study: Angela, age 16

Student information

Name: Angela

Age: 16

Year in school: 11

Included in school year: 11

School: Catholic girls' secondary (Years 7–12)

School region: Metropolitan; lower socio-economic area

School outcomes: Small percentage of graduates attend university. The majority enter the workforce after secondary school, or pursue studies in a technical or community college setting.

Family background: Family immigrated to the city from a non-English speaking country prior to Angela's birth. Family maintains cultural and language ties to country of origin, while also making an effort to integrate into a multicultural society. Parents employed in 'blue-collar' jobs. Both were supportive of Angela furthering her education in an inclusive environment and pursuing leisure interests typical of teenage girls.

Noteworthy individual differences: Standardised assessments indicated significant developmental delays from early infancy. Full-scale IQ of 60. Receptive language ability measured at 8-year-old level, with reading level at Grade 4. Difficulty experienced in most academic areas, particularly language tasks, visual processing and problem-solving. Moderate deficit in short-term auditory memory. Verbal response time of 15–60 seconds (possibly the result of seizure medication).

At the time this study was conducted, Angela took a reduced number of subjects towards completing a regular Year 11 course of study. These subjects were English, mathematics, materials technology, and information technology. Six double periods per week were set aside as private study time to allow Angela an opportunity to catch up on her work. She used this time either to work on her own or to seek assistance from the special-education teacher. As the school did not employ paraprofessionals, the special education teacher also attended some of Angela's classes with her to provide support. Interviews indicated that untrained volunteers were also sometimes used in classes to provide extra assistance for the entire class, including Angela. Angela was described by her teachers as a pleasant and patient student to teach, although her disability did mean that she frequently required extra attention in class. Once she felt comfortable with a new teacher, she would politely request help as required.

Both Angela and staff made mention of the good relationship between students and staff at the school. One staff member remarked: 'Learning, or part of the platform of learning, is that young people develop good relationships with their teachers and with each other. That, I think, is fairly strongly an element of the school.' It appeared that the positive relationship between students and teachers extended to the wider school community, not just those with diverse needs. Comments made in a recent survey of past students compiled by the school recognised the support and kindness shown to students by school staff. Angela's mother also recognised the effort school staff had made in supporting her daughter. She remarked: 'She has got the help of [special-education teacher] always, and she is having some extra help at the moment. I can[not] say anything about that school because there is not the money in the world that I can pay them.' While building a good relationship and offering staff support were seen to be important elements at the school, support for Angela also came from her classmates. Angela, her teachers and her mother all remarked on how her class supported her. One participant remarked that 'all the girls have been very supportive with [Angela]. They care about her.' This support from the class ranged from understanding that Angela sometimes needed more help from the teacher to actually helping her themselves through informal peer tutoring.

Angela had a very positive attitude toward her school, her classmates and her teachers. She said she enjoyed going to school and was interested in what she was learning. So positive was her attitude to school that she made the comment: 'I don't like holidays that are too long. I get bored . . . I was bored in summer. I just wanted to go back to school.' According to her teachers, she was also prepared to attempt difficult tasks before asking for help. When asked what she liked about each of her subjects, the common denominator was that she felt some sense of achievement in each class. She enjoyed making things in materials technology, solving problems in mathematics and typing successfully in computers. Some staff at the school indicated that an effort was made to treat Angela the same as the other students and to not make her feel she was different. They indicated that, although her work was modified, an attempt was made to provide Angela with an experience as close to the rest of the class as possible. Some teacher interviews indicated that Angela took responsibility for her own work and would ask for help only after trying to do it herself first. This idea of giving Angela the responsibility of work was also supported in her home.

Angela also viewed the extra help she was getting at the school in a positive light. In particular, she felt that the help given to her by the special education teacher was a pivotal element in her success at the school, and this view was supported in the interviews with other participants. Angela indicated that spending time with the special education teacher helped her to understand difficult concepts and pieces of work. At no stage did Angela mention any kind of perceived stigma associated with getting extra help at school. The special education teacher at the school performed a number of roles, all of which were reported to be helpful by both Angela and the staff. These included acting as a consultant to teachers, coordinating and training volunteers, assisting with modifying curriculum, support in the classroom and direct teaching.

The school claimed to operate within a culture of caring, kindness, and mutual respect and support. When asked about how this culture came about and why the school was a caring environment in which to work and learn, participants in the study had more difficulty in answering. The principal remarked: 'It does come back to relationships. We don't tolerate people shouting at kids and we don't tolerate people being unkind to each other. At the base of that is probably some sort of a notion of justice.' The principal also cited an emphasis on teamwork at the school as a contributing factor to the school culture:

You're going to use team-based approaches to things. You're going to use . . . group learning settings that are going to recognise the mix of abilities that are within any learning setting. You're going to recognise that the differences amongst people are things that should be celebrated. After all, in a group some are going to be able to contribute really well and provide leadership and rich insights into certain things, where some aren't. Flip the activity around and do something else and it all might be quite different.

Other reasons given for the positive culture in the school included the selection of a caring staff, good leadership from the principal, and the fact that the school was a girls' school. One participant felt that because it was a school for girls, more feminine qualities of cooperation and understanding were emphasised. Whether being a Catholic school made a difference to the culture of caring was a matter for debate. Some participants felt the pastoral aspect had no influence at all, while others believed that there was a moderate and positive effect on the school culture.

Angela received a significant amount of help with schoolwork at home. In particular, her mother frequently helped her with her daily homework. Her mother also tried to relate what Angela learned at school to home where possible. One example of this was getting Angela to help with cooking or asking her to read road signs when they were out in the car. Staff from the school reported that this extra support at home gave Angela a significant advantage at school. Angela's mother saw her role as being a support to Angela with her work and also a source of encouragement: 'My role is to try to encourage her. That is what I try to do always . . . to encourage her to learn.'

The school received special funding in a conventional manner through the Catholic Education Office. Being a Catholic school, and therefore considered by the government to be a private school, the extra funding provided to Angela amounted to about 25 per cent of what she would have received had she attended a public school. The school could not be considered wealthy, and this funding was perceived to be inadequate by only two teachers. Most teachers, however, indicated that resources were adequate to support the learning of Angela and other students with diverse needs. Given the low level of special funding teachers were often expected to work with Angela with no extra staff support. Generally staff felt that they were able to cope with the specialised assistance required by Angela and meet the needs of the class without this support. This was confirmed by brief classroom observations, where teachers were seen to be coping with directing the rest of the class while helping Angela. A peer tutor was used in one class, while Angela received some support from a group of her peers in another. One teacher was not even aware that Angela had a disability at the start of the year, but managed to include her successfully into the class with little assistance once she had discovered what her specific needs were. Some staff mentioned time as being a limiting factor. They felt that they could have been better teachers both for Angela and the rest of the class if they had more time, because it took quite a lot of time each lesson to assist Angela and to get her started with work. Sometimes, if the topic was challenging for the entire class, there was less time to spend with Angela. At the time of the study, the school was working on some organisational changes to try to assist teachers in dealing with issues of time.

After experiencing difficulties making friends and being teased in her primary school years, Angela finally made a friend in her first year of secondary school. While she was described by her mother and teachers as always being shy and preferring the company of adults, Angela managed to make more friends her own age as she progressed through secondary school. According to Angela, this was achieved by her making a conscious decision to approach other girls in the schoolyard and through proactive support from school staff. At the time of the study, Angela had one 'best friend' whom she saw outside of school, as well as a small group of acquaintances at school. Her best friend was described as being very different to Angela—very outgoing and confident. The girls spent their time involved in common teenage activities such as going to see movies or listening to music. Interviews indicated that Angela was the victim of teasing from other students in primary school and from one student in her first year at secondary school. Teachers dealt with this at the time following a parent complaint. At the time this study was conducted, Angela did not get teased and was left alone by students who were not her friends.

The most likely post-school options were seen by Angela, her mother and her teachers as continuing education through a program for people with disabilities at the local community college prior to entering the workforce. This program has a focus on social and life skills. Concern was expressed by staff members at the school at the lack of post-school options for students with cognitive disabilities such as Angela.

Box 1.4: Ways in which Angela's school was inclusive

- Welcoming environment for students with differing learning needs
- Flexible scheduling available, allowing private study sessions
- Angela's available subject choice was the same as for all other students
- Assistance provided by special-education teacher and volunteers only as required
- Opportunities for formal and informal peer tutoring
- Positive staff attitudes towards inclusion
- Positive school leadership from principal
- School fostered an ethos of caring and respect for individual differences
- Curriculum was modified as required
- Friendship development supported by staff
- Team-based approach to inclusion was used
- Parents involved as partners

How to include all students in regular schools and classrooms

The remainder of this book is dedicated to providing you with background information, practical advice, tools and strategies to assist you to include students with diverse learning needs in your classroom. As can be seen in Angela's case study, whole-school commitment is an extremely important element of inclusion, and is a preferable context within which to teach, but we understand that the level of commitment to inclusion varies from school to school. This does not mean, however, that you cannot try your best to be inclusive in your own classroom. We hope that the information in this book will prove helpful to you even if you operate in a school that is not particularly committed to inclusion.

As you read further, be reminded that inclusion is context dependent. Your experience with a particular group of students will be different from the experience of others. There is no single 'correct' way of including all students; however, as suggested previously, there is a general process that you can implement and that will help you to be successful. The following chapters in this book detail that process.

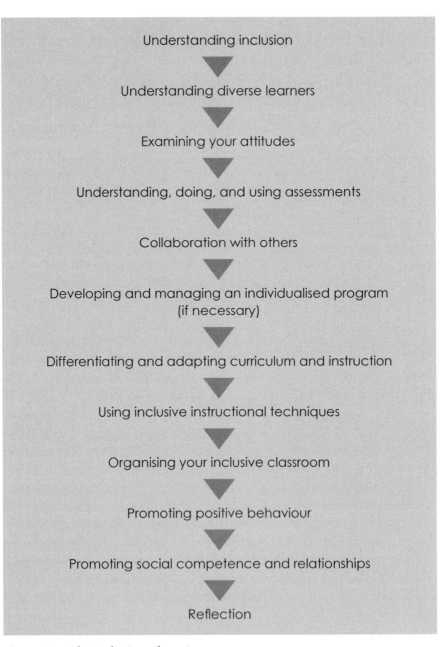

Figure 1.1 The inclusive education process

Key terms

Inclusion. Full inclusion of all students in all aspects of schooling.

Integration. A practice that preceded inclusion and aimed to involve students, generally with disabilities, into existing classes and structures within a regular school.

For discussion and reflection

1.1   Some writers have argued that even if there was no research supporting its effectiveness, inclusion should be pursued because it is morally right. What are your views on this?

1.2   Considering that research has shown that inclusion is an effective approach, why do some parents not choose it for their child?

1.3   Many people believe that inclusion becomes more difficult the older a student gets. Based on your experience, is this the case? Why or why not?

Further reading

Connor, D.J. & Ferri, B.A. (2007). The conflict within: Resistance to inclusion and other paradoxes in special education. *Disability & Society, 22*(1), 63–77.

Foreman, P.J. (2007). *Inclusion in action* (3rd ed.). Sydney: Thompson Learning.

Jorgensen, C.M. (Ed.). (1998). *Restructuring high schools for all students: Taking inclusion to the next level*. Baltimore, MD: Paul H. Brookes.

2
Who are our students with diverse learning needs?

Key ideas in this chapter

- Defining diversity
- Discrimination
- To label or not to label?
- Labels and teaching the full spectrum of diverse needs
- How do I talk about students from diverse backgrounds?

International standards on human rights are based on the idea of full participation of all persons in society on equal terms and without discrimination (UNESCO, 1994, 2000). Over almost three decades, equity legislation throughout the world has significantly affected how schools provide education for all students. These laws make discrimination on the basis of most types of diversity against the law in most circumstances. In education, this means that all students must have the same educational opportunities. This chapter discusses definitions, labelling, criteria for determining learning needs, and the various purposes for diagnosis.

Defining diversity

The term 'diversity' is in itself a difficult concept to define, and indeed is multifaceted. An internet search of the term 'diversity definition' produces over six million hits, and includes widely disparate ideas of what diversity actually means. One problem common to many definitions of diversity is that they do not go far enough in their description of the different facets of diversity that are apparent. There seems to be common agreement in some areas, but not others. Furthermore, many definitions seem to mix ideas of inclusion with ideas of diversity, which for those seeking a clear focus on the topic can cloud the issue (Zepke, 2005). The Calgary Board of Health (2008) in Canada presents a broad definition of diversity that in part resonates with our views, which form the foundation of much of this book. This definition includes the following:

> *All the ways we are unique and different from others. Dimensions of diversity include, but are not limited to, aspects such as: ethnicity, religion and spiritual beliefs, cultural orientation, colour, physical appearance, gender, sexual orientation, ability, education, age, ancestry, place of origin, marital status, family status, socio-economic circumstance, profession, language, health status, geographic location, group history, upbringing and life experiences. (2008, para. 1)*

Obviously, with respect to education and individual contexts, some of the dimensions of diversity described above do not apply (for example, most school-age students have not yet entered into a profession and most are not married); however, the above definition is broad enough to include a wide range of types of diversity. Further, it does not assume that these types of diversity are known, and so lists them specifically in a relatively comprehensive way.

A discussion of definitions of each of the types of diversity listed by the Calgary Board of Health and their historical and current context would result in a long and possibly rather monotonous litany of issues pertaining to each. While in another context such a discussion might have some value, for the sake of succinctness we will discuss further only one type of difference: disability. We have singled out disability for further discussion for a number of reasons. First, there are few if any areas in the world in which people with disabilities are seamlessly accepted and included in all areas of society, meaning that issues regarding this type of difference are of broad international importance. Second, many of the ideas in this text have been derived from the context of disability, as we as authors have a background in this field. Therefore, out of all the different types of diversity that exist, this is the area in which we have the most expertise. Finally, the issues connected with disability, including discrimination and segregation, are common to many other types of difference. In singling out disability for further discussion with respect to difference, we are hoping to let the part tell the whole, inasmuch as that is possible.

The issues behind definitions of disability

Historically, policy and legislation changes have been influenced by the redefining of disability, particularly during the 1970s and 1980s. Three categories of definitions of disability have been used in education: functional limitations; medical; and socio-political (Bernell, 2003; Hahn, 1985; Jeon & Haider-Markel, 2001). Each definition has a different emphasis and type of policy; therefore, each has different support implications for those with disabilities.

Functional limitations definitions emphasise the limitations or inability of the person to perform a particular activity or activities. Definitions can be broad (limited in daily living activities) or narrow (the specific type and amount of employment-related skills the person can perform) (Bernell, 2003), and also call attention to the need for occupational training and income support (Jeon & Haider-Markel, 2001). *Medical* definitions emphasise the person's condition, involve an assessment of their medical condition and describe each disability in a separate category (e.g. cerebral palsy, spinal cord injury). Medical definitions require objective measures that determine who does and does not meet the specific criteria for each category. Medical definitions of disability have implications for increased expenditures for health care and research, and are often supported by philanthropic groups with an interest in particular disabilities (Bernell, 2003; Jeon & Haider-Markel, 2001). *Socio-political* definitions emphasise the failure of the environment to adapt to persons with disabilities. From this perspective, policy attempts to impact the external environment so that persons with disabilities do not face discrimination (Jeon & Haider-Markel, 2001). 'Disabilities are regarded as no different than other bodily attributes such as skin colour, gender or age, all of which have been used as a means of differentiation and discrimination throughout history.' (Hahn, 1985, p. 93)

Definitions make a difference

Definitions of disability influence how problems are defined and what evidence is collected. They determine the alternative solutions that are considered along with who participates in the decision-making. Inclusive educational policies are consistent with socio-political definitions—a student with disabilities should be viewed no differently from any other student with different attributes including race, gender, size, and so on. Obviously, the presence of a disability cannot be ignored because it forms part of who a person is. However, this amounts to only a part of who a person is. An inclusive environment acknowledges difference and caters to it, while at the same time emphasising that all people are both unique and similar in many ways.

Using medical definitions: Special education model

Schools in which policies reflect medical definitions may view a student with a disability as having a problem. Evidence gathered typically involves medical and health professionals in psychological or other general assessment and takes place outside of the context in which the learning takes place (Deppeler, 2003). A professional, such as a special education teacher or psychologist, who is considered to have *expertise* with the problem typically suggests alternative solutions. Solutions are often similar across schools and involve programs suggested for the particular disability. Finally, the adopted solution may be a program that is delivered separately from the rest of the student's peers. Many of these programs are not consistent with curriculum models being employed within the school, and are therefore unlikely to transfer easily to classrooms and integrate with existing school programs.

We believe strongly in the principles of inclusive schooling. We therefore have *not* included the criteria used to define the multitude of categories of disability from a medical approach. When individual students do not make academic progress or continue to be marginalised, the process can often be repeated several times throughout the student's schooling. The process is separate from the school community and therefore has very little chance of success (Deppeler, 2003).

Using socio-political definitions: Inclusive education model

In inclusive schools, communication and collaboration amongst teachers, parents, students and sometimes others from the wider community can determine how to reduce barriers for students with disabilities and increase facilitators for learning.

First, priorities are established for the student. Evidence-gathering typically involves interviewing, observing the student in various contexts in the school, and examining student work. Evidence collection may also involve the teacher critically reflecting on his or her classroom practices through video-recording or feedback from a colleague. Evidence-gathering could also include policy-document analysis or observation of school practices for determining the participation of students in social aspects of schooling. In every instance, the evidence is critically examined, alternative solutions are generated, and decisions are made collaboratively. Solutions are likely to be different from school to school as decision-making occurs in response to the specific priorities and variables important for that particular school context. 'This model also can involve "expert" professional input but it becomes part of the shared decision-making and in response to the collaborative process—but is not reliant upon it.' (Deppeler, 2003, p. 19)

Discrimination

It is an unfortunate aspect of human nature that we tend to discriminate against others. Some discrimination—such as not employing someone because of the colour of their skin—is overt, while other forms of discrimination—such as principals encouraging a student with a disability to choose to attend a school other than their neighbourhood one—are more subtle. McCoy and Major (2007) argue that in Western societies such as the United States, advancement and the attaining of higher levels of status are perceived to be based on merit. Those who hold this view can become blind to the impact of discrimination, believing instead that certain groups deserve their lower status because it is their lower ability or lack of effort, rather than discrimination, that keeps them at a lower status. The discrimination, then, remains and continues unchecked if status is psychologically rationalised in this way.

Few people believe that discrimination of some form or other has been entirely eradicated, and in truth this is unlikely ever to be the case. With that in mind, lawmakers in many countries have enacted laws and policy forbidding active discrimination. Anti-discrimination legislation and policy aim to eliminate discrimination against people on the basis of difference, and to ensure that people from diverse backgrounds have a right to equal treatment before the law and the same fundamental rights as the rest of the community. The Australian Human Rights Commission through the Disability Discrimination Act (1992) outlined two types of discrimination: direct discrimination (less favourable treatment); and indirect discrimination (unfair exclusion). Direct discrimination usually amounts to more obvious types of discrimination such as girls' sporting teams receiving lower levels of funding than boys' teams, or non-admission to certain aspects of schooling. Indirect discrimination, however, can be far more insidious. One way in which indirect discrimination can be achieved is through the categorisation and labelling of students according to their differences.

Further, it cannot be assumed that legislation forbidding discrimination actually achieves that function. Levels of compliance with such legislation differ, and sometimes loopholes in some legislation permit discrimination to continue in some circumstances. For example, the Australian *Disability Discrimination Act* of 1992 indicates that in some circumstances adjustments do not need to be made for people with disabilities if these adjustments are unreasonable:

An adjustment is reasonable if it meets the needs of the student with disability without impacting too much on other people. To determine if an Adjustment is reasonable an Education Provider must consider:

- *The barriers, needs or challenges that face a student with disability.*
- *The views of the student or their Associate.*
- *Whether the Adjustment will impact on the academic standards or requirements of the course.*
- *What advantages or disadvantages the Adjustments might have on the people affected by it.*
- *The costs of making the Adjustment. (Australian Government Department of Education, Employment, and Workplace Relations, 2008, para. 17)*

Loopholes in legislation and policy similar to the one quoted above exist in the United Kingdom, Canada and many other areas of the world. What does or does not constitute a reasonable adjustment, however, is generally not up to the individual teacher or even school. With such legislation, the courts decide what is reasonable and what is not based on cases that come before them, and the results of these cases set precedents for future action. For example, the *Purvis v. New South Wales Department of Education and Training Case* examined a situation whereby a student was excluded from school due to behaviour that was felt to pose a threat to the health and safety of others in the school. The eventual finding was that this was a valid ground for exclusion in this particular case (Dickson, 2005). In this instance, the decision of the school to exclude the student was vindicated by the courts, within the terms of the legislation. However, decisions such as this should not be seen as meaning that schools can exclude whoever they want to by claiming that the presence of a particular student represents an undue hardship on the school. Such court cases generally outline decisions in relation to more extreme cases, and as a general rule schools may not discriminate on the basis of disability or any other form of individual difference. Changes to the physical environment, adapting and modifying curriculum and assessment, assistance from support staff, the provision of specialised equipment, and other forms of support commonly found in schools are all viewed as reasonable responses to diversity under the terms of most legislation and policy.

Legislation aside, it is important to consider other forms of discrimination that can occur to various groups in the context of school and classrooms. Some of this is subtle, and it is possible to discriminate unintentionally. For example, what percentage of questions asked of students in your science classes are answered by girls? What sorts of stereotypes about certain groups influence your expectations? We all like to think we are free of bias, but sometimes the cultures we have been raised and live in, in combination with school cultures, can result in forms of discrimination that can occur without us even realising it—hidden in plain view, as it were. Langhout (2005) argues that public school structures are oppressive for all students, especially those from minority groups including those based on race, social class and gender, and that discrimination on the basis of stereotypes is ingrained in school structures and systems, the end result of which is a silencing of students from various backgrounds. Amid such accusations there is a tendency towards defensiveness. As individuals, most teachers are not explicitly discriminatory in their attitudes, and to be associated with such discrimination might be viewed as offensive. However, Langhout is not necessarily accusing individuals of wanting to oppress certain groups. Rather, her analysis and others like it (for example, see Slee & Cook, 1994) are helpful in that they can open our eyes to what is occurring in the systems in which we function, therefore allowing us to work towards changing such systems.

To label or not to label?

The labelling of students by category according to the nature of their diversity is controversial. In order to understand this controversy, we must first ask why and for what purpose students are identified by a label. Many parents and educators argue that labels are necessary because they provide a common understanding of the needs of the student, and therefore students who are not labelled may not be supported adequately. Further, this group argues that labels promote additional funding for students and their families that is not available to students without significantly diverse learning needs, and for targeted research programs. Other parents and professionals believe that labels are associated with negative stereotypes, harm students' views of themselves, and do not directly contribute to the planning of teaching or curriculum for individual students. Further, this group views disability as a socially and culturally constructed concept and sees the categorisation and labelling of students according to medical and psychological definitions as disabling. For example, Slee and Cook (1994) have argued that we categorise and label students so as to create cultures of disability that allow us to more easily argue for the exclusion of certain groups based on notions of what is best for them as a group. The intent of labelling someone as having a 'behaviour disorder', for example, is sometimes to group them with other students with the same diagnosis in a segregated educational setting. Categorisation and labelling may sometimes be helpful, but there is significant risk of such a practice becoming detrimental in the long term. The cases below illustrate some of the possible advantages and disadvantages of labelling.

Case study: Ben, aged 9 years

Ben's mother was concerned that her son was being bullied at school and that he didn't seem to have any friends. She believed Ben was gifted and that because of his advanced development he found many classroom activities boring. She blamed the school for not providing sufficient challenges. She also believed that it was his giftedness that caused him difficulties in relating to his peers and in speaking in an adult manner. Ben's teacher was also concerned that Ben had very few friends. She observed that he only related to his peers on his terms and could be very bossy and inflexible. She believed that his peers thought of him as 'odd'. She believed that because Ben was an only child and his mother was a single parent, he didn't have any appropriate male role models and was 'spoiled'. Although he wasn't skilled at any sport, she had encouraged him to participate in team activities. She noted he often became upset when he felt the other children were not playing by the rules. She noted Ben was generally well behaved in class and completed his work. In some areas, his performance was of a very high standard (for example, his general knowledge was excellent—he knew lots of facts) but he was very slow with written work and his handwriting was particularly poor. She also noted that he had regular but infrequent episodes where he became very upset and would scream and cry. When this occurred, it was very difficult to calm him down. The teacher indicated that she did not know what caused these episodes. Ben was referred for a psychological assessment.

The psychological assessment report indicated that Ben's test performance was at average to advanced levels of cognitive development, but his verbal abilities were substantially higher than his non-verbal abilities. It was also noted that Ben had some difficulties in solving socially meaningful problems.

Based on these results, and in conjunction with the background information provided by Ben's mother and teacher, further assessment of his social competence was recommended. Using the Gillian Asperger's Disorder Scale (GADS), the psychologist reported that Ben's pattern of behaviour indicated a number of features characteristic of Asperger's Disorder. This includes difficulties in relating to peers as well as other people, the presence of obsessive behaviours such as routines or preoccupation with certain topics, and difficulties in the use of language to communicate flexibly with other people. Delayed motor milestones and clumsiness are additional characteristics. Overall, the disorder causes significant impairment in social functioning, yet because of good language and cognitive skills it is frequently not recognised until later in childhood. Ben's mother and teacher felt the diagnosis was helpful in understanding why Ben was having difficulties in school. A change in direction occurred. Rather than blaming Ben and his mother for his 'odd' behaviour, or the school for not providing sufficient challenges, emphasis was placed on *how* the school and home might support Ben in processing information about people and their emotional and social responses, and in further developing his social competencies.

Case study: Jeff, aged 8 years

Jeff enjoyed school and had many friends in his classroom. He played with them outside during breaks, and saw them after school and on weekends. Jeff was generally regarded as a 'popular' member of the class by his peers. He was liked by his teacher and was regarded as a classroom leader. Academically, Jeff had many great ideas for projects and always actively participated in class discussions. He was verbally fluent and loved to give oral reports, entertaining his classmates with his humour. Jeff disliked reading and rarely brought books home. He tended to avoid most reading and writing tasks in class. Samples of his writing revealed he could spell only a handful of words other than his name. As a consequence, his written work did not often reflect his understanding of the subject and he was experiencing difficulties completing library research for projects. Jeff was referred for a psychological assessment.

The psychological assessment report indicated that Jeff's pattern of performance was consistent with a diagnosis of 'learning disabilities'. As a consequence, further resources were provided to support him. A paraprofessional was funded to work with Jeff in his classroom for two half-days per week. Jeff was scheduled to join a small group for reading support for one hour a day, three times a week, during class time. Jeff indicated to his parents he hated going to the 'dumb readers' group. He complained that his friends never got to sit with him when the paraprofesional was there and asked why he 'couldn't do the same group work—like he did before'. Jeff started complaining about stomach pains before school—needing to stay home because he was sick. In class, Jeff avoided doing literacy tasks by telling jokes and disturbing others, or by not having the necessary materials. He began to feel disconnected from what his friends were doing in class when he missed large sections of regular classroom work due to his remedial classes. He was less enthusiastic about class projects and rarely participated constructively in class discussions. Jeff's teacher no longer regarded him as a leader in the classroom. Although Jeff was still popular with many of his classmates, he was viewed by others as a 'boy who was always getting into trouble'. Jeff was involved in several fights in the playground with boys who had apparently teased him about his reading and called him 'stupid'. Although Jeff made some specific measurable reading gains, his label of 'learning disabilities' resulted in a loss of confidence and social status that went far beyond any reading improvement.

Case study: Carl, aged 11 years

Before I had an assessment and they said I was gifted or somethin' . . . I was always gettin' in trouble. After me Mum got me tested the teachers let me do some different work. I got to use a video camera for my report and 'cause my writin' and spellin' aren't very good, I also get extra time on the computer. I used to hate school . . . I like some of the science stuff. Hey! I did a real cool project with capacitors an' resistance and I won a prize at Science Talent Search.

Case study: Narissa, aged 14 years

Gifted and talented. *The three words that, in the past two years have turned my life upside down. Since being assessed, expectations of me have never run so high. Teachers who had never paid too much attention to me started watching me like hawks. My parents to this day continue to quip 'all we ask is that you do your best'. Nevertheless, the fact is that what they consider to be 'my best' has changed. I have found myself pushed into extension programs, seminars and workshops for able students. I now live in constant fear of Individual Differences Departments, who have given me too much attention and too much extension . . . So parents and teachers alike, my advice to you would be to let your kids be kids. Nobody needs to live with a label. Use extension only if it is sought, or else it will be wasted.*

Be prepared to help extend your child but don't pressure them to achieve any more than they have been. Encourage, but don't push. I lived the first thirteen years of my life without a label and for that I am truly grateful. (Krongold Centre, 1995)

Labels and teaching the full spectrum of diverse needs

The very act of labelling may have come about—and indeed is possibly continued—because it represents an attempt to try to make sense of the vast array of differences that confront families along with schools, educators and other professions. Medical and psychological science is at the point now where literally thousands of different syndromes can be identified and a label attached. Add to this issues of gender, culture, religion, sexual orientation, and so on, and this vast array of difference can seem daunting: How am I going to cater to this wide variety of needs in the classroom when I have never even heard of most of the labels attached to my students?

As we noted in Chapter 1, some texts try to address this difficulty by grouping students with similar labels under broader headings (e.g. high-incidence disabilities, low-incidence disabilities, giftedness) and outlining specific ways to teach these groups. In our view, this still complicates the matter unnecessarily. While there are some strategies that are helpful in working with specific groups of students, there are too many individual exceptions to these ways of working—and in any event, there is a single process that we argue will work for all students, ranging from those with significant impairments to the highly gifted and talented. That process is what is described in this text. We believe this is not an over-simplification, but rather a sensible response to the myriad differences faced in the modern classroom. Focus on the process. As a teacher, you should find some measure of comfort in knowing that once you are conversant with the process approach to inclusion suggested by this book, with an emphasis placed on student needs and strengths rather than labels, then you should have a higher chance of finding success with inclusion—whatever the demographic makeup of your class.

As an example, let us consider two students who might be considered to be at opposite ends of the spectrum in terms of their label, as well as their actual strengths and needs. How might the process approach to inclusion outlined in Chapter 1 be appropriate to helping include both students in a meaningful way?

Student 1: Owen, aged 11 years

IQ and achievement testing indicates Owen is intellectually and academically well in advance of his peers. He is a reflective adolescent and a highly talented artist who also enjoys and excels at music and sport. Owen generally has a very high rate of productivity and is inclined to complain of having 'nothing left to do' in class because he finishes his class assignments early. He is highly motivated, but consistently demonstrates gifted performances in only a narrow range of art, music and sporting activities despite his advanced ability in other academic domains.

Student 2: Miranda, aged 11 years

Miranda's disability is such that it has not been possible to conduct comprehensive and accurate IQ or academic tests on her. She has severe spastic cerebral palsy, uses a motorised wheelchair, and her verbal communication is limited to 'yes' and 'no', which she seems to use inconsistently when expressing herself. She demonstrates awareness of those around her, and seems happiest when working in groups with others. She can hold a pencil in her right hand and is capable of writing five letters of the alphabet. Her parents report a great affinity for animals, particularly the family dog, who is her 'constant companion' at home.

This comparison shows that while Miranda and Owen have very different needs and strengths, the questions one might ask relative to the education of both students are the same. In Owen's case, the answers to the questions would be about how best to challenge him academically and to meet his 'advanced' needs. In Miranda's case, the answers might be more about how best to support her in order to improve communication and other skills of that nature. In both cases, the considerations are really about taking account of the preferred learning style of each student and challenging them so that their learning is at a level just beyond where they are currently at, with support if needed (a process known as scaffolding). This applies to students who are performing ahead of expectations for their age, and those performing below such expectations. In both cases, it involves making adjustments to the way in which teaching is done. Stepping outside of the disability–giftedness comparison, the same set of questions can be used when considering the inclusion of students who present with any form of diversity (see Figure 2.1).

Owen	The process approach	Miranda
Knowing about the forms and issues of and around diversity	Understanding diverse learners	Knowing about the forms and issues of and around diversity
What preconcieved notions do I have about giftedness?	Examining your attitudes	What preconcieved notions do I have about disability?
What do Owen's assessments say? How will I conduct and use classroom assessments to best serve Owen?	Understanding, doing, and using assessments	What do Miranda's assessments say? How will I conduct and use classroom assessments to best serve Miranda?
What can a team contribute to meeting Owen's needs?	Collaboration with others	What can a team contribute to meeting Miranda's needs?
Does Owen need an individualised program? If so, what are the priorities?	Developing and managing an individualised program (if necessary)	Does Miranda need an individualised program? If so, what are the priorities?
How do I plan to meet Owen's unique instructional needs and those of the class?	Differentiating and adapting curriculum and instruction	How do I plan to meet Miranda's unique instructional needs and those of the class?
What specific instructional techniques are needed for Owen?	Using inclusive instructional techniques	What specific instructional techniques are needed for Miranda?
What organisational considerations need to be made to support Owen?	Organising your inclusive classroom	What organisational considerations need to be made to support Miranda?
How can the classroom community support Owen?	Promoting positive behaviour	How can the classroom community support Miranda?
What social support (if any) does Owen need?	Promoting social competence and relationships	What social support (if any) does Miranda need?
How do I plan to reflect on the inclusive processes I have used?	Being a reflective practitioner	How do I plan to reflect on the inclusive processes I have used?

Figure 2.1 Practical example of the process approach

How do I talk about students from diverse backgrounds?

The language we use when talking about learners with differing needs matters. The sort of subtle discrimination discussed earlier can be found in some of the language we use when talking about groups of people. We need to think of the individual person first, rather than the differences that exist. While there are some exceptions to this (for example, many students of the Jewish faith do not mind being called 'Jewish students' when the need to use this identifying term arises), as a general rule it is always safer and advisable to use 'person-first' language, especially in situations where you are unsure. Further, some terms—such as 'mentally retarded'—are outdated and frankly offensive to many, no matter how they are used.

Box 2.1: When talking about difference . . .

In most cases, use expressions that put the person ahead of the difference. For example:

Use:	Rather than:
the man who is blind	the blind man
the woman who is gifted	the gifted woman
the student with disabilities	the disabled student
the student for whom English is a second language	the ESL student
the boy with a cognitive (or intellectual) disability	the mentally retarded boy
the boy who uses a wheelchair	the wheelchair boy
people with and without disabilities	disabled people and normal people

Society can place barriers in the way of people who are different, impeding their achievement and full participation. Handicap is the social or environmental consequence of difference, and it frequently amounts to exclusion. If the societal environment is inclusive, then those with differences will not have a handicap. The field of inclusive and special education is changing. Our conceptions of what constitutes difference have changed along with a shift in focus: from categorical labelling and separate education to a more responsive approach to individual students within the social context of their neighbourhood schools. The challenge is to respond positively to *all* student performances, including individual excellence, within a context that values diversity.

Key terms

Diversity. All the ways in which we are unique and different from others. Dimensions of diversity include, but are not limited to, aspects such as ethnicity, religion and spiritual beliefs, cultural orientation, colour, physical appearance, gender, sexual orientation, ability, education, age, ancestry, place of origin, marital status, family status, socio-economic circumstances, profession, language, health status, geographic location, group history, upbringing and life experiences (Calgary Board of Health, 2008).

Discrimination. Less favourable treatment or unfair exclusion on the basis of a person's difference.

Person-first language. Language that mentions the individual person first, rather than the differences that exist.

For discussion and reflection

2.1 To what extent is meeting the needs of a gifted student the same as meeting those of a student with a cognitive impairment?

2.2 Consider the media. How do they represent students from diverse backgrounds? Does this contribute to stereotyping and discrimination?

2.3 To what extent are labels helpful? Harmful?

Further reading

Katzman, L. (2003). Minority students in special and gifted education. *Harvard Educational Review*, 73(2), 225–39.

Loreman, T. (1999). *Respecting childhood.* London: Continuum.

Seigel, L.S. (1999). Issues in the definition and diagnosis of learning disabilities: A perspective on Guckenberger v. Boston University. *Journal of Learning Disabilities*, 32(4), 304–24.

3
Attitudes and inclusion

Key ideas in this chapter
- Attitudes—what they are
- Values
- Ideologies
- Facing disability
- Realistic planning

Teaching is one of the few professions that brings the professional into contact with the whole range of students aged from 5 through to 16–18 years. Since the policy of inclusive schooling, and its forerunner policies of 'integration' and 'mainstreaming' were implemented, some of those same young people who formerly would have been educated in a special facility will now have been enrolled in their local, regular school. The result is that teachers have a much wider range of students with whom to deal.

Teachers can build up expectations of behaviour within the age groups because they interact and observe them over long timespans. Other professions know how clients or patients are likely to behave only within their narrow realms of focus, but teachers are second only to parents in terms of observing students in their natural environments. Their opinions about students therefore should be both realistic and informed.

Is history repeating itself?

The policy of inclusion is in a sense a return to the original concept of universal compulsory education for all. In the state of Victoria, Australia, for example, the 1872 *Education Act* made it mandatory for all youth of a certain age to be enrolled in a school. The Act stipulated that it should be *all* children, and that education should be free, compulsory and secular. Regrettably, the Act also set out that students were to progress through the grades following an end-of-year examination on the work that was supposed to have been covered during the year. If a student failed to progress, they were held back to repeat that year, and so on until they passed. Further to be regretted was the policy that teachers would be paid according to how well they had done their job—a payment by results system. The outcome was that students with differences, especially those with issues that affected their learning, were not progressing, and teachers were becoming frustrated by the lack of progress and its consequent effects on their salaries and promotion prospects.

The Act was amended in 1874 and students who were deemed 'ineducable' could be excluded from the requirement that they attend a school. A medical doctor in Moonee Ponds, a suburb of Victoria's capital city of Melbourne, had a daughter who was included in the group who could not attend a local school. After failing to win government support, he set up a private special facility in 1881 for his daughter and other children in similar situations. Only after the success of this venture became evident did the idea of special education facilities to cater for those excluded from the normal provisions become officially accepted in Victoria—in 1907. It took almost a century to see the original concept of the importance of education for all in regular schools to be reintroduced and once again become official policy.

This increase in range confirms the fact that teachers are now likely to see more diverse range of students. This is almost unique amongst professional groups. Of the other professions, one could say that dentists see the range, but only when dental treatment is called for; GPs see the range, but only when the children are sick or injured; only teachers see the same students for significant amounts of time, five days a week.

Despite the changes in official policy, the changes in enrolment patterns in most schools have been relatively small. The majority of the population of students develop according to well-known processes and in predictable patterns. Even if there is a significant element of difference, it will often affect only part or one aspect of the person. For example, intellectual disability may affect learning and social competence but physical development is unlikely to be affected seriously. Nevertheless, two important questions need to be asked:

- What barriers are likely to prevent a teacher addressing the educational needs of the one or two students who differ significantly from the majority, and how can a teacher make sure they then progress?

- What is the key to ensuring that a teacher is comfortable or professionally secure in approaching the task of running an inclusive classroom?

The answers to these questions come back to thinking about the attitudes with which teachers approach their tasks. There is obviously a need to consider the professional aspects associated with practical organisation of the classroom, the planning of lessons, modification of curricula and the evaluation of learning (see Chapters 4, 6, 7, 8 and 9), but most important is the need to consider the attitudes of teachers towards those who are different.

Positive teacher attitudes are essential to making inclusion work (Sharma & Desai, 2002), but our attitudes are based on a number of underlying components discussed in this chapter. If we are to maintain a positive attitude ourselves, and assist others with whom we work to develop positive attitudes too, it is important to recognise and understand these components.

Attitudes

Attitudes are basic and pervasive aspects of human life. Without the concept of attitude, we would have difficulty construing and reacting to events, trying to make decisions, and making sense of our relationships with people (Vaughan & Hogg, 2002). Our attitudes are made up of the groups of feelings, likes, dislikes, behavioural intentions, thoughts, and ideas we all have about the people and things we encounter in our everyday lives. They can, however, be thought of as a threefold entity comprising thoughts, feelings, and actions. How widespread this grouping of the three aspects is in our thinking is commented on by McGuire (1989):

> The trichotomy of human experience into thought, feeling and action, although not logically compelling, is so pervasive in Indo-European thought (being found in Hellenic, Zoroastrian, and Hindu philosophy) as to suggest that it corresponds to something basic in our way of conceptualisation, perhaps . . . reflecting the three evolutionary layers of the brain: cerebral cortex, limbic system, and old brain. (1989, p. 40)

Irrespective of their source, our attitudes clearly affect our thoughts, our feelings and what we do—indeed, it could be said that they actually determine what we think, feel and do. They are relatively permanent, and the more we know about a person's attitudes the more we can predict how he or she will behave in relevant situations. Allport (1954) suggests that an attitude is basically a readiness to respond in a particular kind of way, but attitudes also are very emotional because they reflect the ways we evaluate people (including ourselves) and things. They guide us in deciding whether we like or dislike someone or something, and whether we are going to approach or avoid whatever has attracted our attention.

Attitudes are very important to us. They serve the same function as stereotyping and categorisation of people or events. They help us make sense of the world. We use them as short-cuts in helping us decide how to react to things that happen in our lives, or to people we meet, or to political questions we must answer.

Attitude-formation is a direct result of the socialisation experiences we have had since our childhood, and comes about as a result of our experiences in life, the information we have picked up from other sources or our own thinking processes. Because they are learned rather than innate, attitudes are just as amenable to change as any other learned behaviour.

Values

Underlying our attitudes is our system of values. Similar to attitudes, values are enduring beliefs about what is right, and about what principles of living ought to guide our behaviours. They exist 'in the mind' but they show themselves in the way we behave and in the way they influence our emotional responses to events.

Values are concerned with life goals rather than being beliefs about the specific things or events or people to which our attitudes relate. They refer to overriding concerns about what is right in life and play a major role in the establishment of personal goals.

Philosopher Richard Robinson (1964) argued that there are five basic values which should guide one's living: life, beauty, truth, reason, and love. Another philosopher, James Griffin (1989), suggested they should be accomplishment, autonomy, liberty, health, understanding, enjoyment, and deep personal relations. There are no universally accepted lists of values but irrespective of whether we can consciously describe them, our values serve to give a structure to the attitudes we hold.

Our values can change. Sometimes events occur that challenge the values we hold—and challenge them in such a way that we just cannot go on living in the same old way. Take the case of someone who suffers a major loss. This loss could be the death of a spouse or a child or a close friend. It could be that one loses control of a bodily function, or loses a limb, or is diagnosed with an illness that is progressive or chronically debilitating. The challenge to us as the person involved is that the value we once placed on the love and comfort of the lost one, or on being independent and healthy, is no longer applicable and we must come to terms with the newly experienced loss or absence. We feel devalued. Accepting the loss means we need to move from the *devaluating* position to one of viewing it as *non-devaluating*. This is not the same as saying we just resign ourselves to the facts, or ignore them. It means that we need to make changes to our value system.

If we take the case where we have to come to terms with significant changes to our physical systems, how can these changes come about? Let us take the example of the loss of a limb and use the fourfold analysis of value change advocated by Dembo, Leviton & Wright (1956) and outlined in Wright (1983).

First, we know that during periods of crisis one's psychological and physical resources are focused on the loss itself. This shock reaction, or period of mourning, is a time when the realisation dawns that the things we once did without thought are now denied to us. How intense these feelings are and how long they last cannot be defined, as the reactions are very personal and deep seated. The period of mourning is, however, important in that it gives time to prepare for the challenges involved in successfully managing the transition from what *was* to what *is now*.

Second, there is a need to enlarge the scope of one's values to see that what has been lost can be replaced by values which are not dependent on the use of the limb; that one's personality need not change; and that values such as kindness, wisdom, effort, and cooperativeness still apply. To achieve this aim, physique and its importance to us must be subordinated relative to other values—that is, the sense of devaluation of ourselves will diminish as personality and other aspects of personal traits become more important.

Third, there is a need to recognise that the newly acquired disability does not necessarily influence everything we do. It may be a physical fact with effects that are far-reaching, but the physical facts relate only to specific things that we can or cannot do. They do not define us, and even if they are an impediment to doing some things, these impediments may well be due to societal barriers as much as they may be due to personal limitations. If the loss means we now need a wheelchair to get around, we have to learn how to negotiate barriers that we could once ignore. Dembo et al. (1956) call this third stage 'containing disability effects'.

Fourth is a demand that we aim for a transformation of comparative status values into asset values. Comparative status values refer to those attributes of a person that are looked at, by them or others, in terms of a scale of better or worse. This means that whatever is being judged (be it beauty, physical strength or intelligence) is seen as being 'below' or 'above' a presumed standard, with the distinct possibility that perceptions of other characteristics of the person are also being judged by the same measure. Therefore, where the focus may be on appearance, there is a tendency to think that where the person is 'above' on the main characteristic—that is, 'more attractive than most'—then he or she must also be brighter, stronger, and nicer than other people. The alternative is to look at physique (or any other characteristic) not in terms of its comparative status but in terms of its usefulness or intrinsic value. The focus is on the value of the attribute, not in comparison to other people but to the person. A prosthesis or a wheelchair can be appreciated for its usefulness without inherently indicating dysfunction. Perhaps the last word on this matter should go to Shakespeare:

> In nature there's no blemish but the mind;
> None can be called deformed but the unkind:
> Virtue is beauty, but the beauteous evil
> Are empty trunks, o'erflourished by the devil.
> (*Twelfth Night, Act III, Scene 4*)

Ideologies

Just as important as values are the ideological views we hold of what life should be about and how society should be organised. Ideological statements, sometimes referred to as philosophical statements, concern the overall goals for a society or group. Two commonly opposed ideologies concern the differences between those who believe that individual freedoms override the demands required by national security irrespective of the political conditions prevailing at the time and those who do not. We can also think about the ongoing debates about private ownership versus government ownership of public services.

Policies of inclusion are related to the ideological view that schools should provide for the needs of all students, whatever the level of their ability or disability, in their communities. These issues are espoused by governments that have introduced the formal policies on which inclusion is based; however, as Foreman (2007) points out, there is no specific requirement that teachers agree with the policy, just that they must be prepared to provide for the needs of all students in their grades, irrespective of any diagnosis of 'difference'. Clearly an attitudinal system and ideology that are in sympathy with the overall aims will make for better outcomes for all concerned.

Just as important in ensuring inclusive practice works is the underlying belief that all students can learn and be taught. This is a major principle that goes right against the ideas that led to the development of special education provisions, and it places major responsibilities on schools to adjust programs to reflect its utility. Previous approaches to education included categorising students as being either educable or ineducable. Behind this system lies the implicit belief that we should not waste education on those who will not profit from our efforts. The principle that all students can learn and be taught, however, must be seen in light of what it does not say as much as in light of what it does say. The principle does not say that all students can learn at the same rate, nor in the same volumes in the same areas. In Chapter 4, on assessment, we make the point that individual differences in many areas can be identified and that these differences are likely to have some effects on how students learn. The tests that show up these individual differences do not say that learning cannot take place. They can guide teachers in determining just what should be taught and establishing the timeframes that may be needed in order to achieve acceptable levels of achievement.

Facing disability

Differences of the sort that set challenges to teachers range from the frankly obvious, as in conditions such as cerebral palsy, spina bifida, or Down syndrome, to the not so obvious, as in learning disability and some forms of intellectual disability developmental delay or giftedness. Racial differences are often more obvious than cultural differences, and differences in another type of diversity, religion, may or may not immediately be clear or important.

Although we can be—or pretend to be—blasé about any or all of the more obvious differences, it is rare for anyone to be able to approach individuals with a frankly obvious significant disability, for example, without pause. So threatening to our self-image are some forms of disability that we can find ourselves trying out any one or more of a series of strategies to deal with our very private and very personal reactions. We may even try to withdraw from interaction.

Take the following very real but uncomfortable scenario. Imagine yourself in a shopping mall in the food hall and you see a friend or reasonably close acquaintance with another person. You begin to walk towards them but suddenly notice the other person is clearly disabled and being fed by your friend. It is not a usual sight and you pause; it is not often you find an adult or adolescent being fed in public. You recall that your friend has taken on a part-time role as a carer of persons with significant disabilities. You begin to wonder whether you will go ahead and greet them. To withdraw in this way is to deny the fact of friendship, but we justify our behaviour by repressing anxious thoughts about being unfaithful to our friend. After all, we really shouldn't interrupt our friends while they are working!

You find that you cannot withdraw but must interact with the person who is with your friend. In that case, it is tempting to go overboard in one's willingness to be introduced and begin a conversation. False bonhomie, effusiveness, and over-reacting are common techniques to hide our own sense of discomfort, and we use them often. Freud called this sort of response a *reaction formation*—that is, an unconscious impulse is consciously expressed by its behavioural opposite. By such means, in Freud's view, 'I hate you' is expressed as 'I love you'. Or we might try to be jokey and look for a laugh—humour can be very close to the truth and it helps deflect our anxieties about how we should react.

Even those who have chosen to go into occupations where interaction with people with disabilities is the norm need time to build up resources and skills to be able to initiate and maintain normal personal relations. How medical students react to seeing their first cadaver in anatomy classes has been the subject of considerable research, but once they get over their initial shock they must get on with their dissections and learning (Dinsmore, Daugherty & Zeizt 2001). In this example, and in any work that involves close interaction with 'difference', the ability to get on with work is accomplished by the adoption of a professional 'distance'. The focus is placed on the task or on an aspect of the individual that prevents the ego of the professional person feeling threatened. With experience, they can cope with making the distinction between the problem and the person—a task made easier for medical professionals because of the constancy of their work.

Medical professionals, though, do not have the last say on how to interact with persons with disabilities. The Medical School at the University of Bristol in the United Kingdom introduced workshops in communication, led solely by presenters who were themselves disabled, in which students were encouraged to talk about their own experience of disability (Wells, Byton, McMullan & Birchal, 2002). The presenters covered a range of disabling conditions, including visual, speech, hearing and learning difficulties, and the direct teaching by presenters with disabilities was said by the students to have been highly valued. Their list of key teaching elements was divided into three sections: attitudes, skills and knowledge. The first topic on the list of subjects dealt with in the seminars was a consideration of the students' own attitudes, including their emotions, values and reactions to disability and persons with disabilities.

Unlike medical students, teachers are not usually accustomed to dealing with frank difference in the same way medical students must be prepared for it, although academics like Chris Forlin and Susan Carrington (Brownlee & Carrington, 2000; Carrington & Saggers, 2008; Forlin, 2003) have made important contributions in this area with pre-service teachers. Our expectations about the young people with whom we deal are that they will be essentially healthy, 'all together' and whole. That is what characterises the majority of persons found in 'normal' populations, and 'normal' populations are the basis of a teacher's regular life. But the policies of inclusive schooling mean we must be prepared to face the fact that, sooner or later, we will find that not all our students meet the standard of what previously might have been considered 'normal' criteria. It is in relation to these students that we need to consider our reactions and personal behaviours in the way we think about them.

How does one react to a frank or obvious difference?

Being brought face to face with obvious and serious difference threatens our sense of security and makes us feel anxious. Being faced with reminders of difference can lead to a desire to ignore the facts and deny the existence of the differences. Our natural reactions in life include screening out disturbing information and focusing instead on something less threatening. Whether it is because we are generally unfamiliar with how to talk with a person who is obviously different, or whether we somehow identify with the person and imagine how it would be to have, for example, the same form of difference (such as a disability), or whether there is some deeper psychological reason for our discomfort, may not be known. What is known is that it is quite common in considering persons with differences to focus on the difference as if it was the only important thing about that person. Warren (1980) comments that 'the testimony of authors writing from the perspective of disability very frequently draws attention to the fact that it is "the other" who creates significant problems; very often physical difference seems to concern the observer more than it does the subject.' (1980, p. 79)

Although these reactions may be common—perhaps even normal—they disguise the fact that we are thinking of ourselves, not of the person with the difference. Our thoughts may cover a multitude of emotions that could include pity, concern, worry, disappointment, or even revulsion, but such reactions are a *projection* of our own insecurities, not emotions the person stirs in us.

Healthy emotions are addressed to the person; they see beyond the impairment to the person (Greenway & Harvey, 1980). The impairment that causes the disability does not define the child; it defines only a part of the child. Bodenheimer (1974) describes a girl who is deaf and with a visible disability in psychotherapy and her progress towards coming to terms with the disability:

> *This fact is of principal importance to the therapeutic attitude in the situation described here. The child was able to attain distance towards*

something, *could talk about* something, *and thereby distinguish herself from* something. *This* something *always meant something that could be casually referred to as 'suffering' only until she was able to convert or transmute that which she herself was into something she* had *or* has *and would from now on and always, irrevocably and unchangeably, have and keep. The basic change lies in the fact that she now* has *it and no longer* is *it. (1974, pp. 107–8)*

This anecdote sums up the experience whereby the child was able to develop a self-image that was not dominated by the impairments, an outcome achieved by the therapist focusing on her and not her appearance. That, indeed, is the key to coping with those first reactions to obvious difference.

Go back to the earlier section in this chapter in which we introduced Dembo et al.'s (1956, p. 42) analysis of value change. That same process applies as much to an observer as it does to the person with the difference. The first reaction of an observer to frank disability is often one of shock, an affront to our expectations as we adjust our perceptions so that we are neither unreasonable nor unrealistic in terms of our expectations for this person. Second, we need to appraise the situation and avoid taking this one characteristic as an indication of all other aspects of this person. Physique, if the problem is physical, must be subordinated relative to other values that characterise this person. Third, the programming side of the teacher must take the physical status and the whole environment into account to see that impediments to learning are not due to the physical structures or systems of the school. The difference may be a fact of life, but countering its effects is the task of the teacher. Fourth, we need to look at asset values pertinent to the student and hold back on conveying to this student or the class any idea that he or she is disabled and therefore 'unabled'.

Once the student is seen as a person who is the same as others in the group, the focus moves from the difference to the person who wants to learn. The teacher's task is to find the ways whereby the things to be learned can be achieved, a task that may require modification of curriculum materials or reorganisation of the room, or whatever. The important issue is that the values underlying one's commitment to the tasks of teaching are not compromised.

Plan realistically

There is no intention here of suggesting that the way to cope with meeting difference is to deny its existence or its effects on a person's capacity to learn or interact in the social setting of the school. No good purpose will be served if the fact of the difference is denied. What is intended is that the student's needs be seen in realistic fashion without the overlay of emotional investment that will disguise the true extent of individual difference or ways in which the difference has led to a disadvantage.

Irrespective of the emotions we may experience in meeting with people with obvious differences or getting to know them well enough to see beyond superficial appearances, when it comes to making classrooms work there are two overriding attitudes that matter most. The first is the belief that all students can learn. The second is that teachers who believe they can make a difference do just that.

Key terms

Attitudes. The groups of thoughts, feelings and actions that affect how we react to individuals and to groups of people.

Ideologies. Our beliefs about what life should be and how society should be organised.

Values. What we think is right and proper and the long-term basis on which we make decisions.

For discussion and reflection

3.1   Are you uncomfortable when you encounter someone who is significantly different to you in background or personal traits? What is the source of this discomfort?

3.2   Imagine you work with a person who has a negative attitude towards a particular group of people. What, if anything, might you do to help improve the situation?

3.3   Is it necessary for all members of an educational team to share the same values and ideology when it comes to working with students from various diverse groups?

Further reading

McGuire, W.J. (1989). The structure of individual attitudes and attitude systems. In A.R. Pratkanis, S.J. Breckler & A.G. Greenwald (Eds.), *Attitude structure and function* (pp. 37–69), Hillsdale, NJ: Lawrence Erlbaum.

Vaughan, G.M. & Hogg, M.A. (2002). *Introduction to social psychology*. Sydney: Pearson Education.

4
Psychological and teacher-based assessment

Key ideas in this chapter

- Intelligence tests—what are they and what are they good for?
- Components of the most common intelligence scales for children
- Qualitative assessment
- Classroom-based assessment
- Assessment for learning
- Curriculum-based assessment
- Specific assessment tools and strategies

Assessment is part and parcel of teaching. In its broadest terms, assessment concerns the determination of whether learning has taken place, or whether further instruction is required. In the case of children with substantially differing learning needs, it is also likely to involve formal assessments of intelligence, language and neurological or motor development. Teachers need to know what to make of the different pieces of information and recommendations emanating from such assessments—information usually provided in the form of written reports, sometimes supplemented by personal communications between the teacher and the person who carried out the assessment.

From the teacher's point of view, reports vary considerably in terms of both content and quality. This wide variation is due to the different audiences writers have in mind and the different reasons for the assessments in the first place. A report by a paediatrician could have been written for another medical specialist or a general practitioner, and contain numerous terms and expressions that mean little to anyone outside those professions, yet the report could still contain information that a teacher could use.

This chapter is divided into two sections: the first deals with formal assessments, which are usually conducted by psychologists; the second is concerned with teacher-based assessment that you can use in your own classroom.

There are two questions that teachers need to ask about the individual students in their classes. They are:

1. How well are my students doing in terms of their learning—what levels of achievement have they reached?
2. What might their potential for learning be and am I helping them get anywhere near that?

In terms of testing, the first question is best answered by the administration of tests of achievement—most often tests based directly on what is being taught in the teacher's school and classroom. These tests can be very formal, or they can be informal. The formal tests may be those demanded by the overall governing body in the form of standardised tests set across all the schools within its jurisdiction, as used to happen in the United Kingdom, but which is now restricted to them being used as entry tests to UK Grammar Schools. Progressive Achievement Tests (PAT) are also given to New Zealand students at various times during their school experience. Although a stated aim of the New Zealand PATs is for them to be 'a guide in providing teachers with information they can use with identified groups of children and provide more effective instruction', their value to classroom teachers is questionable. The results are really a check on overall standards and our experience in talking with teachers is that the major interest is in seeing where their classes are in relation to the national norms, and not in any individual child's performance.

Of much more value and interest to parents and teachers are tests that are informed by or take into account individual circumstances, and not only provide information about achievement at the time but also identify ways in which teacher, student and parents, can address areas in need of further attention. The concept of national tests, with their emphasis on separating students into predetermined categories either above or below the average for the group to which they are addressed, undermines the philosophy of inclusion. Such tests do not normally serve any immediately useful purpose for classroom teachers. They show only where an individual student sits in comparison with same age, or same grade, peers but not much else; there is no information about where strengths may be and no inbuilt guidance as to where the next teaching advances should be targeted.

The second half of this chapter addresses the question of how teachers may use the information from class- and curriculum-oriented assessments to improve their teaching. This kind of assessment is commonly referred to as formative assessment, and is an integral part of good teaching.

As teachers, we need to be realistic about the achievement levels of the students in our care, and their standards in relation to their peers, but there is no circumstance when a teacher can sit back and say: 'That's it, no more to do!' The writers are all graduates of a university that has as its motto *Ancora Imparo*—a phrase attributed to Michelangelo that translates into English as 'I am still learning'. The motto is one that can be applied to many fields, and that of the profession of teaching is one to which it certainly applies. Indeed, we can with some justification paraphrase and extend the intent of the original motto to read: 'Our students, and we, always have more to learn'.

Along with the opening question about how well our students are doing comes the question that focuses attention on what the potential of individual students might be as we get to know them in our daily work. When is this question important? The answers will vary but could include one of the following situations.

Example 1: Jenny

Jenny is in her second year of secondary school but wants to do fourth-year mathematics next year. She has done very well in all her earlier schooling and is known as a very smart and very quick learner; however, her teachers are a little concerned about the sudden jump she wants to make and are worried that it might be too much for her. They agree her history suggests she can do it but also want more objective information before they will approve such a move.

Example 2: Johnny

Johnny is viewed as quite a naughty boy who exhibits behaviour problems that the teachers find quite challenging. Every now and again, however, he displays behaviours that suggest to the teachers that despite the problems he may be very bright. The concern for the teachers is that his behaviour is preventing learning and/or concentration on regular school work.

Let us look closer at Johnny and consider the question his teacher will now need to ask: Are we asking too much of Johnny? Consider the possible reasons:

1. Is Johnny intellectually capable of doing what is asked of him—that is, do we need to change our teaching styles and modify our expectations to meet his needs?
2. Has Johnny a physical or medical problem that affects his ability to sit still, or concentrate, or spend extended times on individual tasks—that is, do we need to make sure these needs are addressed in order to allow him to concentrate on the tasks we set for him?
3. Is Johnny just bored with whatever is put before him, either because he is not capable of understanding the work or can already do it?

These are all quite different questions and the achievement measures talked about above and explained later in this chapter will not help us at all. There is, however, a form of assessment that may answer these and similar questions about boys like Johnny and girls like Jenny. The form of assessment that might do these things for us are standardised tests of intelligence.

Intelligence tests: What are they and what are they good for?

Intelligence tests come in two forms. The first are group tests that are usually timed tests—that is, students are given sets of specially designed questions and asked to complete as many as they can in the specified time. There is no talk, no conversation with the examiner, and no questions can be asked of the examiner once the test has started. These tests are usually helpful in putting students into groups based on individual scores but in terms of learning much about how an individual solves problems or goes about getting tasks done, they are of no more use than group tests of achievement.

The second form of intelligence test can be useful in answering questions teachers sometimes need to ask about individual students. These are standardised, individually administered tests where a child (or adult) sits in a one-to-one relationship with an examiner and together they work through the requirements of that particular test. There are no interruptions, the focus is on the child, there is opportunity for talk and the experience can be a mutually enjoyable opportunity for a child to show what they can do on a variety of puzzles, or general knowledge questions or intrinsically interesting but challenging tasks.

There is no need for every student in the majority of classrooms to be given an individual intelligence test, but in many classes there will be some students for whom the information a test of this sort yields may be helpful. For teachers, the question is: 'What information can arise from such an administration?'

However, before considering what intelligence tests say, there are some cautions that must first be taken into account, and other aspects that might not be immediately obvious:

1. Intelligence test results are usually reported as a numerical score most often called an Intelligence Quotient or IQ, and at other times as a Standard Score. Never forget that this is just a *score* and it is not a fixed amount that will be relevant or true for ever. It is a score that was obtained at a particular time and under particular conditions. There is every chance that the same test administered on another day will yield a slightly different score. If, of course, the student has had some major upset in their home or personal life or suffered a physical injury to the head for example, then the chances of obtaining the same score are very remote. However, even if there have been no major changes to the individual's situation in all likelihood there will still be minor variations, which is why many psychologists will only report the numerical results in terms of a ten-point range—that is, if the final IQ is 105 they will report it as 100–110.

2. Intelligence tests are intrinsically linked to school learning—not totally so, but very closely associated. This should come as no surprise if one knows the history behind the development of the tests. Many of the questions they contain were developed in consultation with teachers, thus producing 'school-type' questions (Richardson, 1999).

3. Intelligence tests can reveal strengths in cognitive ability that are not immediately obvious, even to people who spend lots of time with a child (see Box 4.1).

4. Intelligence tests must be administered by persons who know what they are doing, can win the confidence and trust of the child, can work within the constraints of standardised instructions and can do so without intimidating the child. These are the reasons why only people with specific training are permitted to use IQ tests.

Box 4.1: What does an IQ tell us or not tell us?

-   An IQ does *not* tell us anything about a person's emotional state— although emotional states can and do affect performances on intelligence tests.
-   An IQ does *not* tell us anything about a person's motivation to do (or not do) well at any given task—although lack of motivation will adversely affect a person's performance on a test.

- An IQ does *not* tell us anything about how a person copes with problems in living, such as relationships, money worries, career aspirations or a host of similar factors.
- IQs indicate, relative to age, how well persons can analyse and problem-solve, how good their memories are, the extent to which they are able to exercise good judgement and how well they can deal with abstractions.
- IQs are important for teachers because the things they tell us about a person's cognitive abilities are about skills and abilities that are important in traditional school-type work.

There are a number of widely accepted, well-credentialled tests available to school psychologists, of which the Wechsler Preschool and Primary Scale of Intelligence (WPPSI), the Wechsler Intelligence Scale for Children-IV (WISC-IV) and the Wechsler Adult Intelligence Scale-IV (WAIS-IV) all yield a full-scale IQ. If the Stanford-Binet Intelligence Scale, Fourth Edition (SB-IV), the Standford-Binet Intelligence Scale, Fifth Edition (SB-V) or the Woodcock-Johnson III Test of Cognitive Abilities (WJ-III) are used, there will be the equivalent of an IQ, termed 'Standard Age Score' (see Box 4.2).

Box 4.2: Some technical, but very important, information

There are some very important technical pieces of information about intelligence tests that all teachers should appreciate and understand. The IQ is an important item, but if not properly understood it can be very misleading—indeed, it is because of its ambiguity that the SB-IV and the WJ-III no longer use it—they have replaced it with the term Standard Age Score (SAS). IQ is a term that has been in use for the past 100 years and it continues to serve the same purpose now as it did in the beginning. The mathematical equations have changed but to all intents and purposes nothing else has. An IQ is a statistical device for identifying where, on a continuum that works in two directions from a mid-point defined as 100, an individual compares with his or her same-age peers on a test of cognitive ability. The 100-point mark is the average of the population on which the test was put together and is itself based on the notion that the results of measuring most naturally occurring phenomena amongst a large population sample will plot on to a normal curve.

The normal curve

The normal curve, sometimes referred to as the bell curve (see Figure 4.1) allows us to make comparisons between people because when we know a person's score (or test result), we can know not only whether that individual is below or above the average but also how far below or above it they may be. In order for this to be true, the test norms must have been based on the results of a properly organised and selected reference group that is similar to the population with which we work. When we are sure the original population is similar to ours, then we can use the norms and compare how well our person has performed relative to others of the same age.

Most people score fairly close to the average point, with smaller numbers of scores tapering off towards the tails of the spread. How far the numbers spread can be found by calculating the standard deviation of scores from the average. Once we know this standard deviation—and in the case of intelligence tests we do—we know more accurately how far from the average an individual's IQ is.

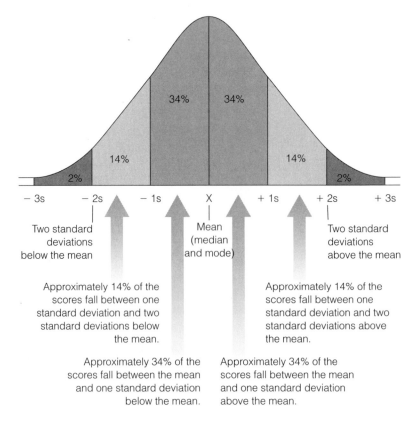

Figure 4.1 The normal (or bell-shaped) curve

Because approximately 68 per cent of the population is within the limits of one standard deviation below or above the average, 68 per cent of the population will have an IQ between 85 and 115. Approximately 14 per cent of the population will have IQs ranging from 116 to 130, with another 14 per cent having IQs ranging from 70 to 86—that is, their scores will be between one and two standard deviations from the average. The remainder of the population, approximately 4 per cent, will be found three (or more) standard deviations either below or above the average, that is, they will have IQs below 70 or above 130.

The reports sent to schools may show single-figure IQs (see Figure 4.2) but the information teachers should take most notice of is the ten-point range—for example, 95–105 rather than 100—that all reports should include. Using this range to report IQs acknowledges that the score obtained at any specific time a test is administered cannot reliably be judged as entirely accurate. If the same test were given on another day, the individual would very likely give slightly different responses, be a little slower (or faster), may be a little more tired (or alert), or may just feel better (or worse) than at the other time. These variations are natural, they are planned for, and they do not invalidate the general trends in cognitive ability that intelligence tests show.

| 0.0 | 1.0 | 2.0 | 3.0 | 4.0 | 5.0 | 6.0 |
| (− 3s) | (− 2s) | (− 1s) | (X) | (+ 1s) | (+ 2s) | (+ 3s) |

Figure 4.2 Single-figure IQ scores

Some reports may talk about 90 per cent or 95 per cent confidence intervals and explain that we can have 90 per cent or 95 per cent confidence that the true score for this person is somewhere within that ten-point range. This information, while correct, need not bother too many teachers. It is a further acknowledgement that all intelligence test results must be treated as indicators of ability, not the final word on what a person can do. The practice of not using a single-figure IQ is important because the single figure hides the fact that there is much naturally occurring variation in human performance. This lack of understanding leads many people to think that an IQ obtained at one point in their life defines their intellectual status, and many other things about them, forever afterwards. This is not so, and there are many reasons why some people's IQs will vary tremendously over time. These reasons could include differences in home life, effects of illness or neurological trauma, changes of country or changes in educational opportunities, to name just a few. An IQ needs to be interpreted in the light of many different factors.

Percentile ranks

Another item or column on the opening page of an educational report based on intelligence tests records the results in terms of percentile ranks. A percentile rank is a way of showing how well an individual has performed on the test compared with others of the same age. This way of reporting assumes that if 100 randomly chosen people from the same population and age took the test, then the result of one person reported as a percentile shows how many people in that group of 100 would score higher, and how many would have scored lower.

- If the IQ was 100, then that person would be at the 50th percentile; half the group would have scored higher and half lower.
- If the IQ was 115, he or she would be at the 84th percentile; sixteen people in the comparison age group would have scored higher and 83 would have scored lower.
- If the IQ was 85, it would be at the 16th percentile; 84 people would have scored higher and fifteen would have scored lower.

Percentile ranks reflect the fact that approximately 68 per cent of the population cluster around the average point, with the spread between scores in that cluster pushing people close together, but as the extremes are reached the distance between points on the scale becomes greater.

- An IQ of 105 is at the 63rd percentile and an IQ of 109 at the 73rd percentile, a difference of ten percentile ranks but only four IQ points.
- An IQ of 127 is at the 90th percentile and an IQ of 145+ at the 99.9th percentile, a difference of ten percentile ranks but eighteen (or more) IQ points.

IQs above 145 are all accorded a percentile rank of 99.9 or >99.9 in recognition of the fact that such high scores are quite rare. It is not normal for percentile ranks to be reported in a range but the same caveats about variation in test results still apply.

The pieces of intelligence

Since Alfred Binet's time, much research has gone into understanding and measuring the development of intelligent behaviour, and the original Binet–Simon test (see Box 4.3) has been extensively revised. Although the global or composite score is usually reported and the information can be taken as a useful indicator of overall ability, it is rarely interpreted as anything more than that. Teachers need specific information about a child's cognitive abilities in planning school activities—much more specific than is available from a single score.

Box 4.3: A little piece of history

The first intelligence test published by Alfred Binet and Theodore Simon in 1905 in Paris yielded a single-figure IQ—all that was then required. Binet's work took place at the time that universal compulsory education for all children was being introduced within the Western world. One outcome of that movement was the realisation that children did not all learn at the same rate and that schools needed to take these different patterns of learning into account. Schools at the time were not able to react to this need and selected individuals were often deemed to be incapable of learning in regular classrooms. For many, it was decreed that they needed to be catered for in special, usually institutionalised, settings.

Binet's test was devised to classify those who should be in regular schools and those who should not, in the light of educational practices of the time, be enrolled.

Binet was not just interested in keeping children out of regular schools if it seemed they could not cope with their demands—he was also concerned with ensuring that children wrongly considered ineducable were not denied the opportunity to learn. In one institution looking after the needs of 25 children in Paris, he identified five who were incorrectly diagnosed as 'idiots', the term then used to describe those with severe intellectual disabilities.

The major individualised intelligence tests give teachers four pieces of information about their student. The actual forms may vary as, for example, the Wechsler Scales yield four Index Scores—Verbal Comprehension, Perceptual Reasoning, Working Memory and Processing Speed—whereas the Stanford-Binet also offers basic scores, namely Verbal Reasoning/Knowledge, Abstract/Visual Reasoning/Visual Spatial Reasoning/Fluid Reasoning, Quantitative Reasoning and Short-term Memory/Working Memory. The four groups give teachers a comprehensive idea of what they know the student should be doing and, where there is a discrepancy between what has been shown on the

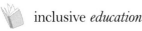

individualised test and school achievement measures, also provide some clues as to where teaching attention needs to be directed.

Verbal comprehension

This section will in most cases apply to students brought up in, or introduced at a fairly early age to, English as a primary or very important secondary language. In the cases where other languages are the prime teaching and community means of communication, then alternative items and norms must apply. It is of great importance, even in English language-based countries, that the concept of globalisation and mass movements of peoples as migrants to new countries mean that there will be few teachers in the developed countries who do not have to consider multicultural issues in their daily work. We have been into English-speaking schools that claim they have enrolled students who were either born in, or have parents who were born in, more than 40 countries or cultural groups. It is, of course, imperative that the results of any testing of students within one or more of these groups be interpreted in the light of these matters. If a student is a product of a purely English-based home culture, then the results of the Verbal Comprehension section of the test can be taken as a very good indicator of ability, allowing for strengths and shortcomings in understanding the basic culture of the student. Where needed, such results can provide a base from which an individual learning plan can be developed.

A key sub-category is vocabulary—being able to explain what a selection of words mean. The selection is quite random, but is graded in such a way that common and easily recognised words begin the test schedule, ranging up to rarely encountered words that only a few students are likely to have seen before—and then only if they have read quite widely.

A second sub-category involves the ability to reason and understand abstract concepts, as indicated by how we use words to describe natural phenomena. One of the ways in which we cope with life, and both understand and communicate ideas, is by using words that have a common and specific meaning but that also allow us to see relationships between phenomena. The basis of scientific development is that no event or thing exists in isolation; everything has its own specific identifying attributes and is also related to everything else. It is a measure of an individual's cognitive ability to be able to recognise and identify the attributes that mean something is different yet also related—the old word game of *Animal–Vegetable–Mineral* exemplifies this capacity.

A third verbal category is the ability to understand social mores and the reasons why we organise our lives as we do. It is a measure of intelligence that we can do things with knowledge of their utility in the way we organise our world. An example of this—not one that appears in any test known to the writer—could be why judges in courts wear black gowns and wigs or similar non-individualistic clothing. One reason is because the wearing of such regalia portrays the individual as fulfilling a real but non-idiosyncratic role in administering justice, and in that sense represents the state or the Crown, or a formal entity removed from personal idiosyncrasies.

The fourth category concerns the amount of information an individual has about their world. The more intelligent the person, the more they will know and the more they will know about it. This sort of information is built up over the years and can come from many sources. Things we hear, things we read, things we think out for ourselves—these all contribute to our knowledge of the world in which we live. The pieces of knowledge may be directly related to our daily life or be quite remote from it, but the popularity of quiz shows on radio and television and the availability of crosswords and other word games, are examples of the way in which we like to have information, manipulate it, and on occasion, display it. The more alert and aware an individual is, and the more efficient the memory banks that daily living builds up in our minds—often without us being aware of the process—the greater are our abilities to learn and recall what we have learned.

In most cases, the responses to the items in the Verbal Comprehension sections of an intelligence test are marked right or wrong, with little opportunity for variation. For example, in the Western world Christmas is usually celebrated on 25 December and so long as the original question specifies which country or culture is being talked about then there is only one answer. But the strength of an individualised test environment is that it also allows apparently incorrect answers to be interpreted as correct. The writer once asked a young five-year-old, 'What is a ball?' The correct answer to such a question could be that it is round, it bounces, it is used in games and other answers of that sort, but this boy gave an answer that was not listed as an example of an acceptable response. He said, 'That is where the prince chooses his wife.' Clearly this was a boy who had been brought up listening to such stories as Cinderella, and this was confirmed later by the parents, who said they had read him stories from all around the world from a young age, including standard fairy tales for children. The answer was graded correct as the boy clearly understood that a formal dance of the sort royalty put on from time to time was called a 'ball', and his response also showed a rather idiosyncratic but correct understanding of a common word that few other five-year-olds would have considered. It shows an 'out of left-field' response that in itself suggests a child whose standards of intellectual reasoning are beyond the normal.

Perceptual reasoning

These test items are of the puzzle type, and have been designed to measure non-verbal spatial or perceptual abilities in ways that are presumed to be culture-fair—that is, their solutions are dependent on perceptual skills rather than understanding of language. The tasks can be explained either by words or modelled (or mimed), with the student copying the physical behaviours rather than responding to words. The actual puzzles involve the manipulation of coloured blocks, puzzle pieces to make up a whole picture and comic strips that need to be properly organised into a coherent story or design.

In every case, the objects can be manipulated, either mentally or physically, in a manner that will allow the student to see when a correct solution has been found. The tasks must be completed within set time limits, and the student is aware that they are being timed. These sub-tests set problems of a kind not usually taught in school, but the information they convey about the attitudes of a student, or the mood at time of testing, and the ability to work within time constraints yet still concentrate on the tasks is important. They also indicate whether there are any major visual/perceptual problems that may need further investigation.

Working memory

This is a very important part of the test results. This index is concerned with the ability to deal with numbers and similar material presented orally, including the ability to manipulate the information mentally and not to be distracted by other noises, movements, or ideas. The numbers or word-based problems need to be handled sequentially, and for successful completion a student must have an adequate non-distractible attention span. The tasks involve working with numbers, such as solving mental arithmetic problems or recalling strings of numbers and repeating them in the correct order. There is a clear link between these tasks and schoolwork.

If this result is significantly lower than the other three, the most probable interpretation will be that this student is being hampered in his or her mental work by competing messages or pressures that are not part of the test activities. If this is typical of the way the student approaches schoolwork, then learning will be affected badly, concentration on the scheduled work will be minimal and the student will always be caught between the external pressures and the scheduled schoolwork. It is unlikely that schoolwork demands will prevail—what, then, will be the value of demanding more and more work when the student has problems that are affecting their ability to concentrate? Teachers in this situation need to understand the student's situation, encourage—rather than badgering the student—build on positives and concentrate on successes.

Processing speed

A key idea in learning is the concept of automaticity—that is, we do things that are common, that we are used to and that we can do without thinking—or at least without thinking too much. Learning to do things automatically is part of cognitive development—students who learn their basic mathematical times tables can solve later arithmetical problems more quickly (and accurately) than students who have not properly learned (or who have over-learned) their basic tables.

This index uses sub-tests that indicate speed of thinking and ability to process information, manipulate whatever is important about it and recall details in order to complete a task. This index is related to concentration on written tasks, an activity closely related to schoolwork. Completing these tasks is linked to the kind of attention and sense of mastery of symbolic material that a successful student needs. Failure suggests that teaching strategies aimed at improving writing speed and planning may be required.

How can all these pieces of information about a student help the class teacher?

Let us consider Johnny again. Johnny is nine years of age, his mother and father are still together and he has an older brother and a younger sister. He's a 'behaviour problem' to his teachers but not so much at home. Johnny has a Verbal Comprehension Index of 125 (range 120–130).

Qualitative assessment

Administering a standardised intelligence test is something educational psychologists do frequently. The concept of standardisation means that the test is always given in the same order, using the same instructions and the same equipment. These rules are needed in order to allow fair comparisons between people in the same age groups.

The same standardised test rules also mean the psychologists administering them are able to note the behaviours of people being tested and to assess whether, in the tester's judgement, there are behaviours that would invalidate the test results. Such observations are more than just a validation or confirmation of the test outcomes, for through making these observations the tester can learn a great deal about the personality of the client. Delaney and Hopkins (1987) describe the administration time as a clinical interview in itself, 'a conversation guided by a purpose' (1987, p. 89). The insights gained from the administration, informed by the experiences of the tester with similar-aged students, can often yield useful information that can be passed on to a teacher. Some examples of the kind of informal assessments that can be made—in this case taken from the SB–IV—include the following:

- Attention—was the student absorbed in the task or easily distracted?
- Activity levels—were they normal or overactive/hyperactive?
- Did the student initiate activity or wait to be told?
- Was the student quick to respond or was urging needed?
- Did the student appear socially confident or insecure?
- Was the student realistically self-confident or distrustful of ability?
- Was the student persistent or easily discouraged?
- Was the student needing a minimum of commendation or did they require constant encouragement?

In many cases, teachers will note the comments in a report and be able to recognise that this is exactly how the student operates in their class. Such confirmation is useful, as are any new insights the report yields. How useful these insights can be is illustrated by Delaney and Hopkins (1987):

> *while testing one child, an examiner made the important discovery that this six-year-old had obviously learned how to avoid the effort of problem solving by manipulating a question-and-answer session. The examinee's teacher later confirmed that she was so sympathetic with the examinee's inability to respond—she looked like she was trying so hard to respond—that she would go on to another child. This examiner's insight was more important to future behaviour modification than the examinee's ability score. And during the test session the examiner used this insight and refused to allow the examinee's strategy to succeed. The examiner eventually determined that the examinee's ability was substantially above that which might otherwise have been assumed. (pp. 89–90)*

Let's go back to Johnny and refresh our memory of the questions, to see what our answers may now be.

1. Is Johnny intellectually capable of doing what is asked of him—that is, do we need to change our teaching styles and modify our expectations to meet his needs?

Johnny was found to have a Verbal Comprehension Index score of 125 (range 120–130), which suggests he is very capable of doing what he is supposed to in class. Have we been too easy, too distracted, or have we allowed our attention to whether he is doing his work to wane?

2. Does Johnny have a physical or medical problem that affects his abilities to sit still, or concentrate, or spend extended times on individual tasks—that is, do we need to make sure that these needs are addressed in order to allow him to concentrate on the tasks we set for him?

Johnny's scores on the Perceptual Reasoning and Processing Speed and Working Memory Indexes, were comparable to those on the Verbal Comprehension Index, suggesting that there are no inherent physical or mental problems hindering his learning.

3. Is Johnny just bored with whatever is put before him, either because he is not capable of understanding the work or can already do it?

This is a question that can best be answered by the use of classroom-based assessments, as outlined in the next section.

Classroom-based assessment

While formal intelligence and achievement tests have their purposes and need to be understood, they often do not help teachers discover what a student already knows, and what that student needs to learn in relation to the curriculum. In order to successfully program for any student, teachers must first know the starting point from which they can teach. The best way for teachers to discover what their students know and can do is through classroom-based assessments. The most effective assessments for the classroom are often those developed by individual teachers themselves.

Assessment at the classroom level can roughly be divided into two categories. The first of these categories is assessment *of* learning. Assessment of learning takes place after learning has occurred, and attempts to quantify that learning. Examples of assessment *of* learning include assignments or classroom tests on a unit of work just completed, for the purpose of a written report for parents and assigning a mark. This might be considered to be the more traditional type of assessment. A second type of assessment is assessment *for* learning. Assessment *for* learning is an attempt to discover what a student knows or can do, and in doing so to provide a starting point for further learning. A class test or assignment might also serve the purpose of assessment for learning, providing that the teacher intends to use the results of the assessment as a basis for further teaching, rather than simply as a mechanism for assigning a grade. You will probably be familiar with the idea of formative and summative assessment. Summative assessment—that used at the end of a segment of teaching to check to see if the outcomes have been achieved—is more akin to assessment *of* learning. Formative assessment, which occurs during the instructional process, has stronger links to assessment *for* learning. Assessments *for* and *of* learning are both important, and indeed some assessment practices can serve both purposes. It is the role of a teacher to decide the purpose of any given assessment; this decision will impact the methods used to assess and the way in which the information is collected and used (Stiggins, 2008).

Gronlund and Waugh (2009) outline eight guidelines for effective student assessment as follows:

1. Effective assessment requires a clear conception of all intended learning outcomes.
2. Effective assessment requires that a variety of assessment procedures be used.
3. Effective assessment requires that the instructional relevance of the procedures be considered.
4. Effective assessment requires an adequate sample of student performance.
5. Effective assessment requires that the procedures be fair to everyone.
6. Effective assessment requires the specifications of criteria for judging successful performance.
7. Effective assessment requires feedback to students that emphasises strengths of performance and weaknesses to be corrected.
8. Effective assessment must be supported by a comprehensive grading and reporting system.

Assessment for learning (AFL)

Assessment information can be collected and used by teachers for many different purposes. Some of the ways already mentioned in this chapter include *assessment of learning*, or summative assessment, which is used for making judgements about students' achievements compared with standards for other students the same age or against curriculum goals for learning. Information gained from summative assessment is often used for reporting to parents. *Assessment for learning (AFL)*, or formative assessment, is used by teachers to understand student learning and the impact of teaching (Deppeler, 2007).

In their now-famous essay *Inside the Black Box*, Black and William (1998) summarised the results of more than 250 studies from nine years of international research. Their review article made clear the powerful impact AFL can have on student learning. They compared the use of AFL with other educational interventions and concluded that effect sizes were larger than most of those found for educational interventions and with the larger gains being realised by the low achievers (Black & William, 1998). The practical effect of these findings means that consistent use of AFL could improve student performances by between one and two grades (Black, Harrison, Lee, Marshall & William, 2003). These findings have been confirmed many times in subsequent research studies (see, for example, Meisels, Atkins-Burnett, Xue, Nicholson, Bickel & Son, 2003; OECD, 2005b; Rodriguez, 2004).

The AFL framework places the learner at the centre of the learning process. AFL promotes the idea that students should be empowered to determine their own learning, and students and teachers should work as partners in the learning processes. In order for AFL practices to be effective, teachers need to:

- believe that every student can improve
- believe that teachers and students should learn together rather than in isolation
- systematically collect and analyse evidence with purposeful aims
- review and reflect on performance and progress with students
- encourage students and peers to interact in reviewing performances and help each other to reach common understandings
- recognise that both motivation and confidence are crucial for effective learning and progress, and that these can be increased by effective AFL practices
- create a learning environment where students feel free to articulate their ideas without fear or embarrassment
- encourage and model the sharing of ideas and active listening to alternative views
- support students' learning by building cumulative successes.

AFL teaching and learning practices are designed to actively involve students in their learning and to maximise their success. The basic AFL premise is that students will improve most if they understand: (1) the specific learning goals—what they are supposed to be learning and why; (2) where they are in relation to the learning goals; and (3) how they can improve their performance to achieve the learning goals. The key AFL teaching and learning practices that emerged from Black and William's (1998) work, which effectively have been introduced by others into classrooms, are described in the following section.

Key assessment for learning practices
Sharing of learning goals and explicit success criteria

A learning goal should state clearly what it is that the student should be able to do, understand, or know as a result of participating in the learning activity. Students need to understand the difference between the learning task (what they need to do) and the learning goal (what they will learn). The learning goal and the explicit success criteria for learning outcomes should be written in a language that a student can easily understand. There are a number of ways to share learning goals and enhance students' understanding of success criteria:

- Use visual cues and wall charts as reminders of learning goals/criteria.
- Have students tell or write a learning goal at the beginning of the learning activity.
- Use rubrics—these are sets of criteria for assessing knowledge, and are the most common form of performance success measures.

Many examples of rubrics are published and freely available on education websites, along with templates and advice for designing your own. When teachers devise and use a common rubric with their students, it helps clarify what is important both the teacher and their students. Some general steps for working with other teachers to design a rubric are listed in Box 4.4.

Box 4.4: Working together to design a common rubric

1. Decide on the specific learning task and level (e.g. student writing of a narrative at Year 5).
2. Collect rubrics relevant to the agreed task—from web- and print-based educational sources.
3. List several expected qualities (from collected rubrics and teacher suggestions).
4. Collate the expected qualities.
5. As a group, discuss and check that the expected qualities are realistic and align with the curriculum learning goals.
6. Decide on the expected qualities for the rubric (e.g. audience, vocabulary, text structure, punctuation) and group into categories if necessary—for example, punctuation, paragraphing and spelling might be grouped under the category of graphic features.
7. Determine how many performance levels should be used.

8. Assign a number range for each descriptive category.
9. Write examples to describe each level (e.g. 1–4). Make sure the examples are explicit and not vague (e.g. avoid using words such as good, better and best). Write the highest and lowest performance levels first. Differences in performance levels can be based on quality, frequency, degree and/or number. For example: Spelling (1–4) Level 1: writing has more than four spelling errors of easy-to-spell words; Level 4: writing has fewer than two spelling errors of more complex words. This might be made more explicit by listing words that are considered 'easy' to spell and those that involve more complex spelling.
10. Test the rubric—teachers should individually test the rubric with students and get their feedback, making sure descriptors are meaningful and that levels are realistic.
11. As a group, compare findings and revise the rubric in light of the feedback.
12. Prepare exemplars and other resources for students and teachers to support teaching and learning.
13. Ensure revision of rubrics is ongoing, to be responsive to a changing curriculum and differing students' needs.

Using strategic questioning

Some questions are better than others when it comes to providing teachers with AFL opportunities. Changing the type of question and the way it is phrased can make a significant difference to the extent to which students are able to reveal their understanding, the language demands made on students, thought processes in which students are engaged, and the number of questions a teacher may need to make an assessment of a student's understanding. Strategic questioning can be used as a tool to:

- analyse students' responses to find out what they know, understand and can do
- identify gaps in knowledge, correct misunderstandings and provide extension work
- identify the most effective teaching/learning activities.

There are many resources available for teachers to improve questioning. Box 4.5 provides a checklist for teachers to reflect upon their own or their colleagues' questioning.

Box 4.5 Checklist: How effective is strategic questioning in the classroom?

Make a note of each time the behaviour is observed.

The teacher . . .

- Makes explicit the key purpose of questions
- Asks closed questions
- Asks open questions
- Asks questions to check students' experiences prior to learning activity
- Asks questions to check students' factual knowledge
- Asks questions that demand higher order thinking
- Asks questions to prompt student reflection on their learning during the activity
- Asks questions to prompt further responses from a student
- Asks questions in different ways
- Waits for students' response after asking a question
- Uses various strategies to allow for thinking time (e.g. *turn to your partner, think/pair/share, hands down*)
- Reacts positively to student responses
- Listens carefully to student responses
- Asks questions to check students' understanding after a learning activity
- Uses students' responses to adjust teaching
- Builds on students' responses, even if they are wrong
- Distributes questions around the class
- Encourages students to ask each other questions
- Provides alternatives for students to answer

The students . . .

- Ask questions of the teacher
- Ask questions of each other
- Ask themselves questions

Feedback

Providing effective feedback can help a student identify *how* to improve their performance. Feedback is most effective when it:

- is made clear to students that the purpose of feedback as well as the feedback itself is to help them improve

- occurs within the context of the specific learning activity
- is ongoing and a familiar part of teaching learning activities
- occurs during as well as after a learning activity
- is oral (telling and talking with the student) rather than written
- uses positive facial expressions, tone of voice and body language
- is clear and focused on the student's learning goals, not on the student
- reinforces the importance and value of a student's attempts
- confirms that what a student is doing is correct and they are on the right track
- provides information as well as appraisal
- gives the student time to reflect and an opportunity to respond
- encourages a student to ask questions to clarify understanding of their performance
- indicates that the teacher is listening to the student
- is focused on the learning strategies and approaches used to improve
- provides direction and the specific challenge for the next step in the learning
- includes sufficient help for the student to move towards independence with the task
- is flexible and changes to adapt to different student responses and learning needs
- is used to encourage and stimulate enthusiasm for learning
- is used in combination with questioning, modelling and explaining.

Peer assessment and self-assessment

Research has shown that students will achieve more if they are fully engaged in their own learning. This means that if students know what they are supposed to learn and can actively access their understanding and any areas on which they need to work, they will learn more than if they passively work through tasks with no real understanding of the learning goal or why the task might be important. Peer assessment helps students to clarify their own understanding of the learning goal and the success criteria while evaluating another student's work. Before asking students to engage in peer assessment, teachers should emphasise that peer assessment is:

- about working in partnership to help each other improve
- *not* for the purpose of comparing themselves with others
- for comparing their current performance with their own previous performance.

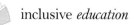

Teachers will also need to model:
- using the explicit language of the success criteria for the peer-assessment process
- respectful language and structure/s for giving feedback to evaluate student work
- active listening.

Self-assessment is a fundamental element of student learning. Once students understand how to self-assess their work performances, they can use this understanding to help themselves learn and progress. What is my learning goal? Where am I now (in relation to my goal)? What do I need to do to get there? Teachers and students work together in setting learning goals. Students then guide their own learning, with the teacher providing support as needed. Teachers can use a number of strategies to enhance and support students in self-assessment:
- exemplars—ask students to look at examples of student work that do and do not meet the success criteria. Exemplars can help students to better understand the success criteria and what is required from a task, and then to identify the next steps they need to take.
- graphic organisers
- portfolios
- reflective journals
- prompts.

Using summative tests for formative understandings

Summative tests such as those used at a national level or by school districts are often viewed as being incompatible with AFL practices. It is, however, possible to use the results of summative testing for the purpose of AFL. The process involves taking the time to analyse and discuss with your colleagues the data arising from these tests. How have students performed on the various skills that the test examined? Are there trends in the data? For example, do a higher number of students experience difficulties with aspects of writing compared with reading? Do a significant number of students do poorly on some individual test items? What do these items purport to test? You will then need to ask further questions to identify why students have performed as they have. Have students been taught the specific skills? Do students understand what the various test items are asking of them? Does the design of the test influence performances? Have students had sufficient practice with test-taking? Delving beneath the total scores in this way will help you and your colleagues to identify how best to improve learning. You might also like to think about how testing in your school has influenced teaching. Can the focus of the summative tests (skills, knowledge and understandings) be used to develop AFL strategies? You may also wish to think about ways you might use feedback from previous tests to involve students in generating questions and analysing their test responses to inform further teaching and learning.

Curriculum-based assessment

Curriculum-based assessment is one of the most effective and relevant means of assessing learning. Formal assessments such as IQ tests, while possibly helpful for providing information with respect to some possible barriers or aids to learning, have limited utility when it comes to finding out what a student knows, and providing a point from which teaching can begin. Curriculum-based assessment involves using curriculum objectives as a basis for measuring what a student is able to do. In some parts of the world, where the curriculum is highly structured and prescriptive, the task of curriculum-based assessment is made easier. In Alberta, Canada, for example, the curriculum outlines what is to be taught in each school year, and breaks the learning goals down into smaller objectives for teachers to teach. In this case, a curriculum-based assessment is made easier because a teacher simply needs to match a student's performance with the criteria outlined in the curriculum. For example, the Alberta curriculum in fine arts for Year 8 stipulates that, with respect to drawing, students will understand that 'parallel lines meeting at a vanishing point create linear perspective in two-dimensional works' (Alberta Education, 1984, Art C7). A teacher using curriculum-based assessment, then, would simply ascertain whether or not a student understands this—probably through asking the student to do a drawing with parallel lines meeting at a vanishing point, and having the student examine pictures and correctly identifying where this occurs. The teacher then 'checks the box' (so to speak) that the student understands this, and moves forward with instruction.

In other parts of the world, curriculum is more flexible and teachers have more scope to devise their own teaching goals and objectives based on contextual factors, which include culture, location, resources, and student background and development. In these instances, a teacher would need to create their own set of criteria in order to conduct a curriculum-based assessment. What you will need to do in order to conduct curriculum-based assessment will depend on your own situation and the requirements of the education authority for which you work.

Salvia and Hughes (1990) suggest eight steps when conducting curriculum-based assessments, which have been slightly modified for use here:

1. Specify reasons for decisions.
2. Analyse the curriculum.
3. Formulate measurable (specific) objectives.
4. Develop appropriate assessment procedures.
5. Collect data.
6. Summarise data.
7. Display data.
8. Interpret data and make decisions.

1. Specify reasons for decisions

Teachers should be able to justify what they do in every area in which they work, including assessment. In order to conduct a worthwhile assessment, a teacher should be able to outline why the assessment is being done, why this method has been chosen for the assessment and how the outcomes of the assessment will be used. Decisions will need to be made throughout the assessment process, and these decisions should always be justifiable in terms of their consistency with good educational practice and the classroom context in which the decisions are being made.

2. Analyse the curriculum

Whether your curriculum is highly structured and prescriptive (as in the Canadian example discussed earlier), or more at the discretion of individual schools or teachers within accepted boundaries, you will need to conduct an analysis of the curriculum you use to determine what is to be measured. This involves methodically working through any curriculum documents and identifying exactly what skills, knowledge and attributes a student is expected to have developed in order to be considered as having mastered that curriculum area or topic.

Depending on the nature of your original curriculum document, these skills, attributes and knowledge areas may need to be listed on a separate piece of paper as follows:

Example: Skills, knowledge and attributes identified from this week's mathematics curriculum topic of 'sorting'

- Students should be able to sort beads according to colour.
- Students should be able to sort beads according to shape.
- Students should be able to sort beads according to size.

- Students should be able to work out which 'odd shape' bead does not belong in a particular group of like beads.

3. Formulate measurable (specific) objectives

Salvia and Hughes (1990) refer to the formulation of 'behavioural' objectives. Their intent is to advocate for the use of objectives that are measurable—a term that we prefer. Once you have analysed the curriculum and determined what students are supposed to have learned, you can begin to set some specific objectives that you will measure. Specific objectives set the parameters for your assessment, and in some cases the curriculum is so worded as to be used without having to be reformulated into objectives by you. In this instance, you simply select the objectives you are going to measure. A good objective will tell you exactly what a student needs to demonstrate, where, when, how often, and under what conditions, in order to be considered to have mastered a skill, knowledge or attribute area.

Taking the example of the sorting activity using beads described above, the expectations for performance are relatively clear. However, even in this instance there are some questions that might be asked. For example, is a single demonstration of sorting beads in this way acceptable evidence that the student understands the concepts? Under what conditions should the student demonstrate this understanding? How many different beads and colours are involved? Other questions also come to mind, of course, and it is your job as a teacher to establish the parameters of exactly what demonstrates acceptable performance and deep understanding of a particular area of learning.

Example: A measurable objective

By the end of the week, students will have demonstrated that they can sort four different-coloured beads according to colour three times during Friday's mathematics class. Colours will be interchanged and will include red, brown, yellow, blue, white, black, green, purple, pink, and orange.

This type of objective can easily be measured. Either students demonstrate the ability to sort the beads three times on Friday, or they do not.

4. Develop appropriate assessment procedures

Once you have outlined *what* you are going to assess, you will need to decide *how* to conduct the assessment. Curriculum-based assessments generally work best when they are conducted within the natural context of classroom activities. Assessments that involve more formal types of approaches, where students are removed from the learning context, tend to be disruptive. As a general rule, students should demonstrate the acquisition of skills, knowledge or attributes in the context in which they have learned it.

Based on a qualitative research technique known as triangulation (Denzin, 1978), it has been suggested that a thorough curriculum-based assessment should involve assessment over different days using different types of measures (performance-based or otherwise) if it is to provide a true picture of student performance (Taylor, 2000). Assessment results should be verified by other evidence, and so a range of different techniques and strategies should be employed if relatively reliable conclusions are to be reached (Gronlund & Waugh, 2009). An example of the development of procedures relating to gathering assessment data for the above example of a sorting activity involving beads might be as follows:

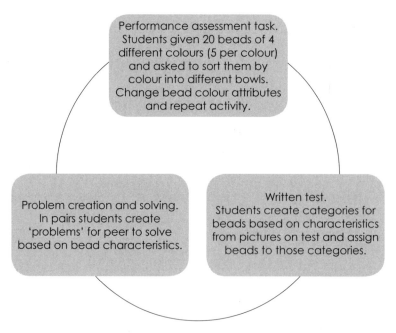

Figure 4.3 Triangulation of assessment data

Box 4.6: Classroom assessment procedures

- When conducting an activity with the whole group, ask all students to demonstrate the skill at the same time. Observe them and check off names on a checklist.
- Organise students to work in small groups. Over the course of a

lesson, visit each group and ask that it demonstrate the learning task. Keep track using a checklist.
- During time set aside for individual work, visit specific students individually at their desks and conduct the assessment.
- Ask students to submit material that demonstrates mastery of the content and/or skills you have been teaching (e.g. models, written essays, drawings, diagrams).

5. Collect data

Up to this point, your curriculum-based assessment has only involved planning. You have identified what is to be assessed, and how it might be assessed. It is now time to put this plan into action by collecting data. Data include the results of any tests or observations conducted in order to assess the performance of students. Examples of the types of data include:
- observational data based on the results of structured observations
- observational data based on anecdotal observations
- written, oral or practical classroom tests
- checklists based on sub-skills relevant to curriculum objectives
- assignments that have been submitted.

According to Deppeler (1998), observation is arguably a teacher's most important tool in planning and implementing curriculum. Regardless of whether background information on particular students is current and detailed, teachers should still undertake their own observations and/or assessment. An intervention program based on background information alone, or information collected by others, will not provide adequate information for planning curriculum. Assessment can be completely or partially based on a range of observational data.

Collecting and recording observations:
- prevents forgetting
- is not affected by previous expectations
- is useful for analysing the relationship between the learning environment and learning behaviours
- is useful for recognising changes in the type or frequency of behaviours relevant to learning
- evaluates the effectiveness of strategies and programs
- provides a basis for setting and modifying objectives and teaching approaches.

Observing a student's learning behaviour and actual performance closely as that student is involved in an activity, and 'best guessing', gives a good indication of modifications that may need to be made, or provides a clearer basis for further observation. The collection of observational data is necessary for program development and implementation, and for ongoing evaluation. It assists in identifying realistic goals that suit the learning needs of students.

6. Summarise data

Once data is collected, it is important to summarise it so that you can begin to make sense of it. Sometimes checklists may run into a number of pages (especially if they have been used for an entire class), and individual students' results will need to be extracted. Summarising the data involves the construction of very brief summaries of any observations conducted and statements reflecting overall performance against the curriculum criteria you have set for students. Some teachers use data summaries as the basis for written reporting of student progress to parents.

7. Display data

If you have collected and summarised data that can be quantified in terms of numbers or percentages (such as test scores, assignment marks or structured observation results), and have been recorded over a period of time, you may consider constructing graphs to demonstrate progress.

Example: Data display for spelling test results

Martin takes a spelling test each week based on lists of ten words with which he has made errors in his own writing. His scores for correctly spelled words can be summarised as follows: Week 1: 3/10; Week 2: 3/10; Week 3: 4/10; Week 4: 5/10; Week 5: 7/10; Week 6: 6/10; Week 7: 9/10; Week 8: 4/10; Week 9: 8/10. Martin's results might be interpreted more easily if expressed on a graph as shown in Figure 4.4. This graph clearly demonstrates an improving trend in Martin's spelling-test results over the nine-week period.

8. Interpret data and make decisions

The final stage in the process is to interpret the data and make decisions based on that interpretation. For example, if a teacher were to interpret the above spelling test results in isolation from other factors, it might be determined that Martin is making good progress on his spelling and whatever teaching methods are being used are effective. If the improvements were sustained over time, it might be determined that Martin no longer requires the extra supports

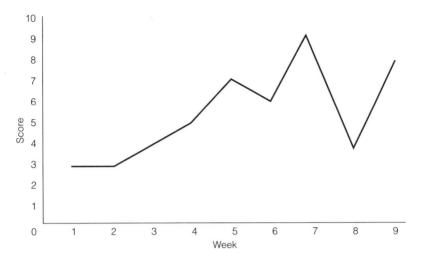

Figure 4.4 Martin's spelling test results

provided to him in order to continue to achieve the same results. Probes into Martin's spelling throughout the year—which might also include checking to see whether there is a general spelling improvement in his writing—would assist a teacher to determine whether spelling continued to be a problem or became an area of strength for Martin.

Specific assessment tools and strategies
Portfolio assessments

Portfolio assessments are an excellent tool for assisting a teacher to conduct curriculum-based assessment. Student portfolios are a simple concept and are commonly used in classrooms, especially primary-level classrooms. They are also an excellent means of demonstrating student performance and achievement at the secondary school level. A student portfolio is simply a collection of key pieces of a student's work that demonstrate progress against defined curriculum objectives.

Portfolios are useful for two main purposes. First, they provide concrete evidence for curriculum-based assessments. When, as a teacher, you are providing written reports of student progress to parents, you may cite evidence for your assessments as being present in the portfolio. They are also useful for times when you meet with parents and students to discuss progress. You can use the portfolio contents as a basis for discussion, and students can show parents examples of their work (see Box 4.7).

Box 4.7: Organising a student portfolio

Student portfolios can be organised according to:
- Chronological order
- Subject or theme
- Specific, predetermined curriculum objectives
- A combination of the above

Some teachers dislike using portfolios for assessment purposes because they view their compilation as extra work. This is true inasmuch as every activity in a classroom requires some effort. However, most students—even the very young—can take responsibility for the upkeep and maintenance of their own learning portfolios under the direction of the teacher. Exactly how much direction is required from the teacher will depend on the students (generally, younger students require more assistance in all things), but in many cases the maintenance of portfolios requires very little input from the teacher. Student portfolios should be treated with some reverence as receptacles of a child's work, and to some extent their academic identity. Further, students will be more likely to treat them with respect and keep them in good order if the teacher assigns value to the portfolios. Strategies teachers can use to ensure that portfolios are appropriately maintained include:
- helping students identify items for inclusion in their portfolio, then making the student responsible for ensuring these items are included
- having students record the contents of their portfolio on the front cover
- conducting brief sessions with the entire class (five to ten minutes) on a regular basis, during which students must update and organise their own portfolios
- conducting brief sessions with the entire class (five to ten minutes) on a regular basis during which students have their portfolios checked for organisation by peers
- using any teaching 'down time' (such as periods when students are completing individual or group activities that do not require significant teacher input) to check up on individual portfolios.

There are many different formats a portfolio can take. Student portfolios can be stored in file folders in a central classroom location, or they might be stacked in boxes (one per student). The 'look' of a portfolio is only limited by what is appropriate to meet the needs of the classroom. One element common to all portfolios should be an index. This can be located on the cover or on a separate sheet within the portfolio. The index should list:

- the date each item in the portfolio was included
- a descriptive title of each item
- a reference to the curriculum objective to which the item relates.

Although there are no limits to what type of format you can choose for portfolios in your classroom, we recommend that you stick to a single, standard format for all the students in your class. This makes maintenance of the portfolios easier (as students can peer-review portfolios), and also produces a more standard format for you to evaluate and base decisions on.

Using Gardner's 'multiple intelligences' as a framework for assessment

Gardner's (1983) 'multiple intelligences' theory is well known to most educators in schools today and, while useful, is a rather lengthy topic in its own right. The theory presents teachers with new and important ways of thinking about classroom-based assessment as an aid to guiding instruction and tracking achievement. The multiple intelligences are a set of capacities including some that have traditionally been outside the scope of most definitions of intelligence. Originally they included visual/spatial intelligence; logical/mathematical intelligence; verbal/linguistic intelligence; musical/rhythmic intelligence; bodily/kinaesthetic intelligence; intrapersonal intelligence; and interpersonal/social intelligence. Gardner (1999) later added naturalistic, existential and spiritual intelligences to this set, although these are yet to receive the same levels of attention as the original seven intelligences.

Gardner suggests that for the purposes of teaching we do not need a highly structured assessment based on the multiple intelligences, and questions the validity of many formalised, structured tests that have been devised to assess multiple intelligences. He argues that:

> For most children, unfettered exploration in a Spectrum classroom or in a children's museum is enough to give a rough-and-ready picture of their intelligences at a given moment in their lives. Nothing more is needed, and as their intelligences are likely to evolve, it is important not to place too much weight on a single profile obtained at a single moment. (Gardner, 1999, p. 137)

With Gardner's recommended 'rough-and-ready' approach in mind, how is a teacher to structure an assessment for multiple intelligences? According to Gardner, an experiment in setting up a preschool 'Spectrum classroom' produced a viable model for useful classroom-based assessment. This classroom was an area in which children were encouraged to play in centres of their choosing. Each centre was designed to encourage the children to use one or another of the multiple intelligences in order to play games, complete activities and solve problems. For example, their musical intelligence was sampled at one centre by inviting them to play with simple musical instruments and learn songs. These assessments were all carried out in their natural context (the classroom), where the children felt comfortable and at ease.

The suggestion that multiple-intelligences assessments can be informal in nature gives teachers who wish to conduct them significant latitude. Obviously, teachers must first be quite familiar with what exactly the multiple intelligences are and what they look like in terms of performance. Teachers who wish to conduct an evaluation of student strengths with respect to the various multiple intelligences could set up a variety of centres, each targeting a different intelligence. For example, a centre measuring bodily/kinaesthetic intelligence may require students to perform some kinds of sporting or dance activities needing coordination and physical skill. A centre measuring logical/ mathematical intelligence may require students to solve problems using a variety of algorithms. What is important is that each centre contains activities that relate almost solely to a single type of intelligence so that the performance of a student is not confused with his or her capacities in the other intelligence areas.

More structured, 'authentic' assessments for the multiple intelligences have been suggested by others (Bellanca, Chapman & Swarz 1994, see Box 4.8). Authentic assessments are those that replicate as closely as possible situations encountered by students in the 'real world' outside of school. Authentic assessment is seen as a hands-on and dynamic way to assess using a variety of traditional and non-traditional approaches.

Box 4.8: Authentic assessments

Bellanca et al. (1994) suggest the following types of assessment under the umbrella of 'authentic assessment':
- **Exhibits.** Using exhibits, students would research a topic then develop some kind of exhibit to demonstrate what they have learned. The most obvious of these would be a poster presentation; however, other types of exhibit can include models, artwork, computer presentations, brochures and advertisements.

- **Performances.** Students demonstrate their learning through some type of performance. They might be expected to write and perform a play, do a poetry reading, participate in a musical presentation, read a short story, produce a short film, put together a mock (or real) radio show or do a creative dance. The audience might be small groups, the entire class or groups outside of the immediate class.
- **Journals and logs.** Students keep a reflective journal that represents their learning journey. This is an excellent way for students not only to document some of the 'hard facts' about what they have learned, but also to be metacognitive and reflect on times they learned effectively and times they did not, as well as how they might improve their learning in the future. Logs and journals do not need to rely solely on the written word. They can also include pictures, audio and video recordings, and presentations on a computer.
- **Demonstrations.** Demonstrations are a particularly powerful way for students to show their learning, and can be an excellent teaching and learning tool as well as an assessment tool. A demonstration can include one student teaching another, or a whole group or class, how to do something.
- **Products.** Teachers have traditionally assessed students based on products. These products have often included essays, or objects that have been produced to demonstrate learning. Products are still a valid form of assessing, especially when used in combination with other approaches. Products can include models, artworks, books produced by students, charts, videos, audio products, textile products such as costumes, maps or computer presentations.
- **Problem-solving process.** This involves having students either solve problems or invent problems for others to solve. When assessing problem-solving, it is important to watch students as they work through the process rather than simply evaluating the finished product. Examples of problem-based assessments include having students write mystery or detective stories for others to solve, solving mathematical problems, solving problems in which they are given a scenario or historical context, or coming up with a different application for a tool.
- **Graphic organisers.** Graphic organisers can assist students to become more metacognitive about their learning. With pen and paper, they physically map out the process their learning has taken,

while outlining points where they have produced a product or developed a particular demonstrable skill. Graphic organisers not only help you to evaluate the pathways students take in their learning, but also help them to see how they learn and how they might improve their learning.

- **Projects.** Projects include the familiar teacher-set papers and tasks, but can also include student-developed research projects about a particular topic. Engaging students in projects assists you to evaluate their research skills and the ways in which they gather, select, and use information. Students may engage in internet research, sharing information with other groups of students, preparing and using surveys, or creating a community group, structure, or event.

Anecdotal assessment

When used judiciously along with other forms of assessment, anecdotal information can be an important component in the development of an overall picture of student needs, strengths, interests and motivations. Here we are not only referring to students with different learning needs: this approach, like all others in this chapter, is applicable to all students. Anecdotal information in the context in which it is referred to here includes information gained from informal discussions with an individual student, his or her peers, past teachers, family members and other school staff. It also includes any notes you take down in class on an ad hoc basis, informal rating scales and checklists.

Interviewing parents

As discussed previously, parents are an essential source of information when conducting assessments, and much of the information teachers gather from parents falls into the 'anecdotal' category. This includes comments made by parents, either verbally or through notes sent in to school.

It is important that you develop a good relationship with parents, as they can be an excellent source of both information and support at the school. Collaboration is the key. The flow of information needs to be two way. Not only can parents provide you with valuable information, but you can do the same for them, offering them an insight into their child's progress at school. Your relationship with parents should begin as early as possible in the school year (or before), and ideally will be friendly, empathetic and productive.

The following list of questions, which may be helpful to you in gaining a deeper understanding of a student when speaking with parents, has been selected and modified from a list suggested by Spinelli (2002).

- What are your child's strengths and need areas?
- What are your child's special talents?
- What motivates your child? What are his/her interests?
- Does your child like school?
- Does your child have any particular fears or worries?
- Does your child have many friends? What are they like?
- How does your child relate to teachers?
- Does your child become involved in group activities or does he/she prefer to work alone?
- Does your child take responsibility for completing tasks?
- What is your child's educational background (schools attended, contexts, etc.)?
- What are your goals for your child this year?
- Is there anything else I should know or any other information I should have?
- What information can I provide to you both now and on an ongoing basis? How can I help you this year?

While these questions can be used as a guide, do not feel limited to them, and omit those that have little value in your own learning context. You want an interview that stays on topic and concentrates on as little extraneous information as possible. This does not mean, however, that the conversation should not digress from the topics you have listed for discussion. There may be more important topics parents wish to discuss that you have not thought of. Any digressions, however, should be focused on the purpose of the meeting, which is to share information about the student. All information from parents, however informal, should be treated with the utmost confidentiality, even amongst other school staff with whom you work. If you wish to share some of this anecdotal information with others, you must first seek permission from the parents to do so.

When interviewing parents, be sure to do so in a place where they feel comfortable, such as a welcoming area in the school. Provide refreshments such as coffee and tea, and make every effort to keep the atmosphere light and informal. Fostering this type of atmosphere should help to elicit better responses to your questions, and it also shows parents that they are regarded as important members of the school, and your classroom, community.

Interviewing students

Eliciting helpful responses from students in interviews can require significant skill. Most teachers have already developed this skill through their past interactions with students, and if a student has attended your school in previous years you are likely to already have developed some form of relationship (even if it is only a face and name recognition), which will assist in making the student feel comfortable in an interview situation.

Interviews with students of any age are best kept informal. You are after candid and honest responses, not the responses students think you want to hear, and the best environment for producing these responses is a casual and relaxed one in which students feel free to speak their mind. With this in mind, any interviews should take place in areas familiar to the student, such as the classroom, school library, gymnasium, or outside on a sporting field or playground. Places that are generally 'out of bounds', such as staffrooms, staff offices and parent rooms, are best avoided. Interviews should be held privately, but all teachers need to be aware of the possible ramifications of being alone in a room with a student.

You may wish to use similar questions to those you used when interviewing the student's parent, but rephrased so as to be appropriate. The following list could serve as a useful starting point.

- What are your strengths? What areas do you sometimes need help with?
- What are your special talents?
- What helps you to want to get your work done at school? What are your interests?
- Do you like school?
- Do you have any particular fears or worries?
- Do you have many friends? What sorts of things do you do with them?
- Do you generally get along with teachers?
- Do you like to work alone or in groups?
- Who is responsible for making sure you get your schoolwork done?
- Tell me about your last school.
- What do you want to learn this year?
- Is there anything else you want to say?
- How can I help you this year?

Interviewing school staff

In many respects, interviewing your colleagues at school should be one of the easiest assessment tasks to conduct. As you probably already know the staff you want to interview, an informal and comfortable situation can be set up in a neutral area in the school, such as the staff lounge or work room. The next chapter is devoted to collaborating with your colleagues; the basic principles of collaboration therefore need not be discussed here. It is enough to say that in most cases your relationship with your colleagues should be warm and professional, and if this is the case then conducting an interview should be a simple matter of taking the time to have a chat.

You will probably want to interview key members of staff, such as previous teachers or support staff. Other staff who have spent more limited time with students in your class may also be interviewed at your discretion if you think the information you gain will justify the time you spend. School staff will doubtless be able to provide you with some 'hard data', such as test results or work samples. This is useful information to have. In addition, you may want to conduct an interview using similar questions to the ones used for parents and students.

- What are the strengths and need areas in this class?
- What are the special talents evident in this class?
- What motivates the students? What are their interests?
- Do the students seem to like school? Who does/does not?
- Do any students seem to have any particular fears or worries?
- Are they used to being involved in group activities?
- Does the child take responsibility for completing tasks?
- What goals could we continue with this year?
- Is there anything else I should know or any other information I should have?

Analysis of your interviews

Once you have conducted your interviews, you can compare the responses using a qualitative-research technique known as triangulation (Denzin, 1978; Lincoln & Guba, 1985). Triangulation involves comparing multiple sources of information and analysing the similarities and differences to give you a more comprehensive view of the subject. Interview data of the nature described above can most easily be triangulated using Form 1 in Useful Forms. It can be copied and modified to record and analyse your own interview responses.

This chapter has examined psychological and classroom-based types of assessment. We hope that the section on psychological assessments has helped you to better understand and interpret any of these formal reports that you might come across. We also hope that the section on classroom-based assessment has given you some ideas on which to base your own assessments and educational decisions. The following chapter deals with collaboration—an essential element of good inclusive practice.

Key terms

Assessment. The determination of whether learning has taken place and/or what further instruction is required.

Curriculum-based assessment. Using curriculum objectives as a basis for measuring what a student is able to do.

IQ. A statistical device for identifying where, on a continuum that works in two directions from a mid-point defined as 100, an individual compares with their same-age peers on a cognitive ability test.

Percentile rank. A way of showing how well an individual has performed on the test compared with others of the same age.

Portfolio assessment. A collection of key pieces of a student's work that demonstrate progress against defined curriculum objectives.

For discussion and reflection

4.1 How are psychological assessments useful to a classroom teacher?

4.2 How can curriculum-based assessments be infused into your daily instructional routine?

4.3 When is assessment for learning appropriate? When is assessment of learning appropriate? What types of assessment serve both purposes?

Further reading

Assessment is for Learning Programme: A national initiative. Available from <www.ltscotland.org.uk/assess>.

Assessment Reform Group, <http://k1.ioe.ac.uk/tlrp/arg>.

Association for Achievement and Improvement through Assessment (AAIA), <www.aaia.org.uk/assessment/assARG.asp>.

Assessment for Learning (AFL): Whole schools training materials. Available from <http://nationalstrategies.standards.dcsf.gov.uk/node/97905>.

Gardner, H. (1999). *Intelligence reframed: Multiple intelligences for the 21st century.* New York: Basic Books.

Gronlund, N.E. & Waugh, C.K. (2009). *Assessment of student achievement* (9th ed.). Upper Saddle River, NJ: Pearson.

5
Collaboration

Key ideas in this chapter

- Professional learning community (PLC)
- Engaging in collaborative inquiry
- Enhancing collaborative discussion
- Collaboration with the wider school community
- Collaboration within the inclusive classroom
- Collaboration with families
- Collaboration with students

> *If everyone is moving forward together, then* success *takes care of itself.*
> —Henry Ford

Inclusive schools regard diversity as a valuable asset that contributes to the social capital and richness of the school community. Democratic processes of representation and collaboration are essential for understanding and incorporating diverse perspectives, and for generating innovative solutions to the unique challenges in schools. Genuine collaboration depends on environments in which teachers work together and with others in the school community to reflect on, analyse, debate and discuss to build upon the collective knowledge and develop practices in their school. The school community includes a range of stakeholders (e.g. students, teachers, leaders, parents, professionals, business owners, policy-makers and educational administrators), all of whom have different perspectives, needs and expectations of the school. Representation in inclusive schools means ensuring all the voices involved in the community are heard. The views and active involvement of every member of the community are valued and important for building shared understanding. This means finding ways to collaborate that involve teachers, parents, and the students themselves, along with support staff and other professionals. This chapter describes some processes that we hope will develop and enhance collaboration, inquiry and sharing of professional knowledge and practices, and that actively support the learning and success of *all.*

Professional learning community
Teachers and teaching matters

In inclusive schools, teachers, students, families, and members of the wider community work together to improve teaching and learning for everyone in the school. Teaching and teacher quality are critical and have an important influence on student learning and the equity of student outcomes. The OECD (2005b) states that:

> It is clear there is not a single set of teacher attributes and behaviours that is universally effective for all types of students and learning environments, especially when schooling varies in many important regards across different countries. (p. 89)

In countries such as Australia, Canada, Finland, France, Israel, New Zealand, Scotland, Sweden and the United States, the quality of teaching has had a substantial impact on students' learning outcomes (Timperley & Alton-Lee, 2008). It seems that if we are to improve the quality of schooling for all, we must improve the quality of teaching. Knowing how to teach has positive effects on student learning (OECD, 2005a) and contributes to improving the equity of student outcomes (Field, Kuzcera & Pont, 2007). However, building the professional knowledge and practices of individual teachers is unlikely to produce sufficient changes to improve student outcomes across a school. Improving the quality of schooling for all will require changes in the collective professional knowledge and practices of teachers who are connected with their school. Programs that encourage teacher collaboration are considered an effective means of improving the quality of teaching (OECD, 2005b). Collaboration supports teachers and leaders to examine the impact of 'new' pedagogy and professional knowledge on student learning in light of the unique understandings and practices in their particular school. In this way, professional learning (PL) has become something teachers and leaders do together as an integral and continuous part of their self-improving work in a professional learning community (PLC) (Dufour, Dufour & Eaker, 2008; Stoll et al., 2006).

Professional learning communities (PLCs) are increasingly popular as a structure for enabling collaboration and for creating a culture of inquiry where systematic investigation and critical reflection are the norm and where everyone participates—teachers, students, parents and other professionals.

A professional learning community is an inclusive group of people, moti-
vated by a shared learning vision, who support and work with each other,
finding ways, inside and outside their immediate community, to enquire
on their practice and together learn new and better approaches that will
enhance all pupils' learning. (Stoll et al., 2006)

Teachers and leaders work together, as well as with parents and students, education and health professionals and other members of the wider school community, to study and improve inclusive practice. What makes a PLC approach valuable for inclusive practice? Well-documented research shows that teaching, learning and educational outcomes for students greatly improve when everyone works together to collaboratively search for and solve problems in their schools (Ainscow & Kaplan, 2005; Ainscow, Muijs & West, 2006; Deppeler, 2006). An effective PLC has the capacity to reduce isolation by supporting everyone to be informed and committed, and by promoting and sustaining the learning of all members of the school community. Many characteristics of an effective PLC (see Box 5.1) are synonymous with inclusive education environments that have a collective focus and shared responsibility for enhancing student learning. Evidence informed processes enable members to critically review practices and generate innovative solutions. Openness, trust, respect and mutual understandings are fundamental requirements for the process and the collaborative learning culture. A PLC depends upon the support and active engagement of the leaders in the school. Leadership supports and contributes to organisational learning through PLC, which in turn influences teacher work and then student outcomes (Mulford, 2008). Professionals outside schools also play important roles in working in partnership with the PLC. The PLC strategy provides members of a school community with opportunities to reach beyond their current practice and to strengthen teaching and learning for diverse students. Resources and practical strategies for creating, building and sustaining an effective PLC in your school are listed in the Further Reading section of this chapter.

Box 5.1: Characteristics of an effective PLC

- Shared values and vision are understood by all members
- Focus is on effective teaching for student learning and equity
- High expectations for *all* students
- Shared responsibility for student learning
- Culture of openness, trust and respect

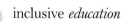

- Leadership is distributed across the school
- Contributions are made by support professionals, parents and others from the wider school community
- Student voices are heard and their input is valued
- Inquiry is valued and evidence is used to inform and improve teaching and learning
- Risk-taking, innovation and professional learning are promoted
- Organisational structures and resources are used to support collaboration
- Sharing critical reflections and practices is common.

Building PLCs holds much promise as a structure for members of the school community to work together to achieve their collective purpose of enhancing student learning. However, realising this means finding real ways to collaborate that involve teachers, parents, and the students themselves, along with support staff and other professionals.

Stoll et al. (2006) encourage teachers to think creatively about how to make the best use of space to promote PLC. How might tables and seating be arranged? Where can food, drink, wall displays and notices be placed? Consider the following examples of reorganising spaces in schools to facilitate professional conversations:

- Combine smaller rooms into larger, shared classrooms where early childhood teachers and support staff can work together and observe one another.
- Remove classroom doors to make primary classrooms into subject specialist bases.
- Use corridor spaces for shared work areas to support team teaching of mixed Year 4, 5 and 6 classes.
- Use the staffroom for daily briefing sessions that include sharing an item of professional learning.
- Create shared work rooms or offices in secondary schools that are physically close to one another.
- Place the coffee machine near the door of a subject department office to encourage conversation among teachers from other departments.

Building professional learning communities holds much promise as a structure for members of the school community to work together to achieve their collective purpose of enhancing student learning. PL communities create real ways of sharing knowledge and practices with others inside and outside the immediate school community. When collaboration involves systematic researching of practice (inquiry), it generates professional knowledge, which is essential for improving teaching quality and enhancing learning.

Collaborative inquiry

Systematic examination of evidence about teaching and learning (inquiry) shows that it is a powerful vehicle for generating collective professional knowledge that informs and improves teaching and learning. Many education systems throughout the world are currently involved in educational reform that is specifically focused on improving the learning outcomes of all students. Accountability, a central feature of reform, requires that schools achieve high standards for all students and demonstrate evidence of progress. Practical inquiry is a powerful approach for empowering teachers and leaders to understand what is working in their context and for demonstrating the effectiveness of their practices in improving student learning (Deppeler, 2007; Groundwater-Smith & Dadds, 2004; Timperley & Robinson, 2001). In the past, teachers and leaders have used their tacit knowledge gained from experience to make decisions about students and schools. Collected evidence played almost no part in these decisions. Although evidence and practical inquiry are relatively new dimensions of teachers' and leaders' work, many professional educators have demonstrated that they can become capable and confident in this area. For some, evidence and inquiry have become an integral part of their work as they plan and implement changes in schools. During the OISE/UT study of the implementation of the National Literacy and Numeracy Strategies in England, Lorna Earl and colleagues (Earl, Watson, Levin, Leithwood & Fullan, 2003), found that many teachers and leaders talked about how they were using evidence to inform their decisions. Similarly, the Project for Enhancing Effective Learning (PEEL) and Perspectives and Voice of the Teacher (PAVOT) projects have been systematically investigating their practice to better understand how they might enhance students' learning (Loughran, Mitchell & Mitchell, 2002). The effects of engaging in inquiry changed teachers' practices and their ability to articulate and share their practice with others.

However, if inquiry is to make sustained changes and impact upon school-wide changes in inclusive practice, it will need to involve collaboration. Collaboration focused on collaborative inquiry (CI) refers to repeated cycles of action research conducted by a group as its members attempt to understand an issue or question of importance to the school community.

Collaborative Inquiry

Action Research　　　**Critical Reflection**

Changing Practice

Figure 5.1 Collaborative inquiry: Working together in repeated cycles of research, reflection and change

CI creates opportunities for a PLC to collect evidence, critically analyse schooling and share practices (Stoll & Louis, 2007). The CI process clarifies and generates knowledge as part of the processes of problem-solving and improving practice. Working together in school-based inquiry, teachers can identify and address the specific circumstances in their schools that may support or impede their reform efforts (West, M.; Ainscow, M. & Stanford, J., 2005). Collaborative discussion focused on evidence has been shown to be particularly effective for identifying and influencing teacher beliefs about students and learning about practices (Deppeler, 2007; Groundwater-Smith & Dadds, 2004; Timperley & Robinson, 2001). For example, in the Learning Improves in Networking Communities (LINC) projects in Australian Catholic schools (2001–05), teachers provided evidence that the improvement in the learning of the lower performing students was a direct consequence of changes they had made to their teaching. Teachers emphasised that the CI processes changed 'not only what they noticed but how they interpreted events', which then raised their expectations for some students (Deppeler, 2007, p. 81). When teachers collaborate in inquiry, they can deepen their understanding of pedagogy and build confidence in their authority to voice arguments and influence change (Deppeler, in press).

There is little doubt that research inquiry developed by teachers and leaders in their own contexts will have the most immediate impact on improving practice in inclusive schools. Supporting teachers and leaders to develop research inquiry will require a PLC, and may be improved through collaboration with universities and other professionals outside the school. In summary, if schools are to make changes that will lead to improvements in student outcomes, their leaders and teachers will need to agree on the need to change what they are doing, critically examine their existing approaches, and be willing to take collective responsibility and put in the time to try out and evaluate new processes. This will mean that leaders and teachers will need to develop skills of collaboration and inquiry, and create a culture in their school community that emphasises collective responsibility for student learning embedded within deep pedagogic principles. Many of the assessment for learning (AFL) strategies outlined in Chapter 4, along with other observation techniques, are basic tools of inquiry. Box 5.2 provides some general guidance and a step-by-step process for introducing collaborative inquiry into your school. The following sections offer more specific advice on enhancing these collaborative processes.

Box 5.2: Collaborative inquiry for school change

Step 1: *Identify a need, improvement priority* or opportunity for change.

Step 2: *Establish a team* to model and lead the CI process and to build PLC, support and readiness for school change. Ask for volunteers and attempt to ensure that membership reflects a range of perspectives relevant to the issue (e.g. teachers in leadership positions, experienced and novice teachers and, where relevant, other stakeholders in the school).

Step 3: *Build commitment.* Clarify the roles of team members in the change process and communicate the priority for change to stakeholders in the school who can influence, or who will directly be affected by, any changes.

Step 4: Schedule *time and spaces* for gathering evidence, for collaborative discussions and for communicating the work.

Step 5: *Audit your practice.* Gather evidence and information about your current practices and the school environment. Evidence can include a wide range of material including, for example, the school's performance on standard measures, and compared with like schools; teacher assessment tasks; policy documents; observations of classroom practice; student work samples; interviews with students and parents; and attendance records.

Step 6: *Analyse evidence.* Working together, analyse collected evidence discussing and debating implications and issues. Capitalise on different members' strengths and expertise in your examination of evidence. For example, some teachers may be more confident or competent with quantitative evidence or have expertise in a particular curriculum area. Balance the need for consensus with timely decision-making.

Step 7: *Use results.* You may or may not need to refine your priority for change in light of your findings. You will now need to decide on an action plan—ask one or two research questions, determine how you will gather evidence to answer questions, plan for the action.

Step 8: *Plan and implement action.* Select strategies for change. You may first need to include a process to skill key teachers in the evidence-gathering processes or in using the specific pedagogy. Before implementing your strategy for change (action), you will also need to plan for how you will manage and respond to resistance and keep teachers focused on the improvement priority, and finally how you will share evidence and outcomes.

Step 9: *Assess progress.* Use findings to evaluate and learn from successes and from errors, make needed adjustments to improve practices or to refine priorities for change, and identify opportunities for further development.

Step 10: *Celebrate successes and communicate findings* to school community. Identify ways to integrate changes or to extend practices as part of the school culture.

Step 11: *Maintain and sustain CI* as an integral part of school culture and professional learning by providing the support, time and resources for both *collaboration and inquiry.*

The CI process may involve several cycles of action research before progress towards the priority for change is evident. The cycles are likely to involve resistance, be bumpy rather than smooth, and will probably raise more questions and issues than they provide answers. Most importantly, CI empowers those who are directly connected with the issues to construct solutions for themselves. The key to success is to go slowly and ensure that you articulate and communicate change as you proceed. Don't allow organisational structures or resistance to dominate or block progress. You may need to celebrate short-term successes to maintain momentum. Most of us who have engaged with CI would agree that the journey is well worth the effort.

Teacher reflection and collaborative discussion

I think a major act of leadership right now, call it a radical act, is to create the places and processes so people can actually learn together, using our experiences. (Margaret Wheatley)

Implicit in the notion of collaboration in a PLC community is a commitment to sharing and improving pedagogical practice. Historically, teachers have often worked in isolation. In developing their practice, they generally worked independently, reflecting on what did and did not work for the students in their classroom. Expert teachers may have made the highly complex processes of teaching and learning seem easy, but the knowledge and skills that they had developed were not made available for their colleagues to examine. This professional knowledge is often described as *tacit,* because it is embedded in teacher's practice without being articulated clearly. An effective PLC creates opportunities for teachers to share knowledge and skills and for professional learning to take place. Collaboratively, teachers articulate their teaching practices and make them clear and explicit. Collaborative discussion helps to clarify beliefs and values, as well as professional understanding, and supports teachers to move from a personal focus of practice to broader educational issues and shared purposes.

Observation of teaching in classrooms is common and essential for building collective professional knowledge. Teachers must trust one another so that they open their classrooms, observe each other and share their practices. Observation is not done to judge or to evaluate teachers. Observation of teaching and students' responses to pedagogy is for the purpose of improving and learning about practice. Teachers observe each other in classrooms, collect evidence (often on a specific aspect of teaching or learning) and then discuss their reflections about the collected evidence with their colleagues. These collaborative conversations are a constructive and integral part of improving teaching and student learning, and building professional knowledge.

Making practice available for others to examine and discuss can, however, pose challenges for some teachers, and will not always be a comfortable process. Discussion protocols are particularly useful for supporting teachers to have professional conversations in respectful and productive ways. Teacher moderation and other protocols (see Box 5.3) structure collaborative discussion processes, enabling teachers to voice, listen with respect to and accept different perspectives. These valuable tools enhance engagement, and help in building trust and the relationships necessary for shared decision-making. Protocols can also be used to guide observations of teaching and to support professional conversations about pedagogy, which is the art and science of being a teacher. It includes the range of strategies an effective teacher uses and the relationship between teaching and learning. Using protocols, teachers can develop a common language to discuss and understand the effectiveness of their pedagogy (Deppeler, 2007). Over time, collaborative discussion supports teachers to align their pedagogical practices more closely and to improve the school's collective ability to help every student succeed. Teacher moderation and an example of a protocol for collaborative discussion are provided in the following sections.

Box 5.3: Protocol for collaborative discussion

This protocol is designed for teachers who wish to share and critically reflect upon their practice. The process is intended to enhance collaborative discussion about teaching and learning, and should take approximately 30 to 40 minutes.

Step 1: **Invitation.** Invite four or five colleagues with a range of perspectives or with specific expertise to participate in the session. With practice, teachers can become skilled in using these processes so it is helpful to include both skilled and novice teachers in the session. As a group, read and discuss each of the steps below. It is best to practise steps with one another before first using the process.

Step 2: **Presentation** (10 minutes). You should present a brief description of one of the following: (1) teaching practice including the intended outcomes, how it is planned to work and why, along with any questions you would like answered; (2) a teaching challenge or you may wish to present some collected evidence (observations, student work samples, video or testing data) and any questions you would like answered. Note that if there is extensive data, you may wish to provide this to colleagues prior to the session and allow more time for collaborative analysis of the materials.

Step 3: **Clarification** (5 minutes). Teachers have a few minutes to ask clarifying questions about your presentation. This is to ensure everyone clearly understands the practice or issue and the reasons for your presentation. Examples: *How was this evidence collected and why? If you do this and then this happens what will you then do? What do you expect to happen? What happened before this? What did the student say?* Teachers should not ask questions that evaluate or judge the practice—for example, *Why didn't you try this?*

Step 4: **Reflection** (3–5 minutes). Teachers individually reflect on what feedback they will contribute.

Step 5: **Feedback** (5 minutes). You now listen and take notes as teachers provide critical feedback on your presentation. Teachers should firstly provide *positive* statements and comments that let you know what they believe is working well and what seems to be effective. Next teachers should provide statements or questions that *improve* the practice or *move forward*. These statements should not be negative but should critique the practice in a way that will support and improve the practice itself or the context within which the work was done. This feedback is *not* personal criticism and should *never* be about you personally or professionally. Feedback should only be focused on the presented material—the practice, or the evidence or the issues or problems that you have presented to be collaboratively examined and discussed. *What if?* or *I wonder what would happen if . . .* questions are more helpful in providing feedback to colleagues than *you shouldn't* or *don't do* statements. Teachers should monitor feedback to ensure there is a balance between positive and more critical comments that attempt to improve or move forward. Little will be gained from the process if teachers contribute nothing but praise, and mutual trust and collaborative relationships will be destroyed if there is personal criticism.

Step 6: **Response** (2–3 minutes). You now have the opportunity to reflect on the feedback and the issues raised, and ask any questions or make comments. Your colleagues remain silent.

Step 7: **Brainstorming solutions and next steps** (5–10 minutes). Teachers can now brainstorm possible solutions, answer the questions posed, or make suggestions for next steps. Depending on what was presented this may involve suggestions for further observation in classrooms or may involve trying an alternative practice or collection of further evidence. For example, teachers might suggest ways in which the feedback could be used to modify the practice.

Step 8: **Evaluation** (5 minutes). Everyone engages in more general discussion of the content for the session as well as how well they felt the process worked. For example, teachers might reveal any insights they have gained regarding their own practice or the presenter may share reflections on how the feedback or discussion moved practice forward.

Teacher moderation

Teacher moderation is another collaborative process that involves teachers in the examination and discussion of student work based on predetermined assessment criteria. In Chapter 4, our discussion of assessment and the work of Black and William (1998) made clear the powerful impact effective assessment can have for improving student learning. An assessment for learning (AFL) framework includes the sharing of learning goals and explicit success criteria with students, and the provision of feedback about their performance in relation to the success criteria. It is therefore important for teachers to be consistent with one another in providing feedback to students. Moderation is a valuable strategy that allows teachers to compare their judgements of student work and align their understandings of the assessment criteria they are using. The shared examination and discussion of student work are often structured with a pedagogic focus. For example, teachers might moderate a piece of persuasive writing using the assessment rubric. The most powerful benefit of moderation is the discussion that arises as a result of the examination of student work. When teachers use moderation, they often find they have different interpretations of the same work and may need to debate their various understandings of the learning intentions. This process helps to deepen understanding of what students are or are not learning, and to identify which practices are working most effectively. It challenges teachers to examine their beliefs about what students can and cannot do. When collaborative critical reflection and discussion are focused on the same students' work over time, teachers can have insights about their teaching strengths and then set goals to improve their practice.

> *When teachers work together to consider the work students have produced, or listen to their presentations or analyse their electronic projects and so*

on, they bring the collective wisdom of all the people in the group to the exercise. More eyes (and consequently more brains) result in more reliable determinations of what students understand. (Earl, 2004, p. 41)

Once teachers see that their assessment practices are closely aligned, they can feel confident about individually assessing students' work. However, when included as a routine practice, moderation will develop collective knowledge, common language and the consistent use of assessment criteria throughout the school. Moderation is an effective tool for improving teaching and student learning. For the step-by-step processes to structure moderation sessions, see the references listed in the Further Reading section at the end of this chapter.

Enhancing collaborative discussion

Encouraging teachers and others to express their ideas and opinions may, in some cases, be very different from a school's usual operational style. Despite the use of protocols for enhancing collaborative discussion, some individuals may remain uncomfortable with these processes. Teachers can be forced to meet, but genuine discussion will only occur if teachers collaborate voluntarily. Collaborative discussion processes will work most effectively when teachers feel free to voice their ideas, beliefs, knowledge and insights, and expect to argue their positions and engage in debate. Collaborative discussion will not be effective if teachers fail to ask critical questions or voice opinions because they may risk damaging working relationships or because of fear of reprisal. Nor will collaborative discussion be productive if it occurs without debate. Critical questioning, comment, and professional argument are vital to shape and deepen collective understanding. Debate must be viewed as a necessary and productive component for improving practice and student success, and needs to be embedded in school culture. CI has advantages for confronting competing perspectives because it involves teachers in articulating assumptions that arise from the critical examination of evidence. Every teacher should feel able and interested to actively contribute and influence collaborative discussion. The key is to ensure collaborative discussion is conducted professionally. The ultimate goal of engaging in collaborative discussion is to heighten critical reflection and expand professional learning to benefit teaching and student learning. Box 5.4 provides some suggestions for enhancing these processes. While these suggestions are most likely to be in relation to teachers' collaborative discussions, they are relevant to, and apply to, collaborative discussions that include any member of the school community.

Box 5.4: Twenty ways to make collaborative discussion more effective

1. Start and finish discussion sessions on time.
2. Arrange seating in a circle so that no one person is seated in a position of authority.
3. Emphasise that decisions are to be made collaboratively and that the process is as important as any of the decisions taken as a part of that process.
4. Promote contributions from all members and parity so that all contributions are considered equal, regardless of position in the school.
5. Make the specific purpose and common goal/s for the session clear at the outset.
6. Ensure all resources to achieve common goals are available to all members.
7. Model and practise respectful listening and trust.
8. Focus discussion and decision-making on improving student learning.
9. Be willing to share ideas, experiences, reflections and practices.
10. Be open to listening to the ideas, critique and knowledge of others.
11. Bring collected evidence and/or student work to the session.
12. Use inquiry to check out differing claims.
13. Ask critical questions based on analysis of evidence.
14. Ask critical questions based on principles of AFL. How will you give feedback to the student? Which descriptors in the rubric need to be made more explicit?
15. Clarify understanding by asking questions and restating information.
16. Take collective responsibility for the outcomes of any decision-making.
17. Create a visual display to summarise and capture the discussion.
18. Check that the recorded information accurately represents what has been said.
19. Conclude each session with a plan and timeline for next steps or the next collaborative discussion.
20. Send a follow-up email to all members outlining the discussion and decisions.

Collaboration with the wider school community

[It] is in the process of making and negotiating shared social meanings that we move imperfectly towards jointly conceived understandings of personhood and community. (Cruddas, 2007, p. 479)

We believe (along with many other educators) that schools can no longer function effectively as separate organisations outside the community. Inclusive schools value multiple community perspectives and the contribution they make both to the social capital of the school community and in tackling complex issues. Collaboration with others in the wider school community can take many forms, from informal relationships to formalised partnerships, and can occur incidentally or as a regular and ongoing part of the work of the school. There are many reasons why leaders and teachers in inclusive schools should collaborate with others in the wider school community. Collaboration is a powerful resource that provides opportunities to hear diverse views on an issue and to find creative solutions. There are many possibilities for collaboration with organisations outside the school, including other schools, businesses, university and other higher education institutions, police and medical services, and health and government organisations. It has been common practice for teachers to work with psychologists and other health or education professionals to support individual students. There is an increasing trend for a wider range of professionals to collaborate to share professional knowledge or to engage in research focused on improving schooling. Along with teachers, collaborators include paraprofessionals, specialist support teachers, medical practitioners, psychologists, occupational therapists, speech/language therapists, physiotherapists, university academics and researchers, and social workers. From time to time, professionals from outside the school may also act as critical friends, supporting and adding new ideas or perspectives to school processes. (See the National College for School Leadership (NCSL, 2006) for suggestions about and examples of the part a critical friend can play in the school improvement process.) PLCs create real opportunities for sharing knowledge and practices with others, both inside and outside the immediate school community.

Challenges of professional collaboration

The ability to collaborate successfully with professionals from health, education, business and the university sector may be challenging. Each professional discipline comes with a unique approach and understanding of students, their learning, and the issues relating to schooling. Negotiating collaborative pathways focused on student success in schooling and the promotion of well-being will not necessarily be straightforward. Old habits can be hard to break and, despite a declared willingness to collaborate, professionals can experience challenges in translating intentions into practice (Burns, 2008). Tension is likely to result from competing perspectives that arise from the different disciplines and professional approaches.

What does it take to be a good collaborator? A willingness to listen to and understand the perspectives of others and effective communication are consistently highlighted as essential competencies (Suter, Arndt, Arthur, Parboosingh, Taylor & Deutschlander, 2009). There may be a tendency to allow school leaders or other professionals with perceived authority to determine what issues are worthy of discussion or to take sole responsibility for decisions (Deppeler, in press). Collaboration will be most effective if it is structured to allow all voices to be heard, not only those individuals in positions of authority. Box 5.4 (above) provides some practical suggestions for making communication and collaborative discussion more effective. Full benefits from collaboration are more likely to arise when professionals:

- take time to understand the roles and respect the expertise of other professionals
- critically examine issues rather than agreeing quickly on a solution
- take collective responsibility for outcomes of any decision-making, and
- structure discussion to enhance effectiveness.

When collaboration with others in the wider school community is working and is positive, there are advantages for:

- supporting and resourcing the school's activities
- providing access to specialised expertise
- better understandings of the needs and priorities of the local community
- helping connect students to work-based learning and employment
- building and extending collaboration with other local organisations and professionals.

Collaboration within the inclusive classroom

In addition to collaborating with professionals and others in the school community, teachers often work with adults within their classrooms. Paraprofessionals, volunteers, and family members can assist and support the teacher with students in the classroom. Support staff—variously known as learning support assistants, teaching assistants, teacher aides, paraeducators, and paraprofessionals—are employed to take on an ever-increasing variety of tasks, with many playing significant roles in teaching and learning (Anderson & Finney, 2008). Many of the issues that have arisen from research examining the experiences of support staff indicate that there is an increasing emphasis on the need for formal training and role prescriptions for support assistants (Richards & Armstrong, 2008). With respect to the support of students with special needs, support staff should have their roles clarified before work begins and should not be left to make decisions for the learning and teaching of individual students. Moreover, Rose & Howley, (2007) suggest there is an increased move towards more flexible arrangements of support in which the assistant supports both the teacher and the students. In clarifying the form and roles for support, the alternatives in Box 5.5 might be considered. The most important thing is to ensure that the characteristics of the support role are clearly defined in advance through collaborative discussion.

Box 5.5: Roles for support staff

1. **Supporting teaching and learning directly.** This may include delivering teacher-planned pedagogy to individual or small groups of students or as a support to the teacher during whole-class learning activities. Support may include the provision of assistance to individual students before, during, or after whole-class activities.
2. **Supporting assessment for learning (AFL)** (see Chapter 4). Support staff can be directly involved in key AFL strategies (e.g. making explicit success criteria, strategic questioning, effective feedback, supporting peer and self-assessment) for individual students.
3. **Inquiry.** On behalf of individual teachers or the school community, support staff can gather, audit or evaluate evidence regarding effectiveness of practices or engagement of students in schooling (e.g. observing classrooms, interviewing students, parents and/or other members of the community, supporting students to have their views heard).
4. **Liaising with families/carers.** As a part of collaboration, support staff can maintain regular communication between teacher, students and families.
5. **Planning and review.** This may include the ongoing and regular recording and maintenance of student responses to pedagogy, shared family communication booklets and memos, meetings, term or half-yearly reviews or computer-based records, and may also involve joint planning based on these data.

6. **Learning materials.** May include preparation of learning materials to support planned teaching or modifying materials to support learning for individual students.
7. **Attendant care.** This may include specialised responsibilities and support for students with disabilities (e.g. eating, dressing, toileting, mobility).

Working effectively with support staff means effective collaboration as a member of the inclusive school community. Ensuring effective collaboration with support professionals is no different from effective collaboration with any other member of the inclusive school community. Collaboration needs to involve:

- the articulation of the perspectives of those involved (e.g. teacher, learner, support staff, family members)
- valued participation
- respect for differences
- shared responsibility
- clear focus on student success
- clearly articulated expectations for involvement
- critical reflection and examination of practice.

In considering tasks or roles for an assistant, it may be helpful to first gather evidence to identify your specific support needs. You might then share and discuss your evidence and reflections with colleagues as part of a team discussion to establish priorities for support. Regardless of the particular roles support staff play, it is critical that the process involves clarification, training, supervision, evidence-gathering, and communication. You will need to schedule regular times to meet, reflect and discuss evidence and examine any issues that arise as part of the ongoing process. Box 5.6 provides a checklist for collaboration with support staff including paraprofessionals and other teacher assistants.

Box 5.6: Checklist for collaborating with support staff

- Have I critically reflected on and used evidence gathered in my classroom to identify a specific focus for assistant support?
- Have I shared and discussed my insights with a colleague and incorporated any suggestions/refinements?

- Have I openly and collaboratively discussed the focus and specific roles of support with the assistant?
- Have I ensured that the assistant is fully aware of relevant school policies and procedures?
- Have I explicitly described the tasks (including both dos and don'ts) of the assistant?
- Have I modelled the required tasks with the assistant?
- Have I ensured that the assistant fully understands and is confident with the specific skills or tasks required?
- Will myself or someone else observe the assistant, and if so when?
- Have confidentiality and ethical practices been discussed with the assistant?
- Is there a schedule for the work, including persons responsible and completion dates for tasks?
- Is there a method and schedule for the assistant or others to collect evidence on the effectiveness?
- Is there a process for the assistant to communicate with me following the work?
- Have I scheduled times to share reflections regarding the evidence and the work with the assistant?
- Has the assistant been introduced to school teaching staff and to the students in my classroom, making clear his/her role, authority over students and indicating any limitations or boundaries?
- Have I included a process for reviewing the role and for the assistant's input into planning changes?
- Is there a process in place if the assistant is unable to attend school for work?

Collaboration with families

Family involvement is a critical component of inclusive education, and the importance of collaboration between the home and the school to the success of students with schooling cannot be over-stated. Traditional parental involvement was led by teachers and often emphasised passive roles for parents. Home–school collaboration emphasises active involvement, where families and schools work together and build relationships as partners. Collaboration involves families, educators and other school community members working together to support students' education and well-being. The increasing diversity of our schools means that we need to expand our understandings of family structures and actions, and work out how to be responsive to students that present diversity in terms of learning, culture, language and backgrounds. When families can collaborate with schools in authentic ways, they will contribute knowledge and valuable insights that might not otherwise be available. Teachers and leaders can use this knowledge to support school decisions about teaching and learning environments that support the unique challenges and interests of their students and best promote success for each learner.

Box 5.7: Home–school collaboration

Schools must take the lead in developing and maintaining collaboration with families. Processes should:

- Provide a welcoming school environment, with a culture of openness to all families
- Promote families as active members of the school professional learning community
- Elicit family perspectives (understandings, opinions and expectations) on all school issues
- Make certain that families are actively involved in school decisions and governance
- Ensure that everyone and everything in the school gives the same message to all families: *Your opinions, knowledge and contributions are valued and respected by our school* (e.g. via teachers, newsletter, activities, policies)
- Promote openness, trust, and shared responsibility for decisions about student learning and equity
- Provide democratic processes, ensuring that all the voices of families are represented and heard
- Confirm that all families understand that the school values collaboration and representation (including families whose primary language is not English and those with limited literacy skills)
- Request volunteers for all aspects of schooling, not just school functions and extra-curricular activities (e.g. support for teaching, sport and as committee members)
- Allocate adequate resources to assist families to collaborate
- Send clear messages that there are high expectations for *all* students
- Create an organisational structure that supports collaboration
- Promote risk-taking, innovation, and community-generated solutions

- Make *sharing* an integral feature of classrooms and school practices
- Create school spaces that encourage collaboration and discussion
- Encourage understanding by celebrating family diversity (forms, backgrounds, ethnicities, linguistically)
- Structure a range of strategies for families to communicate frequently and about their expectations, their child's learning progress and well-being that reflects their preferences
- Encourage participation in adult educational opportunities offered by the school
- Structure opportunities for families to share knowledge and diversity at the school
- Gather and collaboratively discuss evidence regarding barriers and facilitators to family collaboration.

Home–school collaboration is not a set of procedures or activities. The processes listed in Box 5.7 are fundamental to PLC and are consistent with inclusive schooling. When collaboration is characterised by openness, trust, and respect, and mutuality, then families and educators can work together in meeting the challenges in their context. This will involve risk-taking and shared responsibility for the decision-making. Over time, respectful home–school collaboration builds understanding and more closely aligns home–school expectations, which in turn supports students to meet these expectations.

Collaboration with students

Collaboration in inclusive schools actively involves students. Engaging with students to seek their perspectives is fundamental to the culture of inclusive schools, where students are valued and treated with respect for their diverse knowledge and experiences (Carrington & Robinson, 2004; Moss, 2003). *Student voice* refers to individual and collective student perspectives with regard to learning, teaching and schooling. Student voice is not the same as student engagement or student participation, which refer to level of student commitment to learning or other activities in school. Student voice can be active or passive participation, but it reflects a valuing of and respect for students' experiences, views and knowledge as part of the inclusive community. There has been an increased focus on student voice, and a growing body of evidence has shown it to be powerful in affecting academic achievement, school retention, curriculum effectiveness and development in school reform (Fielding, 2007; Flutter & Rudduck, 2004). Every student in every classroom has a voice that should be heard by every adult working in inclusive schools. We believe students are in the best position to give an authentic voice to their concerns and experiences regarding schooling. Student collaboration is about empowering students to voice what they value and believe is important and why, and who they are, and to have an active stake in their schooling. When students have a voice and a stake in their schooling, there is a strong sense of collaboration, and they are respected and consulted at the classroom and school levels. Student collaboration should be an integral part of inclusive schooling. Students have unique insights, and when they are offered opportunities to collaborate with educators in authentic ways there can be benefits for inclusive schools. Many activities can purposefully engage students as collaborators in teaching, decision-making, school planning and inquiry. This chapter highlights a few ideas. More suggestions can be found on student voice websites such as *SoundOut: Promoting student voice in schools* (<www.soundout.org>; see also the Further Reading section at the end of this chapter).

Students collaborate in negotiating curriculum

This means students have a voice in classroom processes, and share in the decision-making and the construction of knowledge. This can include ascertaining what knowledge students have and what they wish to find out. It means students may have input into classroom activities and assessment, and that teachers may allow curriculum to develop from student questions and interests. This may have particular importance for students' voices that may be under-represented or devalued by the curriculum. A curriculum that represents students' cultures, languages, perspectives, and experiences as valued sources of knowledge supports learning that can result from active student engagement. In Chapter 4 we discussed some of the many ways students can collaborate with teachers as they actively develop their potential for learning. Collaboration is a social process that supports learners to develop their capabilities—they learn to do independently what initially they could do only with assistance from teachers and peers. In particular, the *assessment for learning* process provides opportunities for students to collaborate in the development of rubrics and success criteria, in determining their own learning goals and needs, and in the assessment of their own and peers' performance against success criteria.

Students collaborate as researchers

Schools have for a long time involved students in 'leadership' roles. Too often, the traditional models of student leadership in schools have been limited to a small group of students (often those who are highly successful) and to issues that are peripheral to the core business of teaching and learning (which are selected by teachers). In these situations, student voice is restricted to students who are compliant and who speak about safe issues and in ways that are acceptable to teachers (Holdsworth, 2008). The concept of students as active researchers is rapidly gaining credence in response to changing perspectives on the status of children in our society. Groups of students are engaged as researchers to investigate issues and develop solutions to challenges that are important to the school community. Students' involvement in 'real' research activities has been found to have benefits for students and for inclusive schools in different countries (Bland & Atweh, 2004; Carrington & Holm, 2005; Cook-Sather, 2006; Lodge, 2005; Moss, Hay, Deppeler, Astley & Pattison, 2007). For example, students as researchers in projects such as Student Action Research for University Access (SARUA) have investigated issues that have prevented marginalised students from aspiring to or accessing tertiary education and have been highly successful in re-engaging these students with their education (Atweh, 2003; Bland & Atweh, 2004). Projects in Australia (Carrington, Allen & Osmolowski, 2007; Moss et al., 2007) and in Ghana (Deppeler, Moss & Agbenyega, 2008) have involved secondary school students working as researchers in collaboration with teachers, using visual methods to view their school community. Students' photographs and discussion combine to represent their views of their social and physical school environments. The projects illustrate how the insights of students have helped to make public assumptions and values that impede progress to achieving more socially just schools. In a similar vein, Leora Cruddas's work (Cruddas, 2001; Cruddas & Haddock, 2003) in London with a group of girls with emotional and behavioural difficulties provides a successful example of ways in which these marginalised students were supported and better understood. The girls were able to identify barriers to learning and participation, but also highlighted how they wanted their schools to change to meet their learning needs.

Adam Fletcher (2005) has created a framework for SoundOut, including a series of essential tips, rubrics and other devices intended to support meaningful engagement of students as collaborators in school change. In the cycle of meaningful involvement, Fletcher (2005) identifies the steps that occur in collaborative activity where students and adults agree there is meaning (see Figure 5.2).

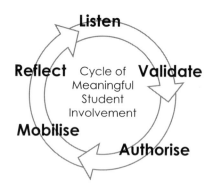

Figure 5.2 Adam Fletcher's cycle of meaningful student involvement

Much like the cycle of collaborative inquiry, students and adults share in learning, acting and reflecting to inform schooling:

1. *Listen*. Student perspectives, ideas, and opinions are shared and listened to by adults.
2. *Validate*. Students are acknowledged as valued and respected members of the school community.
3. *Authorise*. Students learn and develop school change processes.
4. *Mobilise*. Students and adults collaborate in school development and action.
5. *Reflect*. Students and adults work together to critically examine what they have learned in order to inform processes.

Authentic collaboration with students as researchers requires planning and structured processes to ensure that the students as well as the school will benefit from this process. Box 5.8 contains a checklist of essential components designed to empower students to engage with the research and to support collaboration processes with student researchers.

Box 5.8: Collaboration with student researchers

The issue

Must be something that:

- is important to the school community
- is open to investigation and action
- the students themselves choose to do
- involves students in the solution.

The students

Must be positioned as:

- the principal researchers
- the leaders of the action
- skilled and motivated to make a difference.

The environment

Must create:

- spaces where students feel comfortable in expressing their opinions and ideas
- a means for marginalised students to engage and contribute their voices
- opportunities for democratic dialogue about issues affecting students' lives
- educational practices that do not privilege some student voices over others.

The process

Should include structures and strategies to support:

- the identification of authentic issues and concerns regarding schooling
- the learning of research processes, including data collection methods and analysis
- the sharing of the research with the local school community and in wider contexts—for example, providing opportunities for presenting and discussing findings from research at school and at conferences or through publication
- communication and providing alternative practices that do not favour adults and that are likely to give students more ownership of the decision-making. For example, visuals, including video and still photography, are ideal for use with students who, for whatever reason, are less able or reluctant to express themselves in a written or verbal form, and for investigating complex or abstract issues that are more difficult to express.

In the best circumstances, student research is part of a range of diverse opportunities for student collaboration within a school. Schools may wish to formally list the collaborative possibilities that exist within the school and promote these to families. In this way, teachers can see who does and does not have access, and develop strategies to ensure that *all* students can collaborate as researchers—not just a few.

Key terms

School community. The school community includes a range of stakeholders (students, teachers, leaders, parents, professionals, business owners, policy-makers and educational administrators), all of whom have different perspectives, needs and expectations of the school.

Pedagogy. The art and science of being a teacher; it includes the range of strategies an effective teacher uses as well as the relationship between teaching and learning.

Collaboration. A cyclic process that involves teachers and other members of the school community working together to reflect on, analyse, debate and discuss in order to make shared decisions that build upon collective knowledge and develop practices in their school.

Paraprofessionals. People who help schools and teachers to provide services to students with diverse abilities.

Health professionals. Psychologists, nurses, physiotherapists, occupational therapists, speech/language therapists, audiologists and other professionals who work in the health industry.

Student voice. The individual and collective perspective and actions of children and youth with regard to learning, teaching and schooling.

For discussion and reflection

5.1 How might the nature of collaboration differ with different groups (e.g. collaborating with teachers versus collaborating with students)?

5.2 What are some of the professional and ethical issues that come to mind when considering teacher–teacher collaboration?

Further reading

Ainscow, M., Muijs, D. & West, M. (2006). *Using collaboration as a strategy for improving schools in complex and challenging circumstances: What makes the difference?* London, UK: National College of School Leadership, <http://networkedlearning.ncsl.org.uk/knowledge-base/research-papers/using-collaboration-as-a-strategy-for-improving-schools-in-complex-and-challenging-circumstances.pdf>.

Ainscow, M. & Kaplan, I. (2005). Using evidence to encourage inclusive school development: Possibilities and challenges. *Australasian Journal of Special Education, 29*(2), 106–16.

Deppeler, J. (2006). Improving inclusive practices in Australian schools: Creating conditions for university–school collaboration in inquiry. Special issue: Inclusive Education Ten Years after Salamanca. *European Journal of Psychology of Education, 21*(3), 347–60.

Networked Learning Group A-to-Z. Available from <www.ncsl.org.uk/networked/networked-o-z.cfm>. Section P has many resources for establishing and working in a professional learning community.

Stoll, L., Bolam, R., McMahon, A., Thomas, S., Wallace, M., Greenwood, A. & Hawkey, K. (2006). *Professional learning communities: Source materials for school leaders and other leaders of professional learning.* Nottingham: National College for School Leadership. Available from <http://networkedlearning.ncsl.org.uk/knowledge-base/programme-leaflets/professional-learning-communities/professional-learning-communities-05-booklet2.pdf>.

Collaborative discussion

Flowers, N., Mertens, S.B. & Mulhall, P.F. (2005). *Teacher views on collaborative review of student work.* Available from <www.cprd.uiuc.edu/research/school-pubs/MSJ Nov05 mertens.pdf>.

Hole, S. (1999). Three ways of looking at a colleague: Protocols for peer observation. *Horace, 15*(4). Available from <www.essentialschools.org/cs/resources/view/ces res/37>.

Looking at student work to target instruction. Available from <www.urbanschools.org/professional/mod 2/academy 3.html>.

Looking collaboratively at student and teacher work. Available from <www.turningpts.org/pdf/LASW.pdf>.

Protocols. Available from <www.ncpublicschools.org/profdev/resources/proflearn/samplepro>, including Art Shack Protocol.

Teacher moderation: Collaborative assessment of student work. The Literacy and Numeracy Secretariat Capacity Building Series (2007). Available from <www.edu.gov.on.ca/eng/literacynumeracy/inspire/research/Teacher Moderation.pdf>.

Student voice

Appendix A: Other ways to turn up the volume on the student voice. Available from <www.robertsandkay.com/tutv/iii a.html>.

Fletcher, A. *50 ways adults can support student voice for SoundOut.* Available from <www.soundout.org/article.101.html>.

Fletcher, A. (2005). *Meaningful student involvement: Guide to student partners in school change*. Available from <www.soundout.org/MSIGuide.pdf>.

Rudduck, J. (2006). The past, the papers and the project, *Educational Review, 58*(2), 131–43.

A summary of research on using student voice in school improvement planning (2004). Available from <www.educationalliance.org/Downloads/Research/UsingStudentVoice.pdf>.

Tools for students as researchers. Available from <www.soundout.org/research.html#tools>.

Young people's voices (2007). Special issue of *Educational Action Research, 15*(3).

6

How to develop and manage an individualised program

Key ideas in this chapter

- Individualised programming
- The role of the Program Support Group in developing a program
- Developing a long-term vision
- Linking assessment to program development
- Establishing long-term goals and learning priorities
- Establishing short-term specific objectives
- Indicators of achievement
- Inclusive strategies

Individualised programs for learners with significant differences can help educators to ensure that these students are making measurable progress at school. Having said that, it should be noted that we feel a little uncomfortable about the inclusion of a chapter on this topic because our own position on their use is at best ambivalent (see Chapter 1 for a discussion of the pros and cons of using individualised programs). This chapter has been included because sometimes legislative, policy and/or contextual requirements are such that using differentiated instructional techniques is not the only strategy that a teacher must employ to assist students with differing learning needs, and an individualised program is mandated. For this reason, we have decided to take a pragmatic approach; if individualised programs are to be used, then in our view they may as well be done effectively, and information should be provided on how to do this. Further, it is true that well-written individualised programs, when combined with differentiated instruction, can help a teacher to systematically structure and sequence learning in specifically targeted areas. This is not to say that everything a student learns at school will or should be included in an individualised plan. Rather, individual programs provide a focus for the main emphasis of a student's learning over a specified period of time. Used properly, we concede that they can be a helpful aid to teaching on a daily basis. This chapter explores ways in which useful individualised program plans for diverse learners can be developed and documented. It discusses how relevant goals can be devised and written so as to make them easy to evaluate during, and at the conclusion of, a teaching sequence.

The individual program plan

Issues surrounding curriculum provision suitable for all students in inclusive settings are central to successful inclusion (Dymond, Renzaglia, Gilson & Slagor, 2007; Giangreco, 2007). As mentioned in the introductory chapter, the use of individualised instructional plans for those students deemed to need a more customised program has become common practice throughout much of the world. There are both advantages and disadvantages to using such plans (see Box 6.1).

Box 6.1: Advantages and disadvantages of individual program plans

Advantages

There are many advantages to planning programs for individuals, as they tend to:

- help to ensure accountability—the person responsible for providing instruction has clear curricular expectations that must be addressed and that are monitored (Goodman & Bond, 1993)
- help compensate for lack of attention in curriculum—often the regular curriculum is not comprehensive enough to target areas relevant to the lives of children with diverse abilities (Clough, 1988; Jung, 2007)
- give parents the opportunity to have input into what their children learn (Strickland & Turnbull, 1990)

- provide a structure that assists educational collaborators to focus on important areas of learning for a child (Goodman & Bond, 1993)
- provide information on how certain aspects of curriculum will be taught to a child (Ryndak & Alper, 1996)
- outline in advance additional resources and support services a child may require (Ryndak & Alper, 1996)
- provide a framework for assessment (Goodman & Bond, 1993)
- be useful records at times of transition (Deppeler, 1998).

Disadvantages

The negative aspects of individual program plans are that:
- they can isolate a child within a classroom (Tennant, 2007)
- they represent additional paperwork and administrative duties for teachers (Gartin & Murdick, 2005)
- often it is unclear how individualised plans relate to learning and achievement (Riddell et al., 2002)
- they perpetuate the notion that children with disabilities are inherently different from other children (Ryndak & Alper, 1996)
- they often involve narrow, mundane learning tasks (Collet-Klingenberg & Chadsey-Rusch, 1991); as well, they are overly behavioural in orientation (Goddard, 2005) and often focus on 'training' rather than 'education' (Goodman & Bond, 1993)
- they are not student-centred; rather, they are prescriptive and provide little opportunity to follow up a student's incidental interests (Goodman & Bond, 1993). Indeed, many children have little clue as to what their individualised plan contains (Tennant, 2007).

Tennant (2007) cites contradictory evidence for and against when discussing the merits of using individualised plans and, citing many of their disadvantages, calls for a re-evaluation of the practice based on a renewed agenda for research on the topic.

While there are many disadvantages associated with the use of individualised program plans, most of these can be overcome if the plan is viewed as a fluid document that operates within the context of the regular class curriculum. Individualised program plans, while imperfect, can assist you to include students with significantly differing educational needs compared with other students in your class if care is put into the development and implementation of these plans.

Role of the Program Support Group in individual program planning

In some school systems, the development of an individual program plan is the responsibility of the classroom teacher, while in others the responsibility is a shared one between a team of educators, parents and, wherever possible, the student. Regardless of where the final responsibility falls, the involvement of what we call a Program Support Group is fundamental in the process of developing an individual program plan for a student. Indeed, it is the primary task of the Program Support Group to not only ensure that adequate assessment is carried out, but also to develop, assist, and monitor the implementation of the curriculum for a student with diverse learning needs (Friend & Bursuck, 2008; Mastropieri & Scruggs, 2007). The names of Program Support Groups vary from region to region, but in this context the term refers to the committee of important people involved, including the student. The membership should include parents, the student (if this is possible and appropriate), teachers, a school administrator, and other professionals and paraprofessionals.

Regular Program Support Group meetings should be scheduled, along with additional meetings called on the basis of need. This will enable you to monitor the implementation and evaluation of the plan, and to respond by making changes to any elements of the plan that require these changes. Program Support Group meetings should be run as formal meetings with an agenda set beforehand and minutes taken and later distributed to all members of the group. An example of an agenda for a Program Support Group meeting (adapted from Strickland & Turnbull, 1990) is shown in Figure 6.1 (see also Form 7 in the Useful Forms section).

Another important role of the Program Support Group is to ensure any medical and physical needs are provided for. An example of the way this can be done is through the use of forms that are signed by each member of the group so that everyone is aware of the children's needs (see Form 8 in Useful Forms as an example).

Compiling an individual program plan

It is often helpful to think of individual program plans as being hierarchical in nature. They begin with broad visions and goals that are gradually broken down into more manageable segments for teaching. The style of the individual program plan we recommend is structured as a flow-chart (see Figure 6.2).

Agenda for meeting of Program Support Group

Child:	Jeremy X	Date of meeting:	April 1
Place:	West Wing, White House School	Time:	2:00pm – 4:30pm

PSG Members:
Mr and Mrs X, Parents
Jeremy X, Child
Mr Smith, Classroom Teacher
Mrs Jones, Curriculum Coordinator
Mrs Williams, Program Aide
Mr Consultant, Programming for Child Differences
Mrs Hunt, Probation Officer

Purpose: To begin the process of developing an individual program plan for Jeremy

Status: First Meeting

Time	Activity	Program Support Group members responsible
2:00 – 2:05	Introduction of committee members.	Mrs Jones
2:05 – 2:10	Review and approval of agenda, and explanation of procedures to be followed during meeting.	Mrs Jones
2:10 – 2:15	Discussion and agreement as to chairperson and 'case manager'. Recommendation of Mrs Jones to the position.	Mr Smith Mr Consultant
2:15 – 2:45	Review of evaluation information and current levels of performance. • Jeremy, insight into own levels of performance in all six subject areas. • Mr Smith, identification of strengths and needs. Data gathered through tests and informal observations. Presentation of work samples. • Mr Consultant, presentation of data from standardised testing. Mr & Mrs X, observations of Jeremy's level of functioning.	Jeremy Mr Consultant Mr Smith Mr & Mrs X
2:45 – 3:30	Identification and agreement of the areas in which specifically designed instruction is required.	All members
3:30 – 4:20	Development of goals, objectives and evaluation criteria and schedules in each designated area. Identification of and agreement on necessary related services. (Another meeting may be required to complete this.)	All members
4:20 – 4:21	Determine placement. Likely that Jeremy will continue at the White House School.	Mrs Jones
4:21 – 4:30	Summary of meeting. Clarification of areas requiring further work at a future meeting. Date set and agreed to by all members for next meeting.	Mrs Jones
4:30	Adjournment of meeting.	Mrs Jones

Figure 6.1   Program Support Group meeting agenda

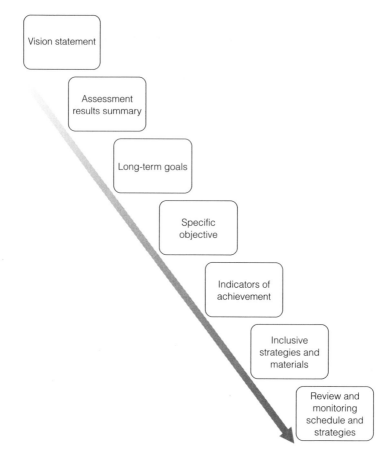

Figure 6.2 Individualised program development process

Blank examples of the forms required to compile an individual program plan can be found in the Useful Forms section. The examples here were completed following the steps in the above flow-chart. We shall now go through these steps one by one to clarify the elements they comprise.

Vision statement

Since the publication of the first edition of this text, the idea of including a vision statement in either the individualised plan or the process leading up to the plan has become increasingly more commonplace. Individualised plans have been criticised for being short-sighted, and a vision statement can be an important part of the process of developing a plan that will possibly be more useful in the long term. The vision statement is a brief message at the beginning of an individualised program plan that, in a very general sense, attempts to convey the 'big picture' of where those involved with the student, as well as the student, hope he or she is headed. The statement should be positive and involves the hopes and dreams of the student, family, and school staff. A good vision statement can help provide direction for the long-term goals being set. An example of a vision statement would be:

> *Our hope for the future is that Jeremy will live independently. We also want Jeremy to be interdependent in the sense that he is connected to and supported by his local community. We hope he will hold down a job he enjoys with an employer who values his contributions. We would like Jeremy to enjoy an active social life and develop close friendships and lifelong relationships with people he loves and values, and whose company he enjoys.*

This statement, while brief and very general, does provide some direction for the setting of long-term goals. It expresses future hopes in three main areas: independent living, employment and social life. Jeremy's goals, then, can be written to reflect these dreams for his life as an adult. This statement should be placed in the space provided on the 'Individual program plan' (see page 122, Figure 6.3 and Form 9 in Useful Forms).

Developing a vision statement may take some time and effort, as the views of all members of the Program Support Group should be taken into account. In developing the vision statement, the following questions—suggested in the work of O'Brien and Pearpoint (2002)—might be asked:

- What does the student enjoy doing now? Does this activity have any long-term implications?
- What are the student's dreams for the future?
- What are the parents' dreams for the future?
- What would you like to see the student do on leaving school?
- What would you like to see the student doing when he/she becomes an adult?
- What are the components of a happy and fulfilled life? What do you think will lead to the student having a happy and fulfilled life as an adult?
- Is there any reason why the student may not attain his/her dreams? How can these be overcome?

Assessment results summary

If you have followed the procedures outlined in previous chapters, by now you should have gathered and understood a range of assessment information about the student for whom this program is being designed. This information

Individual program plan

Child name:	Jeremy	Age:		Grade/Year
Coordinating Teacher	Mr Smith	Date:	April 15	

Vision Statement: Our hope for the future is that Jeremy will be able to live as independently as possible, with minimal assistance from others in daily living activities, shopping, and personal care. We hope he will hold down a job he enjoys with an employer who values his contributions. We would like Jeremy to enjoy an active social life and develop close friendships and life-long relationships with people he loves and values, and whose company he enjoys.

Assessment Results summary:

Assessment Type	Description of Results
WISC-III (psychologist)	• Full-scale IQ of 58. • Global difficulties across each subset but particularly in reading comprehension, spelling and written expression.
Vineland ABS – Expanded form: Interview and Classroom Editions (psychologist analysed)	• Below-average performance in all domains. • Difficulties particularly acute in socialisation and motor skills domains. • Socialisation: does not interact well with others, tends to play alone. • Motor skills: gross motor particularly acute. Slow, difficulty with obstacles, tends to lose balance.
Structured observations at school (teacher and aide conducted)	• Difficulty maintaining positive social relationships: plays alone or argues/fights. • Does not respect 'personal space' during social interactions.
Anecdotal information (teachers, parents, aide, Jeremy)	• Does not recognise opportunities for positive social interactions. • 'Personal space' an issue.
Curriculum-based assessment (teacher)	• Counts to 1000, adds, subtracts, multiplies, simple division. Simple graphing OK. Basic understanding of fractions. Uses concrete aids. • Reads phonetically. Comprehension poor on books over about Grade 3 level. Frequent spelling errors. Difficulties with written expression. • Excels in art. Primarily interested in painting. Has mastered advanced techniques including shading and use of oils & canvas. Aptitude is emerging in other areas such as sculpture.

Figure 6.3 Individual program plan

should tell you a lot about his or her background, interests, strengths, needs and progress in terms of the curriculum. This information is vital to the successful development of an appropriate education plan.

Prior to the Program Support Group meeting, each member of the group should be given adequate time to thoroughly read and understand the reports of each assessment. Further, the teacher should have met with key members of the group (especially the parents) prior to the Program Support Group meeting in order to outline the teacher-based assessments for and of learning that have taken place. The consideration of assessments should not take place immediately before the meeting, as it is better to take time to review the reports and other information in detail and reflect on them. If some members do not understand particular aspects of assessment reports, these should be explained to them at or before the Program Support Group meeting by the person who wrote the report or by someone who understands the type of assessment that has been undertaken.

The assessment results summary is exactly that. It is a summary of the results of all assessments carried out prior to the Program Support Group meeting. The purpose of the assessment results summary is simply to *remind* members of the Program Support Group about the most significant findings from each of the assessments. It is not supposed to be a comprehensive description of every aspect of each assessment. By the time the Program Support Group meeting is held, it can be assumed that each member of the group is familiar with the original reports. It is the task of the person or group responsible for the coordination of the individualised program plan to complete the assessment results summary prior to the first Program Support Group meeting. An assessment results summary should be no longer than one page, and where possible should be written in point form. An example of an assessment results summary for Jeremy follows. It comprises the bottom half of the 'Individual program plan' (see Form 9 in Useful Forms). You will note that it contains a variety of assessments, including formal psychological assessments, observation, work samples, and other curriculum-based assessments. Note also that this assessment results summary contains some information that is deficit-based. This, unfortunately, reflects reality. Most standardised assessments have this tone, and so are included here. This does not mean, however, that the assessment information that you as the teacher include, or that the goals and objectives the Program Support Group set, necessarily need to follow this same deficit-based way of thinking.

Jeremy's assessment results summary

Child name: Jeremy

Age:

Grade/year:

Coordinating teacher: Mrs Smith

Date:

Vision statement: Our hope for the future is that Jeremy will live independently. We also want Jeremy to be interdependent in the sense that he is connected to and supported by his local community. We hope he will hold down a job he enjoys with an employer who values his contributions. We would like Jeremy to enjoy an active social life and develop close friendships and lifelong relationships with people he loves and values, and whose company he enjoys.

Assessment results summary

Assessment type

WISC-III
(Psychologist)
Vineland ABS—Expanded form: Interview and Classroom Editions
(Psychologist analysed)
Structured observations at school
(Teacher and aide conducted)
Anecdotal information
(Teachers, parents, aide, Jeremy)
Curriculum-based assessment
(Teacher)

Description of results

- Full-scale IQ of 58.
- Global difficulties across each subset but particularly in reading comprehension, spelling, and written expression.
- Below-average performance in all domains.
- Difficulties particularly acute in socialisation and motor skills domains.
  - Socialisation: does not interact well with others, tends to play alone.
  - Motor skills: Gross motor particularly acute. Slow, difficulty with obstacles, tends to lose balance.
- Is generally well organised in class.
- Enjoys and is good at musical activities.

- Difficulty maintaining positive social relationships: plays alone or argues/fights.
- Does not respect 'personal space' during social interactions.
- Does not readily recognise opportunities for positive social interactions outside of the family.
- Is a caring and gentle 'big brother'.
- Engages in arts and crafts in his spare time.
- 'Personal space' an issue.
- Performance in music is well above grade level.
- Counts to 1000, adds, subtracts, multiplies, simple division. Simple graphing OK. Basic understanding of fractions. Uses concrete aids.
- Reads phonetically. Comprehension poor on books over about Grade 3 level. Frequent spelling errors. Difficulties with written expression.
- Excels in art. Primarily interested in painting. Has mastered advanced techniques, including shading and use of oils and canvas. Aptitude is emerging in other areas such as sculpture.

Long-term goals

Long-term goals are an important part of any program. They should describe what is to be achieved with a student over an extended period of time. The length of time a long-term goal should cover varies from context to context, but generally speaking a long-term goal should cover no more than a one-year period. This one-year timeline is very common in schools today. In some cases, long-term goals have been known to cover periods as brief as six or even three months where the teaching sequence has been intensive.

Long-term goals should result from elements of the vision statement, along with the information that is included in the assessment results summary. Long-term goals can be quite general in nature. They paint a broad picture of areas in which the student is to develop over an extended period. It is important to keep them simple and clear when writing them so that anyone involved can understand them.

Indeed, simplicity is the key to effective individualised program plans. Not only should goals be stated simply, but they should also be few in number. Each long-term goal will eventually be accompanied by a number of specific objectives, and those developing the plan need to keep in mind what is realistic to achieve in a regular classroom over the specified time period, given levels of staffing and resources. Remember that the purpose of an individualised program plan is not to cover everything a student will learn at school, but rather to create a focus on some of the most important areas of learning for that student. Generally speaking, there is rarely any need to go beyond three long-term goals for any one student.

Example: Well-intentioned but unsustainable practice

Sally was a dedicated and hard-working teacher. She wanted Albert, a student in her class from a refugee background, with little comprehension of English, to develop and grow in a wide variety of areas. The Program Support Group agreed, and together they set seven long-term goals for Albert. To each of these goals they attached five specific objectives to be achieved. This made a total of 35 objectives for the year.

Being a diligent teacher, Sally ensured that she reflected each of these objectives for Albert in her regular classroom program. She soon found, however, that there were so many objectives she couldn't keep track of them all. She also found that there was never enough time during the week to adequately address each of these objectives with Albert. She kept up with the paperwork involved in monitoring each of the objectives by working late into the night.

At the end of the year, Sally's assessments demonstrated that none of the goals for Albert had been fully achieved, although partial progress had been made towards some. The failure to achieve Albert's goals was the result of too many goals. Instead of focusing on a few important areas, Sally was 'spread too thin' by trying to achieve too much. Despite her hard work, by trying to accomplish everything she succeeded in accomplishing little.

After the careful examination of the vision statement and the assessment results summary, each member of the Program Support Group should individually list what they consider to be important areas where goals could be set in order of priority. When each member of the group has done this, the Program Support Group should then discuss and agree on what they consider to be the main priorities as a group. This may involve some debate as to which learning areas are most important. These priorities should then be written up on a separate form and used as the basis for writing the goals. Figure 6.4 shows two completed forms for Jeremy (see also Form 10 in Useful Forms). The first form is an example of what an individual member of the Program Support Group might list, based on Jeremy's vision statement and assessment results summary. The group list is an example of what priorities might have been agreed on for Jeremy after some discussion by all members of the Program Support Group.

Long-term goals

Individual list   Group list   (please circle whichever applies)

Child name: Jeremy X	Date:

Learning Priorities
(in order of most important to least important)

1)	Learning social skills
2)	Employment-related skills
3)	Foster artistic talents
4)	Improve mobility
5)	Improve academic performance

Long-term goals

Individual list   Group list   (please circle whichever applies)

Child name: Jeremy X	Date:

Learning Priorities
(in order of most important to least important)

1)	Developing social skills
2)	Fostering artistic talents
3)	Improving mobility/motor skills
4)	Improve academic performance
5)	

Figure 6.4 Long-term goals

Once priorities have been established, the Program Support Group can begin the task of wording the long-term goals. In devising long-term goals, it is important to remember the points in Box 6.2.

Box 6.2: Hints for establishing long-term goals

In devising long-term goals, it is important to remember the following:

- There should be a focus on the strengths as well as the needs of a child—it is unfair to expect a child to always work in areas in which he or she is weak.
- Goals should be based on the Program Support Group's priorities.
- Goals should be written in terms of learning outcomes and they need to be student centred—a long-term goal stating something like 'To include Jill in all art classes' is based on what school staff intend to do with Jill, not on what Jill will actually accomplish; a better goal in this instance might be 'For Jill to improve her level of participation in art classes', which outlines what Jill needs to do in order to accomplish her long-term goal.
- Goals need not be too specific—the objectives that follow this section will deal with this.
- A time should be provided at which it is expected each goal will be accomplished.

The first point in Box 6.2 deserves further discussion. The uncomfortable truth of individualised programs is that they are generally written for students who are struggling in a particular area, and are often based on the input of education, psychology, and rehabilitation professionals who have generally been asked for their input in the first place because the student is having difficulties. For this and other reasons they naturally focus on the deficits—what a student is in need of rather than what they are good at. The implications of this are that students can end up spending large portions of their time at school working in areas in which they have a history of failure. This surely sets them up for a miserable school experience! While common sense dictates that such needs should not be ignored, the Program Support Group should be cognisant of the fact that not every need has to be addressed through an individualised program, and that some allowance for working in areas of strength should be made. This means that one or more goals in an individualised program should possibly be aimed at improving an area of strength. This can be helpful to the overall program. For example, a student with communication difficulties but excellent social skills might benefit from developing those social skills even further. Not only will that help the student to further excel in an area in which they are already strong, but it might also have the extra benefit of helping to compensate for the communication difficulties in some contexts. Examples of goals for Jeremy are shown below. Because his Program Support Group wanted to avoid crowding his program with too many long-term goals, they chose to focus on the three highest priorities only. Note that one of these priorities builds on a pre-existing strength. His goals are as follows:

Example: Long-term goals for Jeremy

1. For Jeremy to improve his social skills and to increase his level of social interactions, both at home and in the community. Timeline: end of year.
2. For Jeremy to extend and further develop his artistic talents and skills. Timeline: end of year.
3. For Jeremy to improve on his current level of mobility and general motor skills. Timeline: end of Term 2.

Notice that Jeremy's goals relate to his top three priorities established by the Program Support Group. They are also limited to a realistically achievable number, are written in terms of what Jeremy needs to do and are brief and clear. A timeline for completion is also provided. One of the goals is clearly focused on a strength.

The final thing to do in relation to goals is to check that they live up to what is hoped for in the vision statement. When we compare Jeremy's goals with the vision statement, we can see that the social skills goal addresses the vision for an active social life in the future. The goal of developing his art skills relates to a possible future career as an artist, given his talent for and love of art. It also focuses on one of his strengths. The mobility goal addresses the future desire for a more independent lifestyle. Each of these goals is a step closer to achieving the overall vision for Jeremy.

Specific objectives

Specific objectives are statements, based on the long-term goals that clearly outline what needs to be done in order to achieve these goals. They are short term in nature, and may take anywhere from a few days to some months to accomplish, depending on the student and the educational context. With specific objectives, a student must clearly demonstrate that he or she can do something in order to be said to have achieved the objective. The objective, then, must be precise and measurable. As with the long-term goals, they must be written in terms of what the student must do.

To devise specific objectives, individual long-term goals must be examined one at a time. Members of the Program Support Group must ask themselves: 'What sorts of things does the student need to do in order to demonstrate that he/she has achieved this long-term goal?' As is the case with long-term goals, Program Support Groups should be careful not to select so many specific objectives that it is impossible to fit them all into a year. As a general rule, we recommend no more than four specific objectives per goal, and if it is possible to achieve the goal with fewer than four objectives, then this should be done. The success of an individualised program is often inversely proportional to the number of goals and objectives needing to be achieved. For Jeremy, the specific objectives for one of his goals could be as shown in the example below.

Example: Establishing specific objectives for Jeremy

Child name: Jeremy S.

Goal for examination: For Jeremy to improve his social skills and to increase his level of social interactions, both at home and in the community.

Timeline: End of year.

What needs to happen to achieve this goal?
1. Jeremy needs to learn to respect the 'personal space' of others.
2. Jeremy needs to better identify instances where he could participate socially with other kids.
3. Jeremy needs to become more involved in community activities with his peers.

Once you have identified what the specific objectives should be, the process of formally writing them up can begin. One form that is useful in writing many objectives is:

By the end of . . . [put date here], . . . [student name] . . . will be able to . . .

This format is useful because it not only provides a timeframe for accomplishing the specific objective, but also sets the objective in terms of what the student needs to do. An example of Jeremy's specific objectives for one goal is shown below.

Example: Jeremy's specific objectives

Goal: For Jeremy to improve his social skills and to increase his level of social interactions, both at home and in the community.

Timeline: End of year.

Objective 1: By the end of Term 2, Jeremy will stand no closer than approximately 50 centimetres from other people during conversations without prompting 60 per cent of the time when under observation.

Objective 2: By the end of Term 3, Jeremy will increase his initiation of positive social contact with other children at lunch and recess by 60 per cent when under observation.

Objective 3: By the end of Term 3, Jeremy will increase the amount of time he responds in a positive manner to social interactions initiated by other children by 50 per cent when under observation.

Objective 4: By the end of the year, Jeremy will select two community activities (such as sport clubs, Scouts, hobby clubs) and will choose to participate in at least 70 per cent of the activities run by these community bodies.

Note that Objectives 2 and 3 both relate to the same priority (point 2) on the 'Establishing specific objectives' example. Given the two-way nature of social interactions, Jeremy's Program Support Group decided that two objectives were required. Note also that the specific objectives are written in fairly precise terms, including a percentage amount of improvement or attainment required in each area. While a percentage is not essential, there needs to be some way of measuring progress, and expressing progress in terms of a number is often helpful in terms of accountability. In Jeremy's case, his Program Support Group thought that a 50 to 60 per cent improvement or attainment in each area was a realistic target.

In some instances, the terms used in specific objectives will need to be defined in advance. In Jeremy's case, the term 'positive' is used in relation to social interactions. It may be necessary to define this term so that all members of the team, and most importantly Jeremy, know what is expected. Defining terms such as this can be done in a footnote at the end of the list of objectives. For example:

A 'positive' social interaction is one that is conducted in a friendly manner involving smiles, reciprocal conversation, and polite social conventions such as greetings and the use of phrases such as 'please' and 'thank you'. Aggressive physical contact, name-calling, swearing, and yelling should not be present in a positive social interaction.

Well-written specific objectives spell out what is required in order to achieve the long-term goal. While they mention targets, exactly how these targets are to be measured is not spelled out. This is the job of the indicators of achievement.

Indicators of achievement

Indicators of achievement are written to assist in guiding the measurement of the objectives. They explain what measurement tools will be used, what level of performance is required with respect to these tools, and the times and methods for use of these tools. There may be one or more indicator of achievement for each objective depending on the context. Indicators of achievement are useful because they require Program Support Groups to think through their measurement strategy before the individual program plan is implemented. They also serve as a helpful guide for teachers once the teaching sequence and busy everyday classroom activity have begun. Instead of having to devise measurement methods during this busy time, previously developed indicators of achievement (see Box 6.3) put them at the fingertips of the teacher whenever they are required.

Box 6.3: Devising indicators of achievement

In devising your indicators of achievement, you need to consider:
- whether the measurement tool already exists (such as a commercially available standardised test) or needs to be developed by the Program Support Group, and whether the observations are going to form the basis of the measurement data
- how often progress will be measured
- who will be responsible for implementing the assessment
- the times during the day when progress measurement will take place
- where the measurement of the objective will take place

When devising indicators of achievement (see Box 6.3) it is important to take note of assessment techniques such as those discussed in Chapter 4. If baseline data have not been taken already as part of the initial assessment process, they will need to be gathered before the teaching sequence begins. This allows you to compare the data gathered during and after the teaching sequence with data recorded before the teaching sequence to see whether progress has been made. Indicators of achievement for one of Jeremy's specific objectives, discussed previously, might be as follows.

Example: Jeremy's indicators of achievement

Goal: For Jeremy to improve his social skills and to increase his level of social interactions, both at home and in the community.

Timeline: End of year.

Specific Objective 4: By the end of the year, Jeremy will select two community activities (such as sport clubs, Scouts, hobby clubs) and will choose to participate in at least 70 per cent of the activities run by these community bodies.

Indicators of achievement: Jeremy will have chosen and joined two community clubs by the end of Term 1. A calendar of activities for each of these clubs will be acquired and Jeremy (under supervision of his parents) will record those he attends or does not attend. In order to achieve this objective, Jeremy will attend 70 per cent of the activities for each group. Jeremy will keep a brief weekly diary (three to four lines) describing his participation in the groups for that week. This will support the data from the calendar.

Notice that a variety of measurement techniques will be used to measure Jeremy's progress on the objective outlined here. The indicators of achievement delineate what sorts of data will be gathered, by whom, when, and where. A variety of data sources are used, including a diary and self-monitoring.

Inclusive strategies and materials

If you have followed the steps we have outlined, you should now have a fairly comprehensive individual set of goals and objectives for a single student. The checklist in Box 6.4 should ensure that all bases have been covered. The key now is to begin to decide how each objective might be addressed in an inclusive way so that the student is not withdrawn from regular classroom activities in order to work on his or her goals. This section of the plan looks at how the goal will be taught. It includes information on settings, groupings, modes of teaching and links to the curriculum.

Box 6.4: Individualised program checklist
Outside meetings
- Gather assessment data/reports.
- Complete the assessment results summary.

During meetings
- Prepare a vision statement.
- Examine the assessment results summary.
- Establish learning priorities as individuals.
- Establish learning priorities as a group.
- Devise long-term goals.
- Establish specific objectives.
- Write up specific objectives.
- Devise indicators of achievement.
- Consider inclusive strategies and materials.
- Set review schedule.

Review and monitoring schedule and strategies

The final section of an individual program plan relates to review and monitoring. It is important that an individualised program plan is regarded at all times as a working document to be changed and modified by the Program Support Group as required. As the individualised program plan is an active document, it should be reviewed as often as possible. As a minimum, we suggest this should occur once every school term, but the more often you review the plan the more effective it is likely to be. Your proposed schedule for review should be set out in the document in advance, but should not preclude the calling of extra review meetings as required.

Prior to each formal review session, any ongoing assessment data should be gathered and prepared for presentation to the Program Support Group. If specific objectives and goals are met earlier than expected, then new ones should be set by the group to replace them.

The final question to be asked is: 'What changes need to be made?' In some instances, modifications to some of the areas mentioned above can result in successful achievement of the goal or specific objective by the student. In other instances, however, the goal or specific objective may need to be abandoned in favour of another, more attainable target. Continuing to work at an unmodified goal or specific objective on which a student is making no progress over a significant amount of time is not only pointless but is often counter-productive (see Box 6.5). Continued work in areas in which no progress is made is both boring and potentially damaging to the student's self-esteem.

Box 6.5: Poor progress?

If no (or little) progress is made on goals during the designated time, the Program Support Group should consider whether:
- the goal or specific objective was inappropriate in the first place
- the expected level of achievement was over-estimated
- enough time for practice and teaching had been allowed
- there was a problem with assessing progress
- the teaching strategies were appropriate
- the materials were appropriate
- the goal or specific objective was important to the child.

This chapter has discussed how to construct an individualised plan of learning for a student. While this type of plan can be an important tool to assist you to focus on the needs of specific students, it should not be used in isolation from the rest of the class and curriculum, and creative ways of including it in daily plans need to be considered. Some of these ideas are discussed in Chapter 7.

Key terms

Individualised program plan. A written plan that provides a focus point for the main emphasis of a student's learning over a specified period of time.

Program Support Group. A committee of important people involved in the planning, including the student. They ensure that adequate assessment is carried out and also develop, assist and monitor the implementation of curriculum for a student with diverse learning needs.

Vision statement. A brief message at the beginning of an individual program plan that, in a very general sense, attempts to convey the 'big picture' of where those involved with the student hope he/she is headed.

Assessment results summary. A summary of the results of all assessments carried out prior to the Program Support Group meeting.

Specific objective. An objective that requires that a student must clearly demonstrate that he or she can do something in order to be said to have achieved the objective.

For discussion and reflection

6.1 What are some of the positive and negative aspects of individualised programs?

6.2 What interpersonal difficulties might arise in a Program Support Group? How might they be addressed in a proactive way?

6.3 Is there a way of writing and assessing specific objectives that reduces the emphasis on behaviourism while still providing the necessary evidence of learning?

Further reading

Goodman, J.F. & Bond, L. (1993). The individualised educational program: A retrospective critique. *Journal of Special Education, 26*(4), 408–22.

Tennant, G. (2007). IEPs in mainstream secondary schools: An agenda for research. *Support for Learning, 22*(4), 204–8

7
Inclusive instructional design

Key ideas in this chapter

- Defining curriculum
- Universal design for learning or curriculum adaptations?
- Universal curriculum design for learning
- Differentiated instruction
- Considerations for the educational environment:
    - materials
    - resources
    - instructional strategies
    - learning outcomes
- Curriculum adaptations and modifications
- Linking individual objectives and the classroom curriculum through:
    - unit planning
    - individual lesson planning

Considering inclusive instructional design in broad terms should be undertaken before designing an individualised program. In many cases, the type of instructional design you adopt in the normal course of your teaching will preclude the need for such specific programs for individual students. This chapter follows the previous chapter on individualised programs, however, because, in addition to discussing more general inclusive instructional designs, we want to explain how these programs can be combined with inclusive ways of teaching to produce the best outcomes for all students. This explanation will follow a more detailed treatment of inclusive instructional design in general. This chapter examines concepts such as universal design for learning, differentiated instruction, and finally program modification to assist you in structuring your teaching and curriculum planning for all students.

Defining curriculum

Central to the teaching and learning that occurs in schools is the curriculum. Curriculum is an umbrella concept that is comprehensive in scope and complex in practice. In broad terms, it has to do with the teaching and learning of knowledge, skills, and attitudes. It embraces issues such as subject-matter, pedagogy, assessments/evaluation, and related resources involved in the organisation, delivery and articulation of education programs (Deppeler, 1998; National Board of Employment Education and Training, 1992). This book discusses each of the elements included in this definition of curriculum throughout the various chapters. This chapter deals largely with the subject-matter and related resources involved in the delivery and articulation of education programs—that is, what is to be taught and how it can be planned for.

We divide curriculum into two broad areas, which seem to be in agreement with the views of Gardner and Boix-Mansilla (1994). These are what we call the 'core curriculum' and the 'elaborative curriculum'. The core curriculum consists of areas judged to be basic and essential for all students. They are basic in that they provide both a foundation on which subsequent learning may be built, and also the conceptual and methodological tools to continue their own learning, and essential because their intention is to equip students for a satisfying and effective participation in social and cultural life. Examples of core curriculum might include basic literacy, numeracy and other more functional and foundational skills and concepts.

The term 'elaborative curriculum' relates to all other aspects of curriculum that could be considered 'non-core'. The elaborative curriculum is important, as it adds richness, depth, scope, and variety to the core curriculum. What constitutes the core curriculum and the elaborative curriculum is context dependent and depends on the views, attitudes and values of everyone involved in the educational process. For some, learning in school subject areas such as the fine arts or music would be seen as non-essential, and therefore could be classified as part of the elaborative curriculum. For others with strong views on the importance of art and music in society, learning in these subject areas might be seen as essential and they would therefore be included as part of the core curriculum. Most teachers already have an idea about what they consider core curriculum and elaborative curriculum—a view that varies from teacher to teacher. Much of what you emphasise in your teaching will be based on these ideas.

We believe that the learning of all students, regardless of difference, should be based on a mixture of both the core and elaborative curriculum. The proportion of time you spend on each of these divisions of curriculum will depend on individual students and the learning context. Some students will require a greater focus on aspects of the core curriculum in order to better prepare them to attain the sorts of learnings associated with the elaborative curriculum. Others may need a greater focus on the elaborative curriculum so that they can capitalise on swiftly attained learning in core curriculum areas. It is important to ensure, however, that no matter who the student is, elements of both curriculum divisions are included in order to allow for a rich educational experience based on solid foundations and the traditional scholarly disciplines—which, it has been argued, are still important and relevant to our lives today (Gardner & Boix-Mansilla, 1994; Loreman, 2009).

Universal design for learning or curriculum adaptations?

We know of no country in the world in which the regular curriculum is automatically appropriate for all students in the form in which it is published for teachers. One activity of professional teachers is to take the curriculum they are mandated to teach, and translate that curriculum into meaningful learning activities that are relevant and accessible to all students in a class. Those teachers who are able to translate the mandated curriculum in this way are said to have engaged in *universal design for learning*. As with many ideas that contribute to successful inclusion, the idea of universal design is nothing new—it is simply what good teachers have engaged in for decades. What is new is the increased recognition that this is an especially effective and important approach to designing classroom curriculum to meet the needs of all learners.

However, employing universal design is not possible—or at least can be very difficult—in some teaching contexts (and some regions of the world where this book is available). In some regions, curriculum is so prescriptive and narrow in its objectives that many teachers would have difficulty in taking too many liberties in their professional translation of the curriculum—and may even face professional disciplinary difficulties if they were to do so. In these circumstances, teachers must consider identifying and making curriculum adaptations that are specific to those students who require a broadening of the curriculum. In this chapter, we discuss both approaches, beginning with the option which is preferred wherever possible: universal design. Which of the two approaches you engage in will need to be a decision you make personally. That decision should be taken after investigating local requirements.

Universal curriculum design for learning

In terms of curriculum, universal design was preceded by the notion that, architecturally, all buildings should be accessible to people with disabilities. This notion of accessibility for all without requiring further modification or adaptation was expanded to encompass many other areas, including curriculum design (Zeff, 2007). Over the past 25 years or so, principles governing what constitutes universal design for learning have been debated and refined to the point where we now have a set of three governing principles upon which most people can agree. Universal design for learning involves the following elements:

1. *Multiple means of representation*—to give all learners various ways of acquiring information and knowledge. This involves presenting information in multiple formats—for example, direct teaching, group discussion, differing assignments, visual, auditory and kinesthetic presentations.
2. *Multiple means of expression*—to provide all learners alternatives for demonstrating what they know. This means offering multiple and perhaps non-traditional avenues for assessment which go beyond written assignments or tests to include verbal and/or visual presentations, performances, etc.
3. *Multiple means of engagement*—to tap into all learners' interests, offer appropriate challenges and increase motivation. Differing needs, learning styles, abilities and interests are taken into account to ensure that strengths, along with needs, are addressed for all individuals. (Center for Applied Special Technology, 2009; Zeff, 2007)

The premise behind universal design for learning is that, like buildings, all students should be able to access the curriculum and activities without further modification. Some curricula are more conducive to this process than others. While not perfect, in New South Wales, Australia, a number of objectives have been placed in the regular school curriculum for Years 7–10, which expand the course of studies into the realm of what is commonly known as 'life skills', with the intent being to better serve the needs of students with cognitive impairments (NSW Board of Education, 2008). In including such objectives within the framework of the regular curriculum, the end result is that teachers can teach it 'as is' without making further modifications to include life skills for some students as they may have had to in the past. While some might argue, with some justification, that this simply amounts to a separate curriculum in a repackaged form, the fact remains that this content is included in the government-mandated syllabus for regular schools. Curriculum such as this might be seen as beneficial because it negates many of the difficulties associated with having to adapt and modify curriculum not designed for use with a diverse range of learners in the first place.

Differentiated instruction and universal design

In an ideal situation, a curriculum that has been designed and prepared under the principles of universal design is one that is suitable for all students without further modification. Closely associated with the idea of universal design for learning is the idea of *differentiated instruction*. While the two ideas are, in a technical sense, different from one another, we believe that they are closely connected—and indeed, when used intelligently, can complement one another. We see instruction and curriculum as being automatically differentiated where universal design has been employed. However, a distinction between the two can be made. Universal design for learning, as the term suggests, refers to the *design* of learning activities—planning curriculum activities in such a way as to ensure all learners are able to access them. Differentiated instruction mostly refers to the *implementation* of this plan—pedagogical techniques used in the classroom to deliver the appropriately designed curriculum to a wide range of learners.

The distinction, however, is not so simple as one might hope. 'Universal design for learning' is not only about planning, and 'differentiated instruction' is not only about implementation. This is because the delivery of the curriculum through differentiated instruction must be taken into account during the planning (design) phase, and the way in which activities are designed impacts implementation (instruction). This point of view is echoed by Tomlinson and McTighe (2006), who point out that 'differentiated instruction offers a framework for addressing learner variance as a critical component of instructional planning' (2006, p. 2). It is clear, then, that when planning for instruction for the inclusive classroom you must bear in mind not only *what* must be taught (activities appropriate for all), but also *how* it should be taught (techniques appropriate to a wide variety of learners).

In the first edition of this text, we discussed modifying the curriculum to meet the needs of all. The basic premise behind this was that the curriculum was unlikely to be appropriate for all students and that teachers would need to modify it in order to cater for the diverse learners present in the classroom. The thinking at that time was that most students would follow the regular curriculum without the need for such modifications and adaptations, which would really be targeted at those individuals with different learning needs. The growing popularity of universal design for learning has helped us to see that such modifications, rather than being applied subsequent to the planning of units of work and individual lessons, need to be considered at the very beginning of the planning phase. Deppeler (1998) identifies five environments in which adaptations and modifications to curricula can be made. While these adaptations and modifications reflect the time in which they were written, and were originally intended to be made to curriculum subsequent to the planning of units and lessons for a whole class—and really only for those with diverse needs—we believe the considerations outlined apply equally well to the context of universal design for learning and differentiated instruction where such considerations are taken into account at the outset of planning.

First, prior to planning units of work and individual lessons, Deppeler (1998) asks us to pose a number of questions to ourselves regarding instruction and the curriculum. These questions encourage us to think about the extent to which the way we teach and the curriculum we are mandated to teach need to be translated in order to be appropriate for all, and the directions to which particular attention should be paid. In short, these questions help us to identify possible barriers to curriculum and instructional access, which should be kept in mind as we proceed with planning (see Box 7.1).

Box 7.1: Questions for identifying barriers to curriculum and instructional access

1. Can all students take part in the curriculum in its current form? If not . . .
   - What environmental barriers exist to the participation of all students?
   - What barriers exist to the participation of all students in terms of implied instructional strategies?
   - What barriers exist to the participation of all students in terms of required learning outcomes?
2. What needs to be done to remove these barriers to learning and participation?

Source: Adapted from Deppeler (1998).

It is useful to use Deppeler's three main domains within which access to the curriculum needs to be addressed as a frame for discussing how, in practical terms, curriculum can be translated from the often impersonal government-mandated documents in which it is presented to a rich, meaningful, and appropriate program for all students using the principles of universal design for learning.

The educational environment

In keeping with the universal design for learning principles of presenting students with multiple means of representation, expression, and engagement, it is important to adjust the educational environment to reflect this. In using the term 'educational environment', we refer to five main facets of a classroom environment that can be adjusted and accounted for in the planning phase so as to assist in making curriculum and instruction appropriate for all. Deppeler (1998) identifies these facets as falling into five main areas: the physical environment; the materials environment; the resources environment; instructional strategies; and learning outcomes. Creating an appropriate physical environment is dealt with in greater detail in Chapter 9; the other four aspects of the education environment that need to be considered in planning and instruction are outlined below.

The materials environment

Deppeler's (1998) suggested considerations for producing materials that are appropriate for all students relate mostly to written materials, but the idea can obviously be applied more widely. This recognises the predominance of language, and particularly reading- and writing-based tasks, in modern classrooms—an emphasis that continues in schools today. The first suggestion is to increase the readability of written passages. For some children, this will entail enlarging the print, while for others it will mean double spacing or using a particular font. Indeed, for those students who might be involved in learning a new language, graphic prompts such as pictures accompanying text can be helpful. Measures such as these can make the decoding and comprehension process easier, as the print becomes more 'user friendly' and students with difficulties in this area do not need to expend energy on coming to terms with the printed format (see Box 7.2).

Box 7.2: Considerations for appropriate print materials

- Increase the readability.
- Highlight critical features.
- Reduce extraneous details and simplify the layout.
- Supplement with visual cues (pictures, diagrams, mind maps, illustrations).
- Supplement with written cues and prompts.
- Reduce the amount of material selected.
- Simplify the language (use shorter sentences and simpler vocabulary).
- Include selected content (essential content, experience based or interest based).
- Use alternative materials (do not rely solely on print—use models, videos, etc.).
- Create new materials.
- Use student work folders for daily assignments.

Source: Deppeler, 1998.

Highlighting critical features is another strategy that can assist comprehension. This enables students to concentrate on the key features of a text, producing a core understanding of the main events or issues in a passage of text. One way of highlighting critical features, besides underlining or colour-coding sections within a text, is to reduce extraneous details, leaving only what is absolutely essential behind. This can involve removing words, sentences, paragraphs or even entire pages of a text. While these approaches usually do not allow for an appreciation of the aesthetics of a written piece, they will help to get the main points across to the reader. Similarly, simplifying the layout of a written piece can be useful. This may involve eliminating any distracting and non-essential footnotes, diagrams, or pictures.

While eliminating extraneous information is one way to enhance understanding of print, taking the opposite approach can also work well for some students. Supplementing print with visual cues can assist some students to gain meaning from print (Phinney, 1988). This is a strategy commonly utilised with young children, who use non-text clues to assist them in reading stories (Higgins, 1985); it is appropriate for use with students at the early and pre-reading stage, regardless of their age. Similarly, supplementing difficult passages of text with written notes simplifying the concepts can be effective for more advanced readers.

Teachers also need to consider content when modifying the materials environment. To meet the needs of some students, it may be necessary to present only the most essential elements of content, or the core curriculum. Deppeler (1998) suggests that there are three types of knowledge:

1. 'must know' knowledge, which is prerequisite or essential
2. 'should know' knowledge, which is important but not essential
3. 'could know' knowledge, which is neither essential nor particularly important.

Obviously, the focus should first be on 'must know' knowledge. 'Should know' and 'could know' knowledge may not be useful until after key knowledge has been mastered, and may also confuse or overwhelm some students. Not only can teachers reduce the amount of content selected in materials, but they can also ensure that what is selected is based on the past experience or interest of the individual student. An example of this might be a piece of creative writing where a student is asked to outline a sequence of events (instead of writing a full story), based on an experience they have had in the past. Expanding this into a full story (which might come under 'should know' skills) might then follow.

It is important to cater for a range of learning styles in the classroom, and in order to do this a variety of alternative materials should be provided to students. While many schools are striving to improve literacy acquisition, an over-emphasis on print should be avoided as some students may learn better in some content areas from alternatives like videos, discussion, models, or movement. This can be especially true for students who have experienced difficulties with print in the past, and whose lack of confidence in this area gets in the way of learning important concepts. New materials may need to be created to provide alternatives to print. This can be time-consuming for teachers, but the approach can benefit all students.

It might be tempting to think that the considerations relative to materials discussed above apply only to some students, and that in a classroom in which instruction is differentiated, only those students who are struggling with the materials will benefit from the preparation of such 'universal' materials. This is not necessarily true, however. We know that in inclusive classrooms even those students without particularly evident differing individual needs benefit in many ways, including academically from such an approach (Cole, Waldron & Majd, 2004). This may be because, in environments where the materials are more broadly accessible, the concepts being taught become clearer even for those not previously thought to be in need of any differentiation whatsoever.

In educational contexts using universally designed materials, everyone benefits. Further, while the focus of the majority of this section has been on print materials, we would not want you to come away with the impression that these are all that need to be scrutinised in terms of their accessibility. All materials need to be universally accessible. For example, how can the video documentary on Japanese culture be made accessible to those students who have visual impairments, or even those who may not be visual learners in terms of their learning style? How can the abacus used to teach addition and subtraction be made accessible to students with fine motor difficulties, or those for whom tasks involving a measure of visual-spatial skill and perceptual acuity become difficult? All materials used in instruction, not just print materials, need to be examined if a classroom is to become truly accessible to all.

The resources environment

Many considerations for the resources environment, such as the provision of support from colleagues, were discussed in Chapter 5. In addition to the provision of these resources, however, the coordination of a range of community and other support services needs to be given some thought (see Box 7.3).

Box 7.3: Considerations for the resources environment

- Provide additional instructional support (paraprofessionals, volunteers, peer tutors, parents, other professionals).
- Coordinate a range of community and other support services.
- Utilise additional technological resources (computers, augmented communication devices, video, audio).
- Collaborate with other teachers.

Source: Deppeler, 1998.

Schools can benefit in many ways from maintaining a close relationship with the wider community, and teachers in inclusive classrooms can also draw on community resources to assist them in their work. Sometimes beginning this process is as easy as opening up the phone book or surfing the internet to locate local associations formed to support people with various disabilities, various cultural groups, various religions, and so on. More general organisations—some specifically targeted at supporting inclusive practice—are also becoming more prominent. These organisations can often provide you with advice and support to assist you in running an inclusive classroom. Depending on their level of resources, other more tangible forms of support, such as the loan of specialised equipment, may also be provided by these community agencies. It is also sometimes useful to approach agencies with no direct connection to education, but perhaps with a vested interest in seeing quality educational practice take place in schools. For example, philanthropic agencies such as Rotary may engage in fundraising activities on behalf of a school to provide specific resources if there is a request and demonstrated need. These organisations are often run by volunteers. The involvement of non-volunteer agencies should also be investigated by schools working towards the provision of inclusive schooling.

Specific to disability, non-volunteer agencies run by the government (sometimes at an arm's length) are frequently available for support. Depending on where you are located, services for those with differing needs and particular disabilities may be the responsibility of the national or local government health department, education department, justice department, or department concerned with social services and welfare. Regardless of where your relevant government agencies are located, they should be investigated as a possible resource. Different levels of support are, of course, provided by different governments, but what is available should be used to its full extent, providing that the support is relevant and helpful. This extra support can come in the form of advice, program coordination and, in some cases, the direct provision of material resources to the school.

It is difficult to write about the use of technology in a specific sense because, as we know, this rapidly changing and advancing field renders the current technology virtually outdated and in some cases almost obsolete in the time it takes to publish a book (or for that matter, even a blog!) regarding its merits. Suffice to say that the use of computer technology in schools to support all learners is now commonplace, at least in most Western schools. Further, other technological aids have been specifically developed, in the main to support students with disabilities, though they have been helpful in the education of all learners. Technology has assisted all students to communicate, meet academic targets and even develop friendships in online environments. This is sometimes known as 'assistive technology' (see Box 7.4 for examples) because its prime purpose is to assist students in completing other tasks. This technology is often expensive, however, and in purchasing items to assist students to learn, schools and teachers need to exercise caution. You should ensure that any technological items purchased are required to meet a specific need. Second (and this seems obvious), you should ensure that students can actually operate the technology in a meaningful way. We have seen some schools fall victim to the lure of assistive technology only to discover that the students for whom it has been purchased are unable to operate it.

Box 7.4: Examples of assistive technology

Assistive technology currently in use in schools includes the following:

- **Switches.** Switches come in different sizes and can be used to activate pre-recorded messages, toys, appliances or anything else that can be controlled with an on/off switch. Some computer software has been designed that allows navigation through different programs using only a switch. The applications of switch technology are almost limitless.
- **Alternative computer input devices.** A wide range of traditional keyboard alternatives is now available, including joysticks, adapted keyboards, trackballs, touch screens, electronic pointing devices, 'sip and puff' systems (activated by inhaling or exhaling), and wands and sticks (that attach to the head). Some adapted keyboards have overlays that change the context and layout of the keys, and some have enlarged keys or are designed to suit differing ergonomic situations.
- **Braille embossers and displays.** These transfer text from a computer to embossed Braille output. Braille displays allow for a tactile reading of on-screen text.
- **Speech-recognition software (speech to text).** Very much improved in terms of precision, this software can enable a student to type or navigate the computer simply by speaking into a microphone.

Source: Microsoft Corporation (2008).

In evaluating the need for assistive technological purchases, it is first worthwhile to ensure that such equipment or software is not merely a replication of what is available on programs commonly used. For example, while Microsoft Word is not necessarily an example of universally accessible software, it is commonly available and does contain a number of features that can be helpful. One useful feature is 'auto summarise', which helps to reduce large passages of text down to smaller, more salient elements. Microsoft Word also has a feature that will read documents out loud with a high degree of accuracy. Features such as this can save both teachers and students much time and effort at no additional expense. Further, it is a mistake to think that adaptive technology is only for those experiencing difficulties. Generally, the nature of adaptive technology is such that all students can use and benefit from it, and it can be applied broadly both in and out of school, and for teachers as well as students. For example, some of this book was written using speech-to-text software, originally developed to assist those who were unable to access a keyboard, for the sake of convenience and preference rather than necessity.

Technology is a rapidly changing field, and advancements and improvements are being made so frequently as to almost immediately outdate any information in a book that addresses technology. It is for this reason that we do not dwell on the topic in any great detail. One of the best sources of information about the latest in assistive technology is the increasingly omnipresent internet.

Instructional strategies

Chapter 8 probes constructivist instructional strategies grounded in student collaboration. Further to this, however, are some general teacher behaviours that research has shown to be effective in teaching to a wide range of needs. Box 7.5 provides an overview of research-supported inclusive instructional strategies—a list that applies to the modern classroom, but is by no means exhaustive.

Box 7.5: Inclusive teacher-oriented instructional strategies

- Use modelling and direct instruction.
- Provide additional demonstrations using a step-by-step approach.
- Pre-teach vocabulary and concepts using concrete experiences.
- Use role-play and simulations.
- Interact more frequently—differentiate the number of practice items set according to the student's capabilities and provide guided practice with frequent feedback.
- Use a variety of means of positive feedback (points, certificates and other reward systems).
- Use more frequent and more specific praise.
- Use cooperative and partnered learning strategies.
- Use a variety of modes for learning activities—do not rely on passive listening. Consider the variety of learning preferences, including visual, kinesthetic, and so on.
- Change the pace of instruction—increase wait time for oral responses as required, shorten instructions and repeat key elements.

- Differentiate the time to complete set work according to individual needs.
- Ask more questions and use different levels of complexity for different students.
- Provide hints or clues (scaffolding) to facilitate student responses.
- Use a variety of modes for responses (do not rely solely on written responses—use diagrams, tape recordings, construction of posters, models, videos, etc.).
- Incorporate personal interests and special talents into lessons.
- Integrate social skills, life skills and applied academics in the curriculum for all students.
- Incorporate metacognitive learning and problem-solving strategies wherever possible (e.g. How can I help myself? How else can I solve this problem?) for all students.
- Incorporate self-management strategies wherever possible (self-monitoring, self-correcting, self-reinforcement).
- Use criterion and performance-based assessment activities (portfolio presentations, demonstrations, exhibitions, etc.).
- Integrate direct observation and evaluation into the design of instructional strategies.

Source: Adapted from Deppeler (1998).

Having read the list of inclusive instructional strategies in Box 7.5, you could be excused for thinking that the strategies we recommend are little different from the strategies used by effective teachers in the normal course of a school day, be they in an inclusive setting or otherwise. This conclusion is absolutely correct. The skill set of successful teachers in inclusive classrooms aligns well with what we know about effective teaching generally. The perception that significantly different, more effective strategies for teaching a diverse range of learners exist is largely false. Importantly, a good inclusive teacher is an engaged one, one who can respond to the needs of all students in the class, and who plans in advance for this.

Learning outcomes

When considering learning outcomes, it should be remembered that this is one area in which differentiation is critical. While it is important for all students to have access to the same learning activities, the expectations in terms of what learning outcomes are to be achieved and to what degree this will occur can be adjusted from student to student. To this end, open-ended activities where a range of responses can be elicited are generally the most successful. Considerations for addressing learning outcomes are provided in Box 7.6.

Box 7.6: Considerations for addressing learning outcomes

- Can all students complete the same learning activity and produce the same outcome?
- Can all students complete the same learning activity but produce outcomes at different levels in the same curriculum?
- Can all students complete the same learning activity but produce different curricular outcomes?

The third question in Box 7.6 moves further from the ideal of universal design for learning and should be seen as a last resort, but is nevertheless unavoidable in some circumstances and is commonly seen in practice. An example of this might occur in a science lesson on flowers. The majority of the class might be expected to compare and contrast the structure of different types of flowers. However, while participating in the same activity, the learning outcome for a particular student still working on more core curriculum objectives might be to name the colours of the flowers under examination. Both the student with differing needs and the rest of the class are doing the same activity, but for very different reasons.

Obviously, the first point in Box 7.6 of all students participating in the same activities with the same objectives is closest to the ideal of universal design. Next comes having students participate in the same activities but producing outcomes from the same curriculum at different levels, which is more akin to what differentiated instruction is all about. For example, some children might be expected to write a one-page story reacting to a picture they are shown, while another student is only expected to write two sentences. This is essentially the same curriculum outcome of 'writing about a picture', but is assessed on very different levels, with different expectations and definitions of success.

It is tempting at this point to include a number of other tools that you can use in order to further diagnose and translate your local curriculum so that it aligns with the three principles of universal design for learning. However, this would be redundant because an excellent resource already exists that not only provides more comprehensive advice and suggestions regarding universal design than space in this book allows, but that does so in an interactive and comprehensive way. Not wanting to reinvent an already superb wheel, we will simply refer you to this resource, designed by one of the originators of the concept of universal design for learning, the Centre for Applied Special Technology (CAST). In particular, the free and easy to use resource *Teaching Every Student*, found at <www.cast.org/teachingeverystudent>, is invaluable.

Curriculum adaptations and modifications

As discussed earlier in this chapter, while engaging in universal design for learning is preferable, this is not always possible in some circumstances—for example, when the local mandated curriculum is highly prescriptive and inflexible. Universal design for learning is about teachers translating the curriculum to cater to the needs of all without further modification. Sometimes, however, teachers are not permitted to take such liberties and must follow the approach suggested by school system authorities. In such systems, teachers are generally required or encouraged to adapt and modify curriculum only for individual students who require this. Further, in some systems where translating the curriculum to the extent required by universal design is permitted, there are some contexts in which teachers are uncomfortable doing this, because they believe it is in the best interests of their students to adapt and modify curriculum for individuals rather than broadening instruction for the class as a whole. It is for this reason that we now turn to what we view as a less desirable, but nonetheless pragmatic, alternative to universal design for learning: adapting and modifying curriculum to link it to an individualised program. Some of the strategies suggested here, however, are also pertinent to those following a universal design approach. Therefore, we believe it is important for all readers to take into account the discussion that follows.

Identifying links between individual objectives and the classroom curriculum

For any individualised program to assist in the process of inclusion, it must be infused into your class curriculum as seamlessly as possible. Many teachers have difficulty reconciling individual plans with the general curriculum, and as a result many individual programs have in the past been taught in isolation (Goodman & Bond, 1993). This has had the effect of isolating some students, even though they are physically present in the classroom—which is not inclusion. What follows is some advice on how you can teach the classroom curriculum while also addressing the individual goals of some students.

Unit planning

It is important to begin thinking about how you might address individual learning goals for those who have them when you are at the stage of planning a unit of work. A unit of work is a sequence of lessons or sessions on a particular topic (or topics) designed with the aim of achieving an identified curricular outcome or number of outcomes. An example of a unit of work might be a series of physical education lessons on hockey. One lesson might address learning the rules, another lesson might address skill development, another might teach about teamwork in hockey, while other sessions might be allowed for practice and consolidation of skills and knowledge through brief games. At the end of the unit of work, it would be hoped that students would know how to play hockey according to the rules, and would have developed the skills to do so.

As you are mapping out your units of work, you should also be aware of aspects of the unit in which the opportunity to address individualised goals is present. You can do this in a structured way. Box 7.7 lists eight essential elements of inclusive unit design.

Box 7.7: Eight essential elements of inclusive unit design

1. A central unit issue or problem
2. An opening grabber or motivator
3. Lessons that are linked to a central issue or problem
4. Richly detailed source material
5. Culminating projects
6. Varied lesson formats
7. Multiple assessments
8. Varied modes of student expression

Source: Onosko & Jorgensen (1998).

These eight essential elements can create units of work that approach the ideals of universal design in being appropriate for all students. Units designed in this way do not differ greatly, if at all, from the traditional view of units of work. In essence, Onosko and Jorgensen are suggesting that units should be built around problems or issues rather than the more traditional approach of basing units around topics. This idea has gained greater currency in recent times, with a focus on 'big ideas' being fundamental to the backwards curriculum design approach recommended by McTighe et al. (2004), and echoed by

Loreman (2009). This does not mean that units of work can no longer teach about certain topics, but rather that emphasis is given to specific problems and issues within those topics as a basis for teaching and learning. For example, rather than basing a unit of work in science on the topic of genetics, the subject-matter may be explored more effectively through a central question or problem such as 'Is cloning animals ethical?'

In using a problem-based approach such as this, students are able to explore the science of genetics from different perspectives and in different ways in order to answer the central question. The role of the teacher in this situation is to provide an appropriate resource environment for students to explore the question or questions, while using their own knowledge to guide the students and provide appropriately focused teaching. Individual—even traditional— lessons could still occur within this framework in order to provide all students with the information and skills they require to answer the central unit question. The advantage of using a problem or issue-based approach in inclusive unit design is that each student can produce results that reflect his or her ability. There is no 'one size fits all' curriculum, with general criteria set in advance that either may never be reached by some students, or may restrict others to a narrow focus. In investigating a problem or issue, students are free to work at a level appropriate to them, and are judged only against their own past performances. This approach, of course, is based on the premise that all students are capable of solving problems, and indeed all are. Humans—all humans—solve problems right from infancy, from crying to elicit attention from a mother to more complex forms of problem-solving as we develop physically, cognitively, and emotionally. In terms of education, teachers must present students with problems that allow for a multiplicity of solutions and ways of demonstrating those solutions. This responsiveness to the level at which students are working is all part of the repertoire of the effective teacher.

Having students complete units of work based on issues or problems results in a more individualised approach for all students and, due to this, infusing elements of a student's individualised program plan into the regular curriculum becomes much easier. We suggest, however, that you first plan your unit for the class prior to identifying common links between the whole-class program and the individualised programs of particular students. The 'unit planner' sheet presented in Figure 7.1 on p. 156 (see also Form 13 in Useful Forms) is based on the eight essential elements of inclusive unit design discussed previously.

The unit planner incorporates the major elements of inclusive unit design with respect to adaptation and modification; however, it should be noted that such unit design is aligned reasonably closely with the sort of design suggested by proponents of universal design. The differences between the two ways of working (adaptation or universal design) are not clearly delineated at all times, and they occasionally share common strategies and ideas. The unit planner states the central problems or issues, provides information on lesson sequence and culminating projects, and outlines an ongoing assessment schedule. You will notice that under 'ongoing assessments' there is scope to schedule a range of different assessment topics and activities that can be implemented according to the different ways in which students can express their learning, once again demonstrating a connection with one of the three principles of universal design. This is included so that teachers can check to see whether students are coping with the content of the unit, and so that adjustments can be made if they are not. This planner is flexible enough to suit most planning contexts, being largely open-ended in nature, while also providing a reasonably structured framework into which you can infuse individual learning priorities for those who require them.

In order to infuse individual goals and objectives into your unit plans, you should first compare your unit plan to your individual program plan to see if there are any points of 'contact' where individual goals could be easily addressed in the course of teaching the unit. The completed form shown in Figure 7.2 on p. 157, based on a World War I unit example, might help you to do this (see also Form 13 in Useful Forms).

You will notice in Figure 7.2 that the relevant long-term goals listed beside the questions serve as 'goals' for the unit in general. The relevant specific objectives derived from these goals are then listed beside the planned sequence of lessons. In doing this, the teacher can keep these specific objectives in mind when planning the individual lessons, and ensure that opportunities to work towards these objectives are provided. Not every lesson has an objective listed beside it. This is because there is no requirement for each and every lesson taught in a unit to address the goals listed in the individualised program plan. It is enough that goals are addressed adequately throughout the year. This can be done by focusing on them during selected 'key lessons' in a unit.

Individual lesson plans

Once you have planned your unit, you can move on to planning the individual lessons that make up that unit. Teachers have different ways of planning lessons, and often use formats adapted to suit their own individual planning style. The planning format we are using as an example (see Figure 7.3) is an expanded version of the 'Single lesson plan' (Form 6 in Useful Forms) demonstrated in Chapter 5. Aside from assisting you to clarify your thoughts and

Unit planner

Dates: March 1–25		Class: Year 9C	

Subject area:
History – World War I

Central issues/problems
Could World War I have been avoided?
What was life like for soldiers?
What influence did this war have on the lives of people today?

Opening grabber/motivator:
Documentary on WWI followed by class discussion.

Summary of series of linked lessons:

1. Introduction to WWI. Causes, human cost, geographical orientation.	2. Avoiding WWI – was it possible? Class debate.	3. Internet research in computer lab – What was life like for soldiers?
4. Library research – What was life like for soldiers?	5. Group presentations – what was life like for soldiers?	6. Field trip to war memorial.
7. 'Chalk & Talk' and video on life during wartime.	8. WWII veterans and civilians visit and discuss their lives during wartime.	9. Brainstorming: What influence did WWI have on our world today?

Culminating projects:
Individual projects answering central questions.

Ongoing assessments (additional to culminating projects):

When?	What content/skills?	What form will it take?	How did student/s demonstrate learning?
Lesson 2	Knowledge of WWI causes.	Class debate.	Submission of written arguments. Verbal presentation of ideas. Partic. in devel. of arguments.
Lesson 5	Understanding of human cost of war. Conditions for soldiers.	Small-group class presentations (5 mins/group).	Groups to provide class handouts. Develop materials for pres. Ability to answer questions.
Lesson 9	Understanding of impact WWI has on us today.	Brainstorming session.	Contributions to brainstorming. Expanding on ideas of others.

Figure 7.1 Unit planner

Unit planner—Infusing individual targets

Dates: March 1–25	Child: Sandra D	Class: 9C

Subject area: History—WWI

Central issues/problems	Relevant goals:
• Could World War I have been avoided? • What was life like for soldiers? • What influence did this war have on the lives of people today?	• To improve verbal communication skills. • To develop fine motor skills. • To develop computer skills.

Summary of series of linked lessons:	Relevant linked individual objectives:
1. Introduction to WWI. Causes, human cost, geographical orientation	
2. Avoiding WWI: Was it possible? Class debate.	By the end of March Sandra will be able to verbally present information to the class as part of a group. (Goal 1, Objective 3)
3. Internet research in computer lab: What was life like for soldiers?	By the end of March Sandra will be able to effectively 'point and click' a 'mouse' on the computer to access the internet. (Goal 3, Objective 1)
4. Library research: What was life like for soldiers?	By the end of March Sandra will be able to turn the pages of a book unassisted. (Goal 2, Objective 3)
5. Group presentations: What was life like for soldiers?	By the end of March Sandra will be able to verbally present information to the class as part of a group. (Goal 1, Objective 3)
6. Field trip to war memorial.	
7. 'Chalk and Talk' and video on life during wartime	
8. WWII veterans and civilians visit and discuss their lives during wartime.	
9. Brainstorming: What influence did WWI have on our world today?	

Suggested culminating project:

Recorded 'radio broadcast' news report from the era.

Figure 7.2 Unit planner—Infusing individual targets

approach to the lesson, we believe it will also assist you to plan lessons for any paraprofessional who might work with you. We have used this format because we believe it is straightforward and can be adapted to suit the planning preferences of most teachers. Depending on your planning style, you might write less or more detailed plans. This is, of course, up to the individual teacher to decide, taking into account the boundaries of local professional requirements. However, by addressing the categories set out in the remainder of this chapter you are helping to ensure that individual goals are infused into the regular curriculum in a meaningful way.

This lesson planning form takes into account individual objectives, and provides teachers with an opportunity to briefly outline how those objectives will be addressed in the context of the lesson. It should be noted that the section for those with differing needs should not just be used when an individual objective is being pursued. This section can also be used to plan for modifications that occur in the course of lessons where no individual objectives are being pursued. This leads us to the question of what student-specific modifications and adaptations can be made in an inclusive classroom. If you have read this chapter closely, you will already be familiar with the types of modifications and adaptations that can be made to accommodate students. The sections in this chapter addressing considerations for the materials environment, the resources environment, instructional strategies and learning outcomes, in addition to the section in Chapter 9 on the physical environment, already provide direction for possible modifications or adaptations to the regular classroom environment. In the same way that a teacher might work through these considerations if following an approach of universal design for learning, those following an approach of making student-specific adaptations and modifications can also work through these same considerations.

The purpose of this chapter, and Chapter 6, has been to provide you with pragmatic advice and tools to plan for inclusion. We have tried to address and point out the practical aspects of two main approaches to planning for inclusion in evidence in today's schools: universal design for learning; and making student-specific adaptations and modifications to accommodate individualised programs. We make no secret of our view that the most inclusive of the two approaches is universal design for learning; however, we also recognise that in some circumstances student-specific adaptation and modification are necessary, and concede that the broad aims of inclusion can also be met through this approach. The next chapter builds on inclusive planning and examines some teaching strategies you can employ to promote effective inclusion in your classroom.

Individual lesson planning form

Subject area/grade   Science—Grade 3 _____   Date and time _____

Lesson topic	Pond study—Tadpoles to frogs. Lesson 3 in unit series of 6.

Lesson goal:	To introduce children to the 'tadpole to frog' life cycle.
Central problem:	What happens when tadpoles turn into frogs?
Materials:	Class fish tank and tadpoles collected last week.
	'Life cycle of a frog' chart. Relevant books.
Procedure:	Teacher introduces lesson topic. Children are asked the question 'What happens when tadpoles turn into frogs?' They are asked to investigate this problem using the internet, books, their own observations from the fish tank, and discussion with one another in small groups. Resulting from their research the children are asked to draw in the correct sequence what happens to tadpoles as they become frogs.
Homework task:	None for this lesson.
Diverse learner objectives for this lesson:	Katie
	By the end of Term Three Katie will be able to visually track an item as large as a coin against a white background for a period of 45 seconds. (Goal 2, Objective 3)
Inclusive materials and procedures:	When her group is observing tadpoles at the tank, one will be removed to the smaller fishbowl, set against a piece of white paper, and Katie will be encouraged to 'track' the movements of the tadpole with her eyes. Other students will also examine this individual tadpole to see if any changes have taken place.
Alternative assessment:	Visual tracking timed and documented.
Teacher does:	Introduces topic; divides class into groups; sets task; engages with each group and provides input as required; facilitates groups sharing; leads concluding discussion on frogs using chart.
Paraprofessional does:	During activities moves from group to group encouraging input from all children. When Katie's group is at the tadpole tank, provide direct assistance to ensure that an individual tadpole is moved to the smaller tank. Encourage Katie to visually 'track' the tadpole—time & document this. Encourage other children to study this tadpole. Encourage Katie to study larger tank.
Assessment:	Resulting from their research the children are asked to draw what happens to tadpoles in the correct sequence as they become frogs.

Figure 7.3 Individual lesson planning form

Key terms

Curriculum. Has to do with the teaching and learning of knowledge, skills and attitudes. It embraces issues such as subject-matter, pedagogy, assessments/evaluation and related resources involved in the organisation, delivery and articulation of education programs.

Universal design for learning. The process of translating relevant curriculum to meaningful learning activities that are accessible to all students in a class, allowing for multiple means of representation, expression and engagement.

Core curriculum. Curriculum areas judged to be basic and essential for all students.

Assistive technology. Technological aids that have been developed specifically to support children with disabilities, but which have broader application.

For discussion and reflection

7.1   What sorts of barriers do you think you might encounter when adopting a universal design for learning approach to curriculum and instruction?

7.2   When do curriculum adaptations and modifications become unreasonable?

7.3   How does a universal design for learning approach differ from modification and adaptation? How is it similar?

Further reading

Goodman, J.F. & Bond, L. (1993). The individualized educational program: A retrospective critique. *Journal of Special Education, 26*(4), 408–22.

Onosko, J.J. & Jorgenson, C.M. (1998). Unit and lesson planning in the inclusive classroom: Maximising learning opportunities for all students. In C.M. Jorgensen (Ed.), *Restructuring high schools for all students: Taking inclusion to the next level* (pp. 273–85). Baltimore MD: Paul H. Brookes.

8
Collaborative student learning

Key ideas in this chapter
- Collaborative learning arrangements
- Cooperative learning
- Peer support
- Peer tutoring
- Reciprocal teaching

Collaboration is fundamental to creating an inclusive learning environment in which responsibility for successfully educating a diversity of learners is shared amongst the members of the school community. Collaborative structures support a school climate of teamwork, cohesion, shared responsibility and sense of purpose (see Chapter 5). In order for diversity to enrich student learning, educators create positive social environments and structure instruction to promote high levels of interaction that is supportive, respectful, and accepting of all students (see Chapter 10). A large body of research has shown that collaborative approaches to learning can be effective in enhancing achievement, critical thinking, and problem-solving. Students achieve more if they are fully engaged in their learning. There are many collaborative learning arrangements that support student engagement and learning.

Along with pedagogy, curriculum, and differentiation, collaborative learning is a way of providing appropriate learning experiences for *all* students. This chapter expands the processes of collaboration outlined in earlier chapters with an emphasis on learning between students within classrooms, and suggests some practical guidelines for enhancing success.

Collaborative learning arrangements

Collaborative learning is not just a classroom strategy. Like other forms of collaboration outlined in Chapter 5, collaborative learning is an approach that respects and highlights each individual's abilities and contributions, as well as the sharing of authority and responsibility. These principles apply to teachers, students, and other members of the community and in classrooms, at committee meetings, within families, and as an approach to working with other people. Research on students working together in pairs and small groups over four decades has investigated many collaborative arrangements that promote engagement and learning. The underlying premise of collaborative learning is that mutual understanding and consensus are built through cooperation by the members. This is in contrast to competitive arrangements in which students are encouraged to better their peers. In collaborative learning arrangements, students work together on an investigation, problem, or other learning task that requires collaboration. The key to realising success is teaching students *how* to collaborate. It is essential to include learning activities that focus explicitly on collaborative skills and processes such as active listening and the handling of disagreements and differences.

Chapter 4 described the use of peer assessment as part of the assessment *for* learning framework. Peer assessment helps clarify a student's understanding of the learning goal and the success criteria while evaluating another student's work. Students attempt to understand and improve their work, using the feedback from a peer and self-reference to determine the quality of their work. Collaborative learning arrangements that explicitly support low-achieving students to use peer explanations to understand and improve their performance have been found not only to increase engagement but also to extend self-monitoring and metacognitive learning strategies (Gabriele, 2007). There has been substantive research over the past 90 years that has compared achievement in collaborative arrangements with achievement in competitive and individualistic learning. These studies have provided strong support for the effectiveness of collaborative instruction for improving social and academic competence for students with different learning needs. The results of a comprehensive review of more than eight decades of research, which included over 17 000 students from eleven countries, indicated that positive peer relationships and higher academic achievement were associated with collaborative arrangements as opposed to competitive or individualistic structures (Roseth, Johnson & Johnson, 2008).

Collaborative learning benefits students in many ways, including higher literacy achievement (Johnson & Johnson, 1989; Slavin, Cheung, Groff & Blake, 2008; Fitch & Hulgin, 2008), mathematics achievement (Slavin & Lake, 2008), knowledge construction (Barron, 2003; Weinberger, Stegmann & Fischer, 2007), and improved self-esteem and relationships between peers (Johnson & Johnson, 1989; Jenkins, Antil, Wayne & Vadasy, 2003) and between students and teachers (Tomlinson et al., 1997). Reviews of collaborative learning research (see, for example, Gillies, 2007; Johnson & Johnson, 1989; Slavin & Lake, 2008; Slavin & Lake, 2008; Wade, Abrami, Poulsen & Chambers, 1995) have provided positive support for the effectiveness of collaborative learning.

Furthermore, these studies demonstrate that, compared with competitive or individualistic learning, students who learn in a collaborative environment are more actively and fully engaged in their learning, demonstrate better critical thinking and reasoning skills, generate more novel ideas when presented with problems, and transfer more of what they have learned to new contexts. Active involvement in learning has been shown to be especially important for students with disabilities and others who tend to be passive in academic settings. Collaborative learning reduces students' levels of stress and anxiety when compared with competitive methods, and promotes more positive attitudes toward the content matter and to the learning experience itself. It also increases retention. Collaborative instruction enables students to develop important peer relationships that contribute to social development. These benefits are particularly important in influencing the participation and learning of students who are at risk of being disengaged from schooling. Together, these studies illustrate the advantages of using collaborative learning arrangements—particularly when *learning* is the central focus and goal for every student in the inclusive classroom. See Box 8.1 for some of the advantages of collaborative learning arrangements.

Box 8.1: Advantages of using collaborative arrangements for teaching and learning

There are many advantages of collaborative arrangements for teaching and learning:

- Interactive and cooperative rather than competitive and individualistic
- Individualised learning goals and individual accountability
- Structured and positive learning in heterogeneous groups
- Active participation and higher levels of engaged time compared with teacher-mediated instruction

- Improvement in self-esteem and attitude towards academic tasks
- Increased participation of all students in classroom learning
- Higher academic achievement and retention
- Ideal learning context for teaching, practising and reinforcing pro-social behaviours
- Improvement in peer and student–teacher relationships
- Increased respect for diversity
- Collaborative skills valued by society for work and leisure

Numerous collaborative learning arrangements have been designed and proven to be effective for teaching the diverse range of students in their classroom. The following section outlines three of the more popular approaches that structure student interaction in heterogeneous groups, encourage mutual interdependence and provide for individual accountability: cooperative learning, peer tutoring and reciprocal teaching.

Cooperative learning

Cooperative learning has been highly successful and has been adopted widely by teachers in classrooms throughout the world for more than 30 years (Johnson & Johnson, 2002; Putnam, 2009). The benefits of cooperative learning for academic and social learning have been validated in hundreds of research studies. The success of cooperative learning appears to be largely as result of the strong foundation of social interdependence theory upon which the operational procedures are built (Johnson & Johnson, 2009). Cooperative learning encourages collaboration through structured interaction in small groups. As the name implies, it involves students working in cooperation for a shared outcome. One of the goals of cooperative learning is to enhance individual student learning through group work. Another is to develop positive attitudes towards subject-matter and towards learning in general. Cooperative learning can further develop interpersonal and social problem-solving skills and build social relationships. A range of procedures exists for formal and informal cooperative learning groups. Web based forms of cooperative learning are becoming increasingly popular; these include online tools that can be used for wikis and forums. There are a number of elements of cooperative learning that are key to enhancing the processes and realising these benefits.

Characteristics of cooperative learning include:
- promotive interaction
- positive interdependence

- individual accountability
- group processing
- interpersonal and small-group skills.

Promotive interaction

When students are engaged cooperatively in work, promotive interaction involves them in promoting and supporting each other's cognitive and interpersonal efforts to achieve the group's goals. This involves students in trusting one another, sharing resources, helping, giving critical feedback, encouraging and acknowledging each other's efforts and perspectives and working for mutual benefits. Promotive interaction depends on the development of a number of cognitive and interpersonal skills—for example, verbal communication, listening, turn-taking, connecting past and present learning, empathy and sensitivity to others. Teachers may need to explicitly model for students the how of promotive interaction—for example, how to explain knowledge to others, how to check for understanding, how to encourage others, and how to discuss. It is through promoting each other's interaction and learning that students become personally committed to each other as well as to their mutual goals. Ultimately, each student should have at least one student who they are committed to helping learn and are supporting as a person; they should also have someone who is committed to them in the same way.

Positive interdependence

Successful cooperative learning activity creates positive interdependence (Johnson & Johnson, 2003) amongst group members who support, assist and encourage each other. This happens when the group's shared goal depends upon the actions of group members. No single student should feel successful until every member of their group is successful—in achieving both their individual learning task and their group-learning task. Interdependence builds group cohesion and improves performance. When positive interdependence is successfully structured (see Box 8.2), it emphasises, first, that each student's efforts are required for group success, and second, that each student has a unique contribution to make to the joint effort because of his or her resources and/or role and task responsibilities. Positive interdependence creates a commitment to the success of *all* group members as well as to each student's own success, and is at the heart of cooperative learning. If there is no positive interdependence, there will be little authentic cooperation.

Box 8.2: Structuring positive interdependence

Some ways a teacher can structure positive interdependence include the following:

- **Goal.** The group has a common goal and every student in the group is expected to achieve it.
- **Sequence.** The learning task is divided into several smaller steps or tasks. Each student must complete his or her individual task as a part of the predetermined sequence.
- **Role.** Each student is assigned a role with specific responsibilities. Each role contributes to and supports the overall completion of the learning task.
- **Resource.** Resources, information and materials are limited so that students need to work together in sharing the available resources.
- **Incentive.** Every student receives the same reward, but only if every student in the group succeeds.
- **Identity.** The group should establish its common identity by members giving the group a name or designing a logo or symbol. They may also wish to have a slogan or song.
- **Competition.** Each group can compete against other cooperative learning groups.
- **Environment.** The students within a group can be confined to a specific physical area within the classroom.

An example of positive interdependence

The group's task is complete when every member of the group can give one rule for a 'good' narrative and when the group has constructed a narrative text. Achieving this group goal depends on the performance of every member of the team. Each student in the group will be a specialist for a different part of the narrative—for instance, one person will specialise in the characters, another on the plot, another on the setting. The group must cooperate on how to put the narrative together. Students can leave the group to join others who are specialists for the same part of the narrative. When they have enough information, they can then rejoin their own group and tell the others what they have learned.

Individual accountability: Individual goals

Positive interdependence ensures that each student's contribution to the task is important for the group's success. Additionally, it is vital that each student accepts responsibility for succeeding with his or her individual contribution (see Box 8.3). Accountability can vary with each student. While each student is responsible for learning something, not every student has to learn the same thing. Individual evaluations are vital for determining what each student has learned. Teachers can also encourage students to evaluate their own learning and the performance in the group.

Box 8.3: Increasing individual accountability

A teacher might increase individual accountability by requiring each student to:
- perform one identifiable part of the group task
- record his or her observations in individual notebooks (to be collected and read)
- record individual work contribution (daily) in a notebook
- report individually on group work
- evaluate their individual performance—the achievement of their goals and how well they functioned within the group.

Another way to support students to be individually accountable is to assign them different roles each time their group meets to complete their task. For example:

Doing this task depends on the participation of every member of the team. Each member of this group will have a different role every time you work together to complete your group task. One of you will be the encourager and will be responsible for getting everyone to state their ideas, another will be the checker and will need to check that everyone is making progress and completing their individual part of the work. One of you will be the writer and record the important points on how the work was completed, the reporter will report back to the class on the group's progress and the timer will make sure. Reward for this group's achievement depends on the performance and the participation of every member of the team in different roles.

Group processing

Group processing refers to the functioning of the group and how well the group works together. Group processing necessarily involves reflection on what was achieved, what worked and what did not, and what might be maintained, modified or changed to enhance future work. What worked well? What could we do better? The close monitoring of group processes during cooperative learning groups is essential for their success. Teachers and students can take an active role in monitoring the progress of the group in achieving their goal and in students' interaction with one another. Monitoring at the beginning of a cooperative learning session may ensure students understand their task, while monitoring during the activity will help to identify any academic or group interaction difficulties. Teachers can structure opportunities to clarify instructions, or to remind students about effective collaboration and answer questions. Observation should be focused on individual students as well as the group performance and the quality of the interaction among the students. Who is participating and who (if anyone) is not? Do the observed actions support successful cooperative learning (listening, encouraging, volunteering ideas, negotiating)? How do students encourage, explain, demonstrate, paraphrase, question and applaud each other? Students' attention should be drawn to the importance of reflection to improve group processing. One way to enhance reflection is to have one or two students act as observers for a group—monitoring encouragement, interruptions and participation. The 'Observation Wheel' (see Box 8.4) is an excellent tool for structuring the observations.

Box 8.4: Observation Wheel

1. Use one observation wheel for each five-minute interval.
2. Place the names of the students on the wheel, exactly as they are sitting in the group.
3. Indicate when a student speaks to another student with an arrow pointing in the direction of the receiver.
4. Indicate further messages with marks across the shaft of the arrow.
5. Place a ✗ against a student's name every time he or she interrupts or talks over another member.
6. Place a ✓ next to a student's name every time he or she encourages another member to participate.

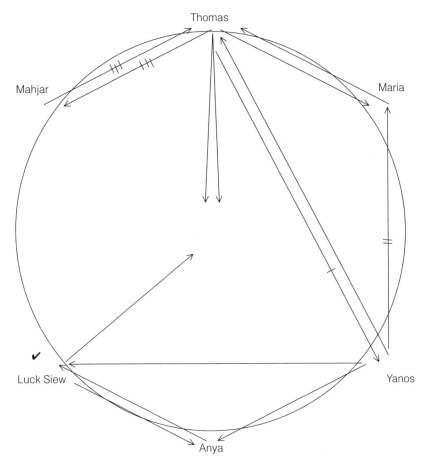

Figure 8.1 Observation wheel

Some things to look out for include:

Patterns of communication within the group

- Did students participate in the group equally?
- Who talked and to whom? Did some students talk more than others?
- Did some students not talk at all?
- How often did individual students talk, and for how long?
- Did some students interrupt others?
- Did some students encourage others?
- Was every student in the group listened to? If not, why not?
- Did the patterns of communication change from the first part of the session to the later stages?

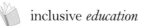

Information-sharing

- How was information in the group shared?
- Was the needed information easily available to every student?
- Did students offer their information to others at appropriate times?
- Did students request each other's information?
- Did students encourage others to share information?
- Did students respond positively to other students' contributions and suggestions?
- Did students ask each other questions or paraphrase to clarify their understanding of other students' contributions?

Decision-making and problem-solving

- Was the information of all group members used?
- How did the group make decisions?
- Was there an obvious leader/organiser?
- Was the problem-solving of the group effective?
- What problems did the group have in working together?
- How could problem-solving be made more effective in this group?

Reflection

Information gained from informal observations or using the Observation Wheel should be used to enhance reflection about group processing. Used constructively, not punitively, this information can support students' reflection, evaluation and interpersonal development. Discussion of observational data with students should help make explicit the group processes, identifying areas for further improvement along with successes. Observations should also inform necessary changes to help the cooperative learning groups work more effectively. It is important that any observational information summarises the work and communication patterns of the group but does not name individual students. For example, in using the Observation Wheel, the observer could say:

> *In this group session some students interrupted several times. More than one student in this group encouraged others to give their views. Some students did not talk at all or only spoke to one other person once or twice. As time went on, only three students were involved in making decisions for the group.*

Group discussion arising from teacher or student observations should also not refer to individual students:

What can we do to increase the participation of all members of this group? Does anyone have suggestions for improving the communication or the decision-making of this group?

Observation can also be used in conjunction with group reflection and evaluation at the end of a cooperative learning session. Students can be asked:

- How did you feel about your participation?
- What helped or stopped you from participating?
- What helps everyone participate in group activities?
- Name one thing someone did that was helpful for the group.
- What is one thing you could do to make the group cooperate better?

Teachers can co-construct alternative forms of evaluation with students (an example appropriate for lower-grade levels is provided in Box 8.5).

Box 8.5: CL group-evaluation questions

1. I liked working with the other members of my group. YES NO
2. I volunteered information or ideas to my group. YES NO
3. I encouraged a member of my group to participate. YES NO
4. I listened to others without interrupting. YES NO
5. I said something positive about another member's idea. YES NO
6. Everyone did something to help get the work done. YES NO
7. Everyone helped in making decisions. YES NO
8. I asked a question when I did not understand. YES NO
9. I thought about how a member felt when they spoke. YES NO
10. I learned something from working with my group. YES NO

Interpersonal and small-group skills

A key element to success with cooperative learning is ensuring that students are taught explicitly *how* to work cooperatively in small groups, as well as explicit skills of relating positively to one another. Teachers sometimes comment that they have tried cooperative learning and that it didn't work. The reasons given often include 'The students didn't get along' or 'One or two of the students ended up doing the majority of the work—the others just went along for a free ride.' If cooperative learning is to be successful, the learning experience needs to be structured to consider the interpersonal and small-group skills of *all* the students involved. All students should be encouraged to actively participate by volunteering their ideas, and to listen to the ideas of others, before selecting a particular solution to a problem. One skill that is very important for students is the ability to respond to a number of different opinions. A range of opinions provides students with an opportunity to question their own views and to search for more information. However, in order for this process to be constructive, students must have developed adequate skills to efficiently communicate their own ideas as well as listen to the ideas of others. They also need to be able to handle praise and criticism, and know how to deal with conflict. Conflict should not be avoided, as it provides an opportunity to learn; however, students need to learn skills to manage conflict as it arises. Students' cooperative learning skill repertoire should be balanced between actions that foster encouragement, sensitivity and friendliness and those that contribute a sense of individual responsibility and control.

In the previous section, we emphasised the importance of monitoring the cooperative learning group processes, particularly through focused observation. Observation can also be used to identify individual students' interpersonal and small-group skills. Teachers can then target particular skills for further development. Explicit teaching should also include rules, expectations for appropriate behaviour and success criteria. Box 8.6 lists some interpersonal and small-group skills. Box 8.7 provides an example of rules for active listening.

Box 8.6: Interpersonal and small-group skills

Interpersonal skills

- Actively listen
- Accept responsibility
- Give constructive feedback
- Contribute ideas
- Participate
- Ask clarifying questions
- Paraphrase others' ideas
- Encourage

Small-group skills

- Share resources and tasks
- Take turns
- Make decisions democratically

- Resolve conflict
- Accept differences
- Show support
- Build trust

Box 8.7: Rules for active listening in a cooperative learning group

1. Look directly at the face of the person who is speaking.
2. Stop writing or any other work and be quiet while the other person is speaking.
3. Keep your mind on the content of what the other person is saying (make mental pictures or repeat key words quietly to yourself to help make sense of what they are saying).
4. Listen to how the speaker is feeling as well as to what is being said, and pay attention to his or her facial expressions.
5. Encourage the speaker with head nods and other positive body language.
6. Do not make a decision until the speaker is fully heard.
7. Ask questions and paraphrase to check and confirm your understanding of both the content and the feeling of what has been said.

Students should and can be actively involved in the development of the success criteria used to assess both individual and group skills. Teaching should always include modelling of good performance of the skill, practice and explicit feedback on performance against the success criteria (see Chapter 4 on assessment for learning and success criteria, and Chapter 10 for resources and teaching social skills). There are also a number of useful resources to help with this process—we have included a few titles at the end of this chapter for this purpose.

Example: Cooperative learning in Year 7

Mr Robinson observed various groups in his Year 7 Studies of Society and the Environment classroom for several weeks. He then made a list of skills needed for further development by all of the students. He also asked students to select a personal goal for themselves from a list of 'small-group skills'. Students could decide whether to share their personal goal with others. Mr Robinson then focused on one small-group skill every week for eight weeks. He began with *participating*, then the following week *accepting* others' ideas at the beginning of group work, then *listening, encouraging, explaining, paraphrasing, asking* clarifying *questions* and finally *giving feedback* to other members.

Each week, Mr Robinson introduced the particular skill with a whole-class discussion of the rationale and purpose of the skill, as well as rules, and modelled examples of the skill. He then gave his students a five-point scale for rating and reviewing their own performance. Mr Robinson also indicated that he and at least one other student would be using this scale for their observations of cooperative learning group work. After participating in several activities each week, students engaged in discussion and reviewed their group processing. Discussion included explicit feedback from Mr Robinson and any student observers. In each subsequent week, Mr Robinson repeated the process, rotating students to observe groups, adding a new five-point scale for each of the skills, providing feedback about performance and involving students in reflection and discussion of their performance. Finally, students reviewed their individual goals and identified particular skills to be included in future class activities.

The five-point scale of listening in Box 8.8 could be used in a similar fashion to Mr Robinson's scale: for observing students and as a basis for providing feedback about their listening, as well as involving them in reflection and discussion of their performance.

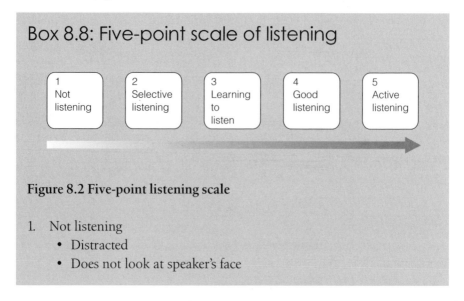

Box 8.8: Five-point scale of listening

| 1
Not listening | 2
Selective listening | 3
Learning to listen | 4
Good listening | 5
Active listening |

Figure 8.2 Five-point listening scale

1. Not listening
    • Distracted
    • Does not look at speaker's face

- Does not respond to what is said in any way
- Fidgets or writes, draws, etc. during speaking

2. Selective listening
   - Only listens to one part of the message (what is said) OR how it is said, but not both
   - Wrongly anticipates what is to be said—interrupts
   - Sometimes looks at speaker, other times tunes out—gazing somewhere else
   - Rarely responds to what is said

3. Learning to listen
   - Maintains good eye contact and looks at speaker's face
   - Shows listening with facial expressions and gestures (e.g. head nod) in keeping with message
   - Listens to what is said and how it is said (content and emotion)
   - Sometimes interrupts and wrongly anticipates what is to be said
   - Does not ask clarifying questions or repeat back what has been said

4. Good listening
   - Waits for key pauses to acknowledge speaker
   - Appropriate level of eye contact and use of gestures
   - Repeats main points of speaker without expanding
   - Does not interrupt
   - Rarely encourages
   - Sometimes asks clarifying questions

5. Active listening
   - Is very involved and interested
   - Verbal and non-verbal acknowledgements are often given as speaker pauses
   - Conveys warmth and interest by positive praise
   - Repeats key points and volunteers more information
   - Conveys an understanding of key emotions or own interpretation of what is understood from speaker
   - Asks clarifying questions
   - Encourages speaker to expand and talk further when appropriate
   - Changes role from listener to speaker only when speaker is fully finished

Enhancing the effectiveness of cooperative learning groups

Using cooperative learning groups as an effective teaching and learning approach requires planning. Not all cooperative learning groups lead to collaboration or demonstrate positive learning outcomes for all students. Research has identified several actions that can enhance the effectiveness of cooperative learning groups. These are listed in Box 8.9 and some are discussed in the next section.

Box 8.9: Twenty ways to enhance effectiveness of collaborative learning groups

Teacher actions:

1. Assign students to small heterogeneous groups (optimal size—four to six students).
2. Vary group composition regularly so that students experience working in a number of different groupings (e.g. ability, gender, friendship, other).
3. Design the task to promote discussion (open or discovery-based tasks).
4. Incorporate manipulative materials to encourage 'hands-on' active involvement.
5. Establish rules and clear protocols for 'how we work together' in groups.
6. Assign and rotate student roles (e.g. writer, encourager, observer, time monitor, runner, checker).
7. Ensure that tasks are clearly defined for students, with an agreed timescale.
8. Check for understanding (e.g. instructions, roles and rules for engagement).
9. Make success criteria (intended academic and social learning outcomes) explicit.
10. Present instructions in visual and auditory ways (in language students can understand).
11. Teach interpersonal and small-group skills (e.g. how to take turns, make decisions, question, listen, paraphrase, give constructive criticism, handle disagreements and conflict).

12. Monitor student interactions within the group.
13. Provide adequate spacing between groups to minimise distraction.
14. Promote interdependence along with individual responsibility.
15. Use some form of individual and group accountability.
16. Individualise success criteria and task requirements so *all* students have an opportunity for success.
17. Provide feedback to students against success criteria for individual and group goals/tasks.
18. Teach explicit strategies for monitoring and critical reflecting on students' skills and group processing.
19. Use peer assessment and self-assessment with success criteria to promote critical reflection.
20. Recognise outstanding group performance.

Assigning students to cooperative learning groups

The first issue in planning a cooperative learning activity is how to constitute the groups. First, what is an appropriate size? The optimum size suggested for cooperative learning groups is between four and six students. Fewer students may not provide sufficiently different points of view. More students may prevent group cohesion or cause some students to withdraw completely from active participation. A larger group requires more time to develop productive collaborative relationships. Heterogeneous groups composed of students of different ethnic backgrounds, genders and races, and with varying learning styles and achievement levels, are preferable. Students of different abilities should be distributed equally in each group. Students at higher levels of competence may be better at explaining concepts to others in the group and may do so more frequently. The process of explaining will improve these students' understanding while other students can benefit from the explanations provided by these peers. Further, the development of intellectual argument and acceptance of a variety of perspectives promote mutual construction of meaning and are vital for the social interaction and development of all students. Grouping students of varying abilities and achievement levels typically leads to a greater variety of ideas and more frequent giving and receiving of explanations in discussion. It is important to remember that forming heterogeneous groups does not mean randomly selecting students and assigning them to groups. Therefore, when thinking about assigning your students to groups, try to view them along a continuum of a number of characteristics. Some characteristics may be important for particular groups or tasks. For example, some students may be particularly proficient at hands-on construction, or dramatic performance or music. Others may be more or less socially skilled or verbal in a group context. Some will be articulate talkers and others introverted; some will be excellent readers but weaker writers; some of the writers will have trouble with expression and others with spelling; some will be great at generating writing ideas but find grammar and expression challenging. Students who work at the same academic level will not be completely alike. Assigning students to groups should as much as possible be tailored to suit their unique profile and to provide challenge for students with different capabilities. For example, grouping students who can stay focused on a learning task with those who find it more difficult to do so may be an effective way to create a group. By observing groups and changing their composition regularly, you can take advantage of individual students' strengths and ensure that the same students are not always the most skilled in the group. Students with disabilities and additional learning needs should be placed in groups and closely monitored to ensure that participation is successful.

Selecting the task

The next step is to construct or select tasks that will engage all students in the content to be learned. Tasks that lend themselves to collaboration are those with more than one solution that can be expressed in a variety of formats and, most importantly, that require discussion and explanations in order to demonstrate student thinking. Discovery-based and open tasks that have no set procedures to follow or specific solutions are more likely to promote student interaction and involve a higher level of problem-solving. Use manipulative materials that can be shared by group members and that can keep students actively involved and focused on the task. The cooperative learning task must be clearly defined so students understand what is expected from them in the assignment. Finally, the way you establish the cooperative learning experience is critical for promoting positive outcomes. Teaching students how to work in groups, and clearly outlining the learning task and expectations of students as success criteria, can have a positive effect on the quality of both the group interaction and the learning experience. Assigning each person in the group a specific role and changing the roles is also very important in order to ensure that one or two students do not dominate or take over the role of leader in the group, and that everyone has the opportunity to function in each of the different roles.

Peer support

Peer support refers to various alternatives that involve students working together to support each other's learning. Students' peer-support roles vary from providing direct instruction and modelling (peer tutoring) to encouraging and monitoring performance. Peer support arrangements vary considerably. Arrangements can involve one or several peers, across ages (Karcher, 2008) and on a class-wide or school-wide basis. The focus of these activities is also varied and can have interpersonal and cognitive as well as academic objectives; it can also be combined with self-management. Peer support has consistently and successfully been used as a practical approach for engaging students with disabilities in inclusive schools (Carter & Kennedy, 2006).

Research has consistently demonstrated that peer support has academic, as well as interpersonal and social, benefits for a range of students, including those with disabilities (Maheady, Harper & Mallette, 2001) (see Box 8.10). As with the other collaborative arrangements presented in this chapter, there is substantial evidence to support the use of peer support in facilitating the inclusion of students with disabilities, with benefits including enhancing academic performance, improving interpersonal relationships, and much greater acceptance of individual differences. However, the potential impact of peer support alternatives depends upon careful planning, collaboration, and evidence regarding effectiveness. Peer support is only one element of a multifaceted approach to supporting the diverse range of students to participate fully in schooling. Peer support should be connected with other school-wide structures and classroom practices to ensure that *all* students are participating meaningfully in their schooling (Choi, 2007; Cushing, Clark, Carter & Kennedy, 2005)

Box 8.10: Advantages of peer support

- Promotes active learning engagement
- Creates learner-friendly instructional environments
- Increases opportunities for students to engage in positive social interaction
- Improves peer relationships and classroom climate
- Increases student on-task time and response
- Reduces teacher:student ratios as students are in effect the tutors for one another
- Increases opportunities for students to receive feedback and encouragement
- Is preferred by students

Like all collaborative arrangements, successful peer support arrangements require teachers to engage in careful planning and explicit teaching. Frequent monitoring of the progress of all students is also vital to determine whether each and every student is making the intended gains (Vaughn, Klingner & Bryant, 2001). Teachers will need to employ many of the same strategies suggested earlier in this chapter for implementing cooperative learning groups if peer support arrangements are to be both successful and effective. In short, careful planning, explicit teaching, and frequent monitoring of student involvement and progress are vital for successful peer support arrangements.

Peer tutoring

Peer tutoring is a general descriptor for cooperative learning strategies that involve pairs of students in teaching and learning on a one-to-one basis. Tutees are the students who receive the instruction or encouragement from the tutors. In cross-age tutoring arrangements, an older student acts as a tutor for a younger student. In reciprocal teaching arrangements, students alternate between tutor and tutee roles. The effectiveness of peer tutoring is supported by substantial research evidence, and provides teachers with another instructional alternative to cater for the diverse range of students in their classrooms today.

As with cooperative learning, reviews of the research evidence make it clear that when peer tutoring is implemented with care, it has been found to have a significant positive influence for both the tutee and the tutor in a number of academic as well as social areas (Robinson, Schofield & Steers-Wentzell, 2005; Rohrbeck, Ginsburg-Block, Fantuzzo & Miller, 2003; Seigel, 2005; Stenhoff & Lignugaris, 2007; Sutherland, Wehby & Gunter, 2000; Topping, 2005) (see Box 8.11).

Much peer tutoring in schools was originally targeted towards academic areas such as reading and mathematics, and sometimes involved drill and practice approaches focused on narrow skills (Topping, 2005). Increasingly, the trend has been to use peer tutoring for more challenging tasks in literacy, mathematics and science, and problem-solving and thinking skills (Gersten, 2001; Topping, Peter, Stephen & Whale, 2004: Topping & Bryce, 2004; Vaughn, Klingner & Bryant, 2001) (see Box 8.12).

Box 8.11: Advantages of peer tutoring

- Access to one-on-one assistance
- Opportunities to learn and interact socially in mutually supportive ways
- Opportunities for extended practice

- Increased opportunities for feedback
- Learning in a supportive context
- Improves self-efficacy
- Heightens engagement
- Flexible, cost-effective and easily implemented along with existing programs
- Provides modelling of academic and social skills
- Enhances social relationships and decreases negative behaviour
- Encourages positive social interaction
- Opportunities for collaborative learning
- Time-efficient
- Effective with all students
- Positive influence on social and academic outcomes for both tutor and tutee

Box 8.12: Success with peer tutoring

As with other collaborative arrangements, the positive benefits can be enhanced by ensuring these key elements are included:

- Intensive and explicit training of tutors before beginning
- 'Active' learning activities
- Structured and carefully prescribed lessons
- Sessions scheduled to occur frequently but to be of short duration (e.g. four to five times a week for no longer than 30 minutes per session)
- Positive collaborative culture
- High levels of positive feedback and encouragement for both tutors and tutees
- Regular monitoring of students' progress, engagement and peer interaction

Reciprocal teaching

Reciprocal teaching (RT) was developed as a strategy to improve reading comprehension in small groups of students (Pallincsar & Brown, 1984; Pallincsar, David & Brown, 1989). The teacher and students take turns leading a dialogue about sections of a text. Students involved in the RT process are checking their own understanding of the material they have encountered. The premise of RT is that by engaging in structured and active dialogue with a peer, students with learning difficulties will increase their participation and improve their understanding (Pallincsar & Klenk, 1992; Rojewski & Schell, 1994). It is expected that the thinking or cognitive processing that is accomplished between learners during RT activities will eventually be accomplished by individual students. This notion that individual cognitive development is constructed through participating in social groups is consistent with the Vygotskian (Vygotsky, 1978) perspective. Research has demonstrated that RT can be effective with widely diverse students and in a variety of contexts (Lederer 2000; Rosenshine & Meister, 1994; Vaughn & Schumm, 1995). RT has continued to be a valuable support for comprehension (Boulware-Gooden, Carreker, Thornhill & Joshi, 2007; Spörer, Brunstein & Kieschke, 2009; Takala, 2006) and has now been extended to be integrated with video and computer technology (Kucan, Pallincsar, Khasnabis & Chang, 2008; Pallincsar, Spiro, Kucan & Magnusson, 2007).

RT activities support students' participation through the practice of four specific comprehension strategies: clarifying; questioning; summarising; and predicting.

- *Clarifying*. When a challenging or difficult text is encountered, questions should be formulated that will make the rest of the text easier to understand.
- *Questioning*. The 'why and how' questions should prompt discussion and generate further questions.
- *Summarising*. Important details are highlighted to support students' understanding of the key idea of the paragraph and to enable them to predict what is ahead in the next paragraph.
- *Predicting*. Students encouraged to make guesses about where the text is going next.

The role of the teacher is to model, scaffold, provide feedback, and collaborate with students in their efforts to understand the material that is being read. Initially, each strategy is modelled then, as students become more confident and competent through guided practice, they take increasing responsibility for mediating discussion with their peers. Sessions gradually become dialogues where students prompt each other to use, apply and verbalise a strategy and comment on the application. See Box 8.13 for guidelines on starting reciprocal teaching.

Box 8.13: Starting reciprocal teaching (RT)

Step 1:   Select a well-structured text
Step 2:   Teach the four comprehension strategies: predicting, clarifying, questioning and summarising.

Step 3: Model each of the strategies using the first paragraph of the text.

Step 4: Form small groups of four to six students with a range of literacy levels.

Step 5: Assign each student in the group one of the remaining paragraphs.

Step 6: Have the student 'teach' one the four strategies to the group, using their paragraph.

Step 7: Provide scaffolded support as needed. The extent of teacher scaffolding will depend upon students' level of skill with each of the four strategies, and their ability to work collaboratively in a group.

Step 8: Encourage discussion within the groups, both during and after the student teaching. Ask students to identify the skills that were most effectively and least effectively used.

Step 9: Increase RT group independence by reducing the level of teacher scaffolding and change the teacher's role to one of facilitator.

Step 10: Monitor comprehension and group processes by observation and by asking higher-level comprehension questions.

Teachers wishing to implement RT in their classrooms should consult the many excellent resources available in print and on the internet. As emphasised throughout this chapter, successful implementation of RT, like all collaborative arrangements, depends on careful ongoing monitoring of the learning group and being ready to intervene when necessary. Altering group membership and/ or providing explicit teaching or modelling may be required. It is also important to encourage students to monitor the process themselves.

We believe that *all* students should have appropriate learning experiences in inclusive schools. The collaborative learning arrangements we have described in this chapter can be highly effective in enhancing students' interpersonal skills, and engagement in their learning. More importantly, collaborative structures are fundamental to creating an inclusive classroom in which responsibility for learning is shared amongst the members of the school community.

Key terms

Cooperative learning. Collaboration through structured interaction in small groups. It involves students cooperating to achieve a shared outcome.

Positive interdependence. When the group's goal or product outcome depends upon the actions of all group members.

Peer tutoring. A general descriptor for cooperative learning strategies that involve pairs of students teaching and learning on a one-to-one basis. In cross-age tutoring arrangements, an older student acts as a tutor for a younger student. In reciprocal teaching arrangements, students alternate between tutor and tutee roles.

Reciprocal teaching. A collaborative strategy to improve reading comprehension, in which teachers and students take turns leading discussions regarding sections of text using four strategies.

For discussion and reflection

8.1   What criteria might a teacher use to decide whether or not it is best to use a teacher-led or a student-collaborative instructional approach?

8.2   Do some areas lend themselves more naturally to a collaborative instructional approach? Which areas? Why?

8.3   What are some of the potential problems a teacher might encounter with collaborative instruction, and how can any risks be reduced or potential problems avoided?

Further reading

General

The Cooperative Learning Center is a research and training centre housed at the University of Minnesota. It provides cooperative learning articles, research, a newsletter and other resources. The research team of Roger T. Johnson and David W. Johnson will even answer questions on cooperative learning sent by teachers, and past answers can be found in their Q&A section. Available from <www.co-operation.orgt>.

Gillies, R.M. (2007). *Cooperative learning: Integrating theory and practice*. Thousand Oaks, CA: Sage.

Hutchinson, D. (2007). Teaching practices for effective cooperative learning in an online learning environment (OLE). *iJournal of Information Systems Education, 18*, 357–67.

Johnson, D.W. & Johnson, R.T. (2009). An educational psychology success story: Social interdependence theory and cooperative learning. *Educational Researcher, 38*(5), 365–79.

Pallincsar, A.S., David, Y.M. & Brown, A.L. (1989). Using reciprocal teaching in the classroom: A guide for teachers by reciprocal teaching. Available from <www.ncrel.org/sddrs/areas/issues/students/atrisk/at6lk38. htm>.

Villa, R.A., Thousand, J.S. & Nevin, A.I. (2008). *A guide to co-teaching: Practical tips for facilitating student learning*. Thousand Oaks, CA: Corwin Press.

Specific applications

Haenan, J. & Tuithof, H. (2008). Cooperative learning: The place of pupil involvement in a history textbook. *Teaching History, 131*, 30–4.

Harper, G. & Maheady, L. (2007). Peer-mediated teaching and students with learning disabilities. *Intervention in School and Clinic, 43*(2), 101–8.

Meadan, H. & Monda-Amaya, L. (2008). Collaboration to promote social competence for students with mild disabilities in the general classroom: A structure for providing social support. *Intervention in School and Clinic, 43*, 158–67.

Nagel, P. (2008). Moving beyond lecture: Cooperative learning and the secondary social studies classroom. *Education, 128*, 363–8.

Petursdottir, A., McComas, J., McMaster, K. & Horner, K. (2007). The effects of scripted peer tutoring and programming common stimuli on social interactions of a student with Autism Spectrum Disorder. *Journal of Applied Behaviour Analysis, 40*, 353–7.

Shamir, A. & Lazerovitz, T. (2007). Peer mediation intervention for scaffolding self-regulated learning among children with learning disabilities. *European Journal of Special Needs Education, 22*(3), 255–73.

Temple, V.A. & Lynnes, M.D. (2008). Peer tutoring for inclusion. *ACHPER [Australian Council for Health and Physical Education and Recreation] Healthy Lifestyles Journal, 55*, 11–21.

9
Organising the inclusive classroom

Key ideas
- Physical layout of the inclusive classroom
- Classroom seating plans
- Classroom procedures
    - student tasks
    - emergency plans
    - substitute teacher plans
- Personal care
- Medication in the classroom

Organising students and staff in the classroom is an issue of prime importance to learning. The development of clear procedures and structures helps to ensure that the day runs smoothly and that learning is optimised. Often having a diverse class means that teachers need to put considerable thought into the structures they implement in the classrooms. Generally, however, this effort pays off in terms of producing a pedagogically sound environment for all, which promotes both community and learning. This chapter presents some ways of organising class structures and procedures so as to promote inclusion. Issues addressed including the physical layout of the classroom, seating plans, classroom procedures, and issues of personal care and medication administration for those students who require them.

Physical layout of the inclusive classroom

A major consideration in an inclusive classroom is the physical layout of the room. It almost goes without saying that all students must be able to gain physical access to a classroom in order to be involved in learning activities with the rest of the class. Physical access is the most significant prerequisite to learning in an inclusive environment; without it, no other type of access—such as curricular or social—can occur. It is the responsibility of school administration and the classroom teacher to ensure that all students are able to access the classroom, and that any required modifications to structures are clearly communicated to the appropriate person in the school and are carried out. These modifications should not be viewed as a luxury for which one should be grateful—they should be seen as the bare minimum of what is required for a school to meet the needs of its students. Many education systems have special funds set aside, as well as contingency plans for the modification of existing buildings. Most new school buildings are now constructed with universal access (access for all) in mind.

When we think of universal physical access, one of the first things that may spring to mind is the installation of ramps in areas where there are stairs. Ramps are important for access—not only for children in wheelchairs, but also for those using walking frames or those with general mobility difficulties, and even elderly grandparents or others visiting the school. The installation of ramps is not necessarily an expensive process. Reasonably priced metal ramps that are easy to move and store are now readily available (for example, many parents use these to assist in loading students in wheelchairs into vehicles). We have also seen examples of ramps constructed from sturdy plywood and painted with a non-slip coating that have adequately met the needs of schools for years in terms of cost, function, and durability. In multi-storey school buildings, the installation of a lift may need to be considered. This might take some time to complete. In the meantime, school administration could timetable all classes for students with mobility difficulties in ground-floor classrooms.

Providing universal access does not, however, stop with the installation of appropriate ramps. Narrow doors may need to be widened. Anyone who has spent a day in a wheelchair can attest to the skinned knuckles that result from doorways being too narrow to fit through easily. How doors open and close also needs to be considered. Doors may be required that are easy to open from a sitting position, and that will stay open long enough for a student with a mobility difficulty to enter a room. While it is important for teachers to be aware of the sorts of general modifications that may be required in a school building, determining exactly what these are generally falls to architects and engineers, who can conduct environmental audits. Your own awareness of this is important, though, because generally such audits are done on request from school staff who are no longer finding the school building suitable for the needs of the student body. Unless school staff bring this to the attention of the relevant personnel, such modifications can be forgotten or ignored, or an assumption can be made that they are not required.

It is within the classroom space that an individual teacher can have a significant impact on physical access. Once in the classroom, all students need to be able to move around freely. For this reason, the bigger the room the better it will be, especially if wheelchairs or other mobility devices are used by some students. Modern classrooms are often cluttered with chairs, tables, benches, shelves, bags and other learning materials, all of which can represent significant problems for some students, including those with mobility issues. Students with visual impairments may also be impacted. For example, for those with visual impairments, doors should always be left either fully opened or fully closed to ensure that these students do not walk into half-opened doors, which can be more difficult to see. Tables may be positioned in such a way to deny all students access to all areas of the room. Clutter at below-knee level, including mats and rugs, may represent a tripping hazard or cause the wheels of a wheelchair to become stuck. A case study by Loreman (2000) involved a 15-year-old student who used a wheelchair, and for whom access was a significant issue. This student was upset by the fact that he was never able to access any other area of a classroom than the front of the room, due to the way the desks had been organised. He indicated that this situation had a significantly negative impact on his relationships with his peers, who generally sat away from the teacher towards the back of the room. Teachers need to consider how their classroom can best be physically structured to meet the needs of all. Obviously, in a larger room with more area in which to spread out, this will be easier. In smaller classrooms, furniture needs and positioning will have to be given more consideration. In classrooms with students who have visual impairments, the frequent moving and reorganising of classroom furniture should be avoided.

Students who seem to be easily distracted should be seated in areas in which distractions are minimised. For these students, a window seat may not be the best position from which they can concentrate on classroom tasks. Likewise, areas of the room that are full of stimulating materials, such as posters, fish tanks, animal cages, and the like, might best be avoided. High-traffic areas such as doors or frequently used shelves are also often not conducive to students being able to concentrate.

Consideration should also be given to the height of tables and benches in a classroom. In secondary school science rooms, for example, all students should be able to access sinks and other aspects of the room, such as gas lines for Bunsen burners. In the inclusive classroom, some benches may need to be lowered and some tables raised. Shelving should also be set at an appropriate height for all students. The lowering of built-in benches may entail some inconvenience but should be undertaken if they are used to aid teaching. The raising of tables to allow a wheelchair to fit underneath them can be done easily. We have seen examples of metal extensions that fit on to the bottom of existing table legs to raise the height, which is a cheap and effective alternative to purchasing a new, specially adapted student table.

For students with visual impairments, issues of lighting and visibility need to be considered. Specific advice for students with visual impairments will vary according to the individual, but in general these students should be seated in a position that is appropriately lit, and from which they are best able to view any instructional materials being used. Students who are deaf or hard of hearing should be seated in a position that best enables them to hear what is being said and to see the sign-language interpreter; if they are lip-readers (also known as speech reading), they should be seated in a position from which they can clearly see the teacher and other students speaking.

Modifications to provide access for all can begin in the classroom, but certainly should not end there. Ideally, all students should be provided with access to all areas of the school (see Box 9.1). This includes the school office, teacher offices, sporting facilities, and the playground. Drinking fountains should also be set at an appropriate height so that all students can access them. Students with visual impairments may require hazards such as poles, rails, steps or benches to be painted in a bright colour such as yellow so they do not accidentally walk into them.

Box 9.1: Physical access to and around classrooms—things to consider

- Ramps where there are steps
- Width and positioning of doors and doorways; opening and closing speed
- Arrangement of furniture
- Classroom clutter such as games, bags, rugs, toys, sporting equipment
- Table, bench and shelf height
- Lighting

- Unobscured lines of vision
- Distractions
- Access to sinks and other specialised classroom equipment
- Access to drinking fountains
- Access to other areas of the school such as other buildings, sporting fields, playgrounds
- The visibility of hazards

Seating plans

There are many ways of organising how students are seated and grouped for learning in the classroom. In some classrooms, especially those with very young children, more time might be spent engaged in activities out of the students' designated seats than in them. In many secondary schools in certain subject areas, students remain seated for the majority of their time. This section examines some common ways of organising students for instruction that can be applied to any age group in any setting (see Box 9.2).

Box 9.2: Advice on seating and space in inclusive classrooms

- Provide preferential seating if physical access problems are still being solved.
- Seat students with 'study buddies' to assist in peer-to-peer support.
- Seat those with difficulties in a particular area near a good role model in that area.
- Place students away from distractions wherever possible.
- Use study carrels or quiet areas as required.
- Match work area to learning styles.
- Keep desks free from extraneous materials.
- Ensure barrier-free access for all.
- Provide adequate space for movement.
- Allow for flexible grouping arrangements.

Source: Adapted from Mohr (1995).

Traditional expository teaching seating plan

Traditionally, students have been seated in rows of tables or desks facing the teacher, who has generally provided instruction from the front of the classroom (see Figure 9.1). This is evident in many early photographs of classrooms. Many teachers continue to seat students of all ages in this way for instruction, and find this approach effective in their context. Many secondary school classrooms are set up this way to begin with, offering teachers who work in the room for brief sessions little scope for change.

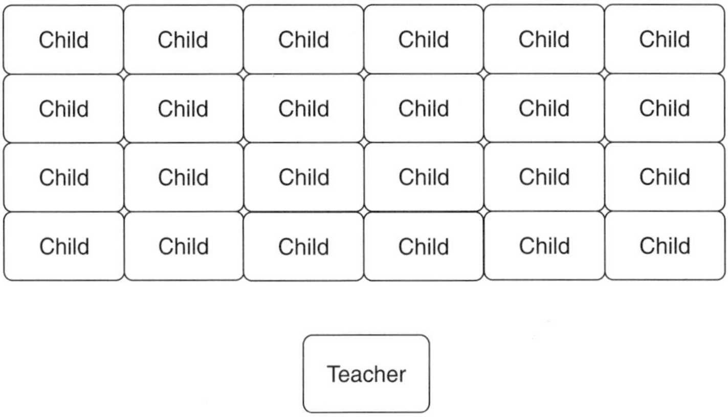

Child	Child	Child	Child	Child	Child
Child	Child	Child	Child	Child	Child
Child	Child	Child	Child	Child	Child
Child	Child	Child	Child	Child	Child

Teacher

Figure 9.1 Traditional expository teaching seating plan

The advantage of seating students in this way is that their attention is naturally drawn towards the teacher standing in front of them. The teacher can also see the faces of all students to help ensure that each one is listening or is 'on task' (McNamara & Waugh, 1993). There are, however, some significant disadvantages associated with teaching in this way. Instruction becomes teacher focused and the opportunities for learning from peers through discussion are significantly reduced. Classrooms set up in this way tend to encourage 'chalk and talk' (or Smartboard and electronic marker!) type teaching strategies, and discourage active involvement in learning (Woolfolk, 2001). Individual needs are difficult to address in this type of teaching situation. Potential exists for students to become passive receptors of knowledge rather than active participants in the learning process.

Students with different learning needs can be especially disadvantaged in classrooms set up in this way. As discussed previously, they may be restricted to sitting in the front of the room under the gaze of the teacher rather than with their friends. While there are some academic advantages to sitting near the front (Woolfolk, 2001), the social barriers it presents are problematic (Loreman, 2001). More significant, however, is the need for many students to be more actively engaged in their learning than this mode of instruction allows. Under this model, students may only be able to interact with the students sitting directly next to them. This curtailed level of social interaction is inconsistent with social constructivist pedagogy, a way of teaching and learning involving social interaction that has been found to have powerful positive effects (Pourdavood, Svec & Cowen, 2005). In addition, a teacher must consider the role of any paraprofessional in a classroom structured in this way. Providing support to individuals would generally entail sitting directly next to those individuals. Given that those with diverse needs tend to need heightened levels of individual support, the tendency might be for paraprofessionals to frequently be seated near these students' desks, thus heightening the curtailing of peer social interaction.

Ability groups

Some teachers choose to seat students in groups according to their perceived ability, knowledge or skills in a range of areas. This is known as *ability grouping*. Students in these groups do not necessarily directly face the teacher, who has more scope to conduct expository sessions or give instructions from any part of the room (see Figure 9.2). There are significant advantages to having groups organised in this way. With the teacher moving around the room, more students can become actively engaged in the teaching session. Students in these groups generally face each other and are able to interact with one another in their learning. Teachers can become involved in small-group teaching situations, which they can adjust from group to group depending on levels of perceived ability or need. Students are also able to interact and learn from one another with greater ease than if they were simply seated in rows. Teachers can also often access students with greater ease when grouped in this way to provide assistance and individual instruction than when students are seated in rows of desks, as it frees up more space in the classroom.

There are, however, some significant disadvantages to grouping students in this way, and these tend to outweigh the advantages listed above. First, there is almost certainly a social stigma attached to members of various groups, especially those in groups perceived to be struggling with classroom work (McNamara & Waugh, 1993). Students might engage in competitive behaviour in order to move up to a higher group, and indeed a negative impact on the social atmosphere of the classroom and school has been noted (Hallam, 2002). Second, we know that grouping students according to perceived academic ability is not helpful in terms of general academic improvement for all. While some might benefit from association with a group of more gifted students, the rest of the class may largely miss out in involvement with this

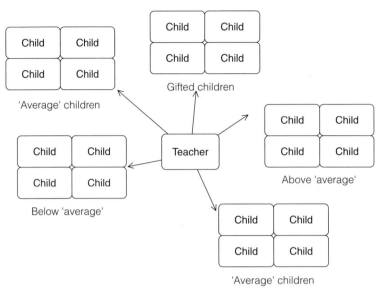

Figure 9.2 Ability groups seating plan

often-positive academic and social influence (McNamara & Waugh, 1993). Further, it is acknowledged that paraprofessionals are most effective when they act as a resource for the entire class (see Chapter 5). In the context of ability grouping, the tendency might be for paraprofessionals to frequently be seated at the group containing the lower academic achievers, given that these students are generally seen to require higher levels of individual support. The presence of this paraprofessional might help to produce a social stigma with respect to the students in the group, who might be viewed by classmates as the 'special' group in the regular class.

Heterogeneous grouping

Placing students in heterogeneous groups means placing students with a variety of perceived mixed abilities and learning needs in the same group (see Figure 9.3). This is increasingly being regarded as a superior way of grouping for learning, as it avoids many of the difficulties encountered with similar-ability groups. In heterogeneous groups, students with different backgrounds, interests, and abilities can interact with and learn from one another. Because they are able to easily interact, a variety of constructivist, student-centred teaching strategies can be employed, such as peer tutoring and cooperative group work (McInerney & McInerney, 2002). Students can also work on individual tasks as required. The advantages to the teacher include being able to facilitate learning for students rather than using teacher-centred instructional techniques, the ability to provide instruction from any point in the classroom, and the ability to move around the room with greater ease to assist individuals. Further, having students with different strengths and needs gathered together means they can assist each other in learning. This enhances the learning experience and contributes to the building of classroom community. With respect to paraprofessionals, having different students with different needs spread throughout the room can be beneficial. The paraprofessional in this circumstance can more frequently visit all groups and make connections with all students, rather than simply focusing the majority of attention on one area of the room, as might be the case in a classroom operating under an ability-grouping model.

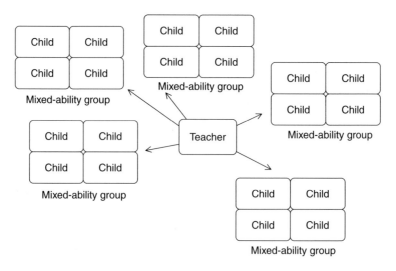

Figure 9.3 **Heterogeneous groups seating plan**

Individual learning spaces

Some teachers set their classrooms up so that students are not grouped at all. Instead, they create a number of small learning spaces to which students can retreat according to their preferences and the task they are supposed to complete (see Figure 9.4). This is more likely to occur in classrooms containing younger children, but even at secondary schools some areas (such as libraries) are often structured according to this model. The advantages of this model are such that the age of the student is largely irrelevant, and it should not be viewed as only useful for younger students.

Under this model, students can choose to work in an area that best suits them. Spaces are available for instruction in small or large groups as well as for individual work. A comfortable couch space can be useful for projects involving reading or informal discussion. The teacher and paraprofessional are free to move around and address individual needs as required within the various learning environments.

The main drawback to setting up a classroom in this way is a very practical one. For students to benefit from this type of seating plan (where they essentially choose where they want to sit most of the time), they need to be both self-motivated to learn and self-disciplined. Therefore, it would not necessarily work for every group of students. Some students may not be able to deal with the lack of structure that a learning environment like this implies. They also need to be able to follow individual courses of study, and to some extent manage their own work (McNamara & Waugh, 1993).

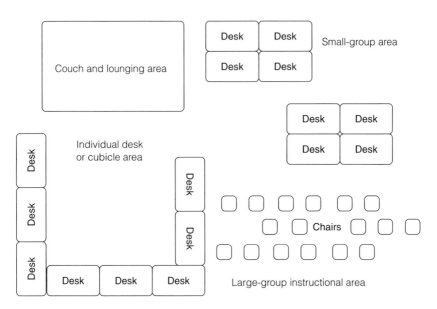

Figure 9.4 Individual learning spaces plan

Using a combination of approaches

In practical terms, many teachers are restricted in how they can group students for any given activity by a variety of factors, which include the size and shape of the classroom, the resources available, the amount of time spent in one classroom and the nature of the students. In all instances, however, flexibility and the need for students to enhance their learning through social interaction should be considered. Teachers might use a combination of the seating and grouping models outlined above as they construct a learning environment for their students. Classrooms of students who are grouped according to the principles of student-centredness and the need for active social interaction in learning will be structured to enhance learning whatever the makeup of the student body. According to Alexander, Rose & Woodland (1992, p. 32), classroom practice will be more effective if teachers:

- have the skills demanded by whole-class teaching, group teaching, and one-to-one work with individuals
- exploit the potential of collaborative group work
- use a combination of these strategies, according to the purposes of the task at hand.

Classroom procedures

Aside from structuring the physical layout of the classroom, effective teachers have established procedures that are clearly communicated to all students. These procedures can range from more mundane, everyday tasks to situations that would only occur in exceptional circumstances. Our experience has been that students of all ages are generally more comfortable within the framework of clearly established routines and procedures. That is not to say that learning itself should become routine, but rather that there is a general framework of procedures that students can reference most times in a classroom.

Student tasks

In most classrooms, there are established tasks that students must perform to ensure the smooth running of a class. In classes of younger children, these tasks can include any number of activities such as taking attendance, running messages to the office, being responsible for maintaining classroom areas, or caring for class pets. Older students, who frequently move from teacher to teacher, are often expected to perform fewer classroom tasks due to the more transient nature of their contact with staff members. There are, however, areas of responsibility that they may still take on, such as organising events or being involved in various school welfare committees. When using an inclusive approach, it should be noted that all students should be expected to perform tasks that contribute to the overall well-being of the classroom and school community. Classroom and school tasks should be voluntary in nature, and should reflect individual skills and interests.

Emergency plans

All schools and classrooms should have a clearly set out and understood contingency plan for emergencies. Most schools choose or are required to practise these emergency procedures on a regular basis. Having a diverse student body requires schools to put extra thought into these plans. Where the evacuation of buildings is required, thought needs to be given to how all students are going to safely and quickly evacuate the premises, with special thought being given to those with mobility issues or who have difficulty following instructions. Once students have left a building, safety also needs to be considered. An example of the outcome of a good emergency plan follows.

Example: The emergency plan

Miss Holly taught a Grade 5 class in an elementary school in Edmonton, Canada. This class of 25 included one student in a wheelchair and one student with a moderate to severe visual impairment. One day in mid-January, with outside temperatures of –15°C and snow on the ground, the school alarm system went off, indicating that all students and staff should evacuate the building. The emergency plan Miss Holly had previously developed and communicated to her class was put into practice.

As the students went about dressing in their cold-weather clothing and lining up at the door, Miss Holly put on her coat and hat and placed the class attendance list in her emergency basket. As she did this, administrative staff entered her classroom and assisted the student with a visual impairment to put on her coat and hat. The staff laid the coat of the student in the wheelchair over her but did not put it on properly. Dressing this student involved removing her partly from the wheelchair and would have taken more time than would have been wise to spend, given the situation. Part of the plan, developed in consultation with this student and her parents, was that this would be the procedure followed in these circumstances. On Miss Holly's instruction, the entire class and staff left the building via the pre-arranged route. One of the administrators pushed the student in the wheelchair. On exiting the building, the class quickly assembled at the designated assembly point. Miss Holly then removed the blankets from her emergency basket and distributed them to the students who indicated that they needed them, ensuring first that a blanket was given to the student in the wheelchair to compensate for the fact that her coat was not on properly. Miss Holly then checked attendance.

Emergency plans should be written and posted in a prominent spot in the classroom so that all students and other adults who may use the room from time to time, can familiarise themselves with the required procedure. These plans should fit in with the overall school emergency plan so that staff are not working in isolation during emergency situations.

Emergencies at schools are not limited to incidents affecting the entire school. Emergencies can and do occur in individual classrooms from time to time, and while it is not possible to anticipate every type of event, contingency plans for emergencies that might conceivably occur should also be considered. These are especially important in classes including students with particular medical conditions that make them more liable to the occurrence of a personal emergency. Should any student suffer a medical emergency, teachers should have a procedure in place whereby other staff members can be contacted for assistance and an ambulance can be called without hesitation. If your classroom has a phone or you have your own cellular (mobile) phone with you, then this is the obvious way to both contact an ambulance and another staff member for assistance. If your room does not have a telephone, a responsible student may need to be designated to go and tell appropriate school staff about the incident and what needs to happen.

Plans for substitute teachers

Almost every teacher will miss days of work through illness at some points in their career. In the inclusive classroom, it is important that any absences are planned for in advance. By its very nature, illness often hits us when we least expect it, so a well-constructed plan for the teacher who will replace you in the short term will assist your classroom to remain inclusive, even when you are not there.

In addition to any plans or information you would ordinarily leave for a substitute teacher, you should also leave some more specific information on any students with different learning needs and what your expectations are for their involvement in the class (i.e. you expect full involvement!). Remember that, even though you are absent, your class is still your class and sensible substitute teachers will attempt to run it as closely as possible to the way you do. Often teachers do not know who will be taking over their class when they are away. For this reason, you should assume in your plans that they know nothing about your students or about inclusion. They might, of course, but they just as easily might not and you have no way of knowing in advance which is the case.

A brief information folder, updated by you from time to time, is often helpful to substitute teachers. This folder should contain the following brief information:
- general information on students in your class
- a brief description of your inclusive philosophy and what this means in practice

- your expectations that this philosophy will continue to be practised in your absence
- any important medical or other information.

It is important to keep the information concise. Remember that most substitute teachers do not have the luxury of a lot of time to prepare for classes and read information. Two pages is probably a good length. Any additional, non-essential information can be included in the folder as an appendix.

If you are lucky enough to work with a paraprofessional, this person can also provide an excellent source of continuity for the classroom and information to the substitute teacher while you are away. Paraprofessionals should be briefed on their role in supporting the class and the substitute teacher in your absence, what sort of information they should relay to the substitute teacher, and at what points of the day extra assistance might be required.

Meeting students' personal care needs

The remainder of this chapter discusses issues of personal care that we concede generally relate more specifically to students with disabilities. These are issues more pertinent to individuals than the class as a whole, but are important practical aspects to consider in organising the inclusive classroom. Although we are uncomfortable about singling out specific groups of students, this aspect should not be ignored. Teachers frequently express concern about their ability to meet the personal care requirements of some students, and often this concern arises from genuinely not knowing what to expect in these situations. Our experience has been—and this is also demonstrated in research—that once teachers gain some experience and get to know the specific students involved on a personal level, such concerns and anxieties are generally considerably reduced. It is best to simply try to set aside your initial concerns and anxieties, adopt a positive attitude, and enjoy the professional and personal learning opportunities offered by such circumstances.

Meeting the personal care needs of students has become a controversial topic within the teaching profession. Some teacher unions and associations are explicit in their view that teachers are in schools to instruct only, rather than meeting personal care and other needs of students. Our perspective runs contrary to this view. Teaching goes beyond the simple transmission of content from a curriculum document from teacher to learner, and we have misgivings about organisations advocating for such narrow definitions of teaching. We believe that most people go into the profession of teaching because they care deeply about students and want not only to support their learning, but also to improve their lives in general. Generally, people do not go into teaching because they want to become one-dimensional transmitters of knowledge. With this in mind, most teachers willingly and enthusiastically take on tasks outside of the narrow scope of curriculum and instruction if it improves the lives of students and assists them to be ready for learning. When viewed in this context, making arrangements for, and being personally involved in, matters of personal care for students is, in our opinion, not asking too much of the modern, caring teacher. Further, involvement in personal care is frequently not a solitary activity; often paraprofessionals, parents, and other school staff are involved where such care is required. The discussion below focuses on the two areas of personal care about which teachers seem most unsure: assistance with eating and toileting.

Helping students who require special assistance to eat

Some students require assistance with eating. As with any area of personal care, teachers and paraprofessionals should ensure that a routine for these students is developed that respects personal dignity and choice. Steps should, of course, also be taken to ensure that snack and meal times take place in an inclusive environment.

In all instances, staff working with students who require assistance with eating should seek specialist advice and training from both the parents of the student and relevant professionals, such as doctors or speech-language therapists who have some expertise in swallowing and chewing, and who are familiar with the student (Jaffe, 1989). Failure to do this can have dire consequences. People can easily choke when being fed, and staff who are unaware of the correct feeding techniques, or what to do in instances when choking occurs, put their students at risk. Some students have gastric feeding tubes (G-Tubes) that look complicated but are easy to set up and connect; however, these also require specialist instruction before a teacher or paraprofessional should use them.

Unless a student requiring assistance refuses food, or has a medical reason for eating at different times, they should eat at the same times and in the same environments as other students. In some countries, all students have lunch at school, while in others they may or may not go home for lunch. In most countries, students eat morning and afternoon snacks outside, weather permitting. Students requiring assistance with eating should be no different unless there are compelling reasons why this should not occur. Staff helping the student can go outside with them, assist them in the areas frequented by their friends and peers, then leave them to their break as appropriate. The emphasis is on doing an effective job in assisting in this area while trying not to interfere too much with the social experience of students eating together. Students being assisted should also have the right to refuse food if they are not hungry, and to make choices about what they eat, insofar as all students have choices about the food they eat at school.

Other students may initially have questions about the sort of assistance that is taking place. These can be answered frankly in order to demystify the process, but in such a way as to emphasise the similarities and differences in the way all people eat. Our experience has been that peers generally get used to the idea of one of their number being helped in this way by a staff member, and the practice is quickly accepted and swiftly ceases to be an issue. In no circumstances should the provision of such assistance be delegated to peers. Not only do they not have the on-the-job training provided by allied health professionals, but allowing one student to engage in such personal care assistance can foster attitudes of dependence that are contrary to inclusive views of all students being equal and capable members of the school community.

Toileting students who require special assistance

Some students require help with toileting. This is usually the result of a physical condition or cognitive issues that have resulted in the student being delayed in toilet training (Boswell & Gray, 1998). Toileting can be a daunting prospect for a teacher who has never had to deal with this before, but by developing a few procedures in the school, toileting issues are more easily dealt with. Early research on inclusion showed that teachers who had never taught children with physical disabilities were most concerned about toileting, while those who had taught these children were much more concerned about other issues (Frith & Edwards, 1981). This demonstrates that toileting is not as frightening as it might at first seem once you have gained some experience. How much assistance you will get with toileting a student will depend on your school context. In some schools, paraprofessionals are assigned the job of toileting those who require it. In other school systems, this task is the responsibility of the classroom teacher. In both instances, it is the responsibility of the classroom teacher to ensure that toileting is done correctly, and with maximum dignity for the student, even if the teacher does not personally do the toileting.

Toileting falls into two main categories. The first comprises those students who are being 'toilet trained', are not in nappies (diapers), but may need to be taken to the toilet and given assistance at designated times. The second category consists of those students in nappies (diapers) who will need to be changed regularly. In both cases, use of a private, specially designed washroom for people with disabilities is appropriate. Careful planning must go into the construction of these washrooms to ensure that there is adequate space not only for a toilet, but also for staff, wheelchairs, lifts, an appropriately sized change table and storage areas for changes of clothes, nappies, and so on. Your school washroom should be set up so that any toileting can be done quickly and with a minimum of fuss. Nappies, cloths, wipes, creams, changes of clothes and other items should be on hand to ensure an efficient and dignified experience. The best way to ensure that student dignity is maintained is, of course, to conduct toileting in private. The washroom, with its highly personal procedures, is the one area of a school where an inclusive environment with other students is not appropriate.

Any staff involved in toileting students should follow what are known as 'universal precautions' in order to maintain the health of all involved. Universal precautions come from a 'worst-case scenario' perspective and operate under the assumption of the presence of disease. This means that even if you think you know that the students you are engaged with have no communicable diseases, when it comes to toileting you should treat them as if they do. Conversely, the adoption of universal precautions also protects the student from any diseases the caregiver may have. In the case of toileting, universal precautions usually only amount to washing hands before and after toileting and the wearing of new disposable gloves with each student. If any other measures are required to ensure that body fluids do not come in contact with others, then they should be taken. Any spills of bodily fluids (such as urine) should be cleaned using gloves and a 1:10 bleach/water solution, and any cloths used disposed of in a plastic-lined bin and professionally cleaned. Surfaces such as change tables should also be disinfected between uses (Tetlow, 1990).

In scheduling regular toilet times, a teacher needs to keep discretion in mind. Toileting should be done at times that draw minimum attention to the student and ensure minimum disruption to the school day. The best times to implement a toileting regime are generally during class transitions. This can mean between classes, just prior to or towards the end of break times, or just before or after school. These times are frequently busy and hectic, and thus withdrawal to use the washroom is less noticeable. In general, students tend to use the toilet at these times, so in this sense the timing is nothing out of the ordinary.

Medication in the classroom

Teachers are frequently called on to administer medication to students. The prevalence of certain conditions means that the administration of medication is increasingly becoming an issue in schools. A considerable amount of debate as to the appropriateness of the practice of teachers administering medication has been taking place around the world for a number of years (Clay, Farris, McCarthy, Kelly & Howarth, 2008; Gadow & Kane, 1983; McCarthy, Kelly & Reed, 2000). Some argue that teachers are not medical practitioners, and thus should not be administering medication. Others argue that when students are at school, teachers must act *in loco parentis*—that is, in the place of parents—and thus should ensure the well-being of students in their care by administering medication (Morse, Colatarci, Nehring, Roth & Barks, 1997). Some schools are large enough to have a school nurse employed, but these are certainly in the minority and the reality is that, like it or not, teachers often have no choice but to administer medication to students during the school day.

Having said that, there are reasonable limits to what a teacher might be expected to do. Administering oral medication, for example, is more appropriate than administering other types of medication. Under no circumstances should teachers administer needles or perform any invasive medical procedures on any student. Further, we recommend that teachers only administer medication if there is no other alternative.

You may also wish to seek advice from your professional association regarding the administration of medication. In some instances dosages and administration times can be adjusted by the family doctor so that all medication can be administered at home, outside school hours. We recommend that in all cases the family doctor be consulted to see if this is a possibility. If this is not possible, then doctors should consider administration times that interfere as little as possible with class times.

Furthermore, procedures at the school and classroom level need to be developed and implemented to ensure that student safety is not compromised. Teachers need to take measures to ensure not only that medication is administered in a safe and appropriate way, but that adequate records are kept of this administration should a problem occur. This is because errors and omissions in medication administration in schools do occur (Clay et al., 2008), and good record-keeping can assist in preventing this from happening. Most school jurisdictions now have procedures in place for the storage and administration of medication, and you should check what rules and protocols apply in your local area; however, general considerations for medication storage and administration can be found in Box 9.3.

Box 9.3: Considerations for schools regarding medication storage and administration of medications

- All medications (including prescription and over-the-counter) should be kept in a clearly marked, locked, secure central area.
- Access to medication should be restricted to a small number of staff members with appropriate training.
- Written parental and medical professional consent must be provided prior to administration (see Form 16 in Useful Forms).
- Medical professionals should provide explicit, plain-language instructions for administration.
- A single, designated member of trained school staff should administer all medication for the school (with a second trained staff member assisting to ensure no errors are made).
- Confidentiality should be respected, and administration should take place in private.
- Appropriate protocols for administration (such as hand-washing and glove-wearing procedures) should be established and followed.
- Accurate and up-to-date records of administration should be kept (see Form 17 in Useful Forms).
- Appropriate arrangements should be made for administration if the class is away from the school building.
- If an error of omission, dosage, medication type, time or method of ingestion is made, seek medical advice and notify parents. Complete an incident report (see Form 18 in Useful Forms).

Source: Based on information from Biggs et al. (1998); McCarthy et al. (2000).

This chapter has examined practical aspects of inclusion, including how to allow for universal classroom access, as well as some important aspects relevant to individual students, such as assistance with eating, toileting and the administration of medication. The next chapter discusses how to promote positive social relationships for all students.

Key terms

Ability grouping. Placing students in groups according to their perceived ability, knowledge or skills in a range of areas.

Heterogeneous groups. Placing students with mixed abilities in the same group.

For discussion and reflection

9.1 What sort of classroom seating arrangement appeals to you? Why?

9.2 What are your concerns about providing personal care to students who need it?

9.3 Are there any realistic alternatives to medication administration at school?

Further reading

Jaffe, M.B. (1989). Feeding at-risk infants and toddlers. *Topics in Language Disorders, 10*(1), 13–25.

McCarthy, A.M., Kelly, M.W. & Reed, D. (2000). Medication administration practices of school nurses. *Journal of School Health, 70*(9), 371–6.

10
Inclusive classroom management

Key ideas in this chapter
- Defining challenging behaviour
- Understanding reasons for the challenging behaviour of individuals
- Developing an action plan for individual students
- Violence and touching
- Building a classroom community
- Class meetings
- Classroom management tips that work

Since the advent of schooling, teachers have had to adopt strategies aimed at keeping students focused on the task at hand. This has become known as classroom management. Classroom management is important because learning becomes a far more difficult, if not impossible, task in a chaotic environment where students and adults do not respect one another's learning, and behave in ways that disrupt learning. More generic strategies for classroom management are outside the scope of this text, and readers are referred to other excellent texts focusing solely on this topic (see Albert, 2003; Bloom, 2009; Jones & Jones, 2004).

The majority of this chapter is focused on positive ways of working with those students who might pose more unique challenges. Previously, students who engaged in what was viewed as disruptive behaviour were excluded through suspensions, school expulsions, special class or school placements, or being removed from the room or sent to 'time out' for frequent or extended periods of time. While in extreme and rare circumstances some of these options might still be necessary, the removal of students viewed as disruptive from regular classroom environments results in poor long-term outcomes for those students (Lane, Wehby, Little & Cooley, 2005), and is inconsistent with the inclusive ideals of acceptance of all and learning together. These students are entitled to our attention and the same standard of education as any other member of the class; however, like all students, they also need to be taught what appropriate behaviour is and to be supported in their efforts to adopt more pro-social behaviour. Challenging behaviour can be viewed as an annoyance and source of irritation in the classroom, or as an opportunity to develop new skills and understandings about teaching and learning. This chapter focuses on positive ways of dealing with students whose behaviour is challenging through a whole-school and an individual-classroom approach.

What is challenging behaviour?

Challenging behaviour can occur as the result of conflict between a student and the environment. When this happens, a student may choose to respond to his or her educational environment in ways that differ significantly from age-appropriate expectations and interfere with his or her own learning or that of others. Challenging behaviour, of course, ranges widely between temporary and relatively minor behaviours, such as talking during teacher-led instruction, to more serious and long-term patterns of behaviour that might include, but are not limited to:

- the inability to maintain satisfactory relationships with peers or adults
- episodes of physical violence towards people or property
- the use of poor or hostile language
- resistance to following rules or expectations
- general unwillingness to follow instructions from those in authority
- self-harming behaviour
- a general mood of anger or unhappiness (adapted from Educational Response Centre, 1992).

These behaviours can present themselves to teachers in the context of a learning situation, and are often a sign that the student is having difficulty coping in that particular situation. It is the job of the teacher and the school to find and address the reasons for undesirable behaviour in order to present all students with an optimal learning environment.

Understanding the reasons for the challenging behaviour of individuals

In order to successfully promote the sort of behaviour required in your class-room to optimise learning, you must first understand why individual students might engage in unacceptable behaviour. First, all behaviour—good or bad—needs to be viewed as a product of student choice (Albert, 2003). This is a very important way of looking at behaviour. If we do not believe that behaviour is a choice, then we are saying that the actions of a student are out of his or her control, and therefore nothing can be done to change that behaviour. We are saying that, as the behaviour is essentially innate and not influenced by the conscious mind, there is no point in intervening or expecting more from the student. While there are some examples of students not being able to exercise choice over the way in which they behave (for example, some medical conditions involving psychosis), these are certainly an extremely small minority and should be addressed by the medical profession as they present. Under most circumstances, we simply must begin with the premise that a student is choosing his or her behaviour if we are to successfully intervene and change the way in which they behave.

Consistent with a wide range of other authors, Albert (2003) presents a useful frame through which to view student misbehaviour, according to which the sources of misbehaviour fall into four categories: attention-seeking; avoidance of failure; power; and revenge. Once these are understood, it is difficult to imagine any misbehaviour that does not have its roots in one of these four categories.

Attention-seeking behaviour

As the term suggests, attention-seeking behaviour occurs when students are trying to fulfil a need for extra attention. Even if you may feel that these students already get plenty of extra attention, they feel they need more—and sometimes this need is never completely addressed no matter what you try! Attention-seekers can operate in two modes. 'Active' attention-seekers are those students who engage in behaviour that often lacks subtlety. These are the students who do things such as making faces at their peers, calling out in class, or pulling the hair of the person in front of them. 'Passive' attention-seekers are those who, as Albert describes it, engage in 'one pea at a time' behaviour. They rarely disrupt in an explicit manner, but rather may work on 'slow, slower, and slowest speeds' (Albert, 2003, p. 24). They get our attention by not cooperating and deliberately not reacting to our instructions. Both active and passive attention-seekers prefer positive attention, but often their behaviour is so irritating to teachers and peers that all the feedback they get is negative. To the attention-seeker, however, negative attention is better than none at all and will only serve to reinforce the misbehaviour. Albert suggests that we deal with attention-seekers by rewarding instances of appropriate behaviour, and by teaching students appropriate ways of asking for extra attention when they need it.

Case study: Chandra the attention-seeker

Chandra was a Year 7 student with a reputation for seeking attention. She was academically capable and successful, however, she spent significant portions of each class passing notes to friends, walking aimlessly around the room, throwing small items to her friends and teasing boys. Her science teacher responded by using a number of techniques, including proximity control, ignoring, asking her to stop, threatening consequences and giving her 'the eye'. These techniques all worked for a few minutes; however, once his back was turned the behaviour often started again. The teacher decided to meet with Chandra privately about her behaviour, and, having established that she liked him as a teacher and was academically confident, came to the conclusion that her behaviour was the result of active attention-seeking. As a result, the teacher decided to provide her with legitimate attention. At the meeting, they established that they held a common interest in basketball, and it was decided that this would be the vehicle through which legitimate attention would be provided. In exchange for appropriate behaviour in class, the teacher occasionally came out and shot baskets with Chandra and her group of friends at lunchtime. The teacher made a point of spending a minute or so before each class discussing the previous night's professional basketball game with Chandra. Over time, the previously negative relationship became more positive, and while Chandra was not completely 'cured' of her attention-seeking tendencies, they were reduced significantly to the point where she rarely disrupted instruction in her science class.

Avoidance of failure behaviour

Avoidance of failure behaviour is another self-evident term. When avoidance of failure is the cause of misbehaviour, students tend to withdraw from classroom activities in order to avoid the possibility of performing poorly. These are students with low self-esteem and little confidence in their own abilities. According to Albert (2003), these students tend to procrastinate, do not complete work, develop temporary incapacities such as headaches, or assume traits associated with those who have learning disabilities. We can help these students through improving their self-esteem by providing them with learning situations in which they can experience success, and by drawing them into congenial relationships with us and their peers. If we can assist these students to reflect on their successes, then their concept of themselves as effective learners should improve.

Case study: Troy avoids failure

When Troy's Grade 4 teacher asked him to put together a PowerPoint presentation on four types of alternative energy, he responded in the same way he always did when asked to complete academic tasks: by sitting at his desk and making no effort to begin the work. On prompting from his teacher, he moved to the computer table. On further prompting, he opened up a fresh PowerPoint presentation. With still further prompting, he collected the books he needed to complete the assignment from the tub at the front of the room. He never did complete that assignment, and this was not unusual. After discussion with Troy and some colleagues, the teacher came to the conclusion that his behaviour was the result of failure avoidance. The teacher decided to tackle this in a number of ways, the first of which was providing Troy with less intimidating assignments. For example, his assignment on alternative energy would be reduced to creating a presentation on only one type of alternative energy instead of four, and he would be allowed to complete this with the assistance of a cooperative peer. Indeed, although Troy was academically capable in the teacher's view, expectations for work would continue to be modified in this way until he began to experience success and feel more confident, at which point the level of modification would be reduced. Before each learning task, the teacher would take a minute with Troy to facilitate some positive self-talk with respect to the task at hand. Further, the teacher decided to put together a portfolio of Troy's successes. When he was feeling particularly disheartened, the teacher would take the time to go through aspects of the portfolio with him in an effort to show him his past accomplishments and future promise. It was recognised that improvement would likely not occur overnight, but with support and vigilance Troy might be able to build up his confidence, improving his learning overall.

Power behaviour

Students who engage in power behaviour are constantly trying to challenge our authority as teachers. They want to engage us in public power struggles and have a need to be seen as being 'in charge'. This can be very threatening to teachers. If we are seen to have lost a power struggle with a student, then from that point on we can feel like our authority is questioned not only by that student, but also by the rest of the class (although whether or not our authority is actually questioned by the rest of the class is a matter for debate). The consequences for a teacher who is perceived by the majority of a class to have no authority are obvious, and once lost, authority is very difficult to rebuild. Albert (2003) lists two types of power behaviour. A student can exhibit *active* power behaviour by throwing physical or verbal tantrums, showing both disrespect and defiance towards the teacher, or demonstrate *passive* power behaviour by quiet non-compliance with instructions while continuing to outwardly act friendly, which is often little more than a thin veneer covering the seething resentment underneath.

Revenge behaviour

Revenge behaviour occurs 'when students misbehave to get revenge . . . they are retaliating for real or imagined hurts' (Albert, 2003, p. 51). Students exhibiting revenge behaviour want to hurt their teacher as much as possible. They do this through physical or verbal attacks, or by deliberately violating the values held by a teacher through their comments or actions. According to Albert, students who are exhibiting revenge behaviour have 1001 ways of saying 'I hate you'.

The principles of prevention for both power and revenge behaviour are similar. The most important—and often the most difficult—thing to do is to avoid confrontation and power struggles altogether with students exhibiting these types of behaviours. You cannot win, as these battles are generally continued until they are settled on the student's terms. Even if you do eventually get your way, you have probably lost your cool and some of your dignity in the process. The best solution is to diffuse any potential confrontations by:

- becoming aware of situations where confrontation might occur and changing your approach to teaching accordingly
- when confrontations do occur, employing strategies that will help you to avoid a pitched battle.

You should also find ways of helping these students to legitimately hold some power or, in the case of revenge behaviour, to express dissatisfaction in a constructive way. You can do this by developing a relationship with these students and negotiating the holding of power through special jobs for which they can be responsible, and by opening up a two-way dialogue for the expression of any real or imagined hurts. In this way, you are not engaging in public power struggles.

Case study: Andre challenges the teacher

Andre's Year 8 mathematics teacher asked him to respond to a question he asked from the front of the room, to which Andre yelled out, '&%$# you! I'm not doing what you say!' A gasp came from the class, which immediately fell silent, watching for what would happen next. The teacher, recognising the situation for what it was (power or revenge behaviour), simply turned away from Andre and calmly asked another student if she would like to answer the question, which she did. The lesson continued, with the teacher deciding to forgo the group activity and instead asking the class to complete a task in pairs, with the exception of Andre who sat with his head on the desk, brooding. The class ended and all students, including Andre, left. The teacher felt that if he had engaged with Andre at any point, a power struggle would have ensued, and this was probably best avoided because it is impossible for either side to win a public power struggle. The teacher immediately informed the school principal, who caught Andre at the end of his next class in a better mood and asked him to come with him to the office. Andre, having no issue with the principal and now in a much calmer mood, complied, and met with the principal and mathematics teacher in the school office. The discussion from this point involved the assigning of consequences for the behaviour, and a plan for ensuring that such behaviour was not repeated in the future. Importantly, due to the teacher's prudent calm non-engagement in a power struggle at any point, along with assistance from a colleague (the principal), the situation was resolved calmly.

Developing an action plan for individual students

Ongoing misbehaviour of individual students is probably best tackled in a positive, but also structured and planned, way. One of the best ways to build this structure is to come up with an action plan to deal with specific behaviours being exhibited by a particular student. It is wise to involve the student in this process so that your action plan also becomes a type of social contract between you and the student.

The first step in this process is to ensure that the student is aware of what the misbehaviour is (an assumption that should not immediately be made), and that the student is willing to commit to improving their behaviour. There are many ways you can make the prospect of behaviour improvement attractive. These can range from discussions about how more positive reports home may improve the atmosphere around the house, to more concrete rewards. Once a student has accepted that a behaviour needs changing and is willing to work on it, then an action plan can be drawn up (see Form 19 in Useful Forms). The stages in drawing up that plan are:

1. identify behaviours
2. identify reasons
3. identify solutions
4. identify consequences and rewards.

Identify behaviours

At this stage, you need to identify what the misbehaviour is. The idea is to extinguish this behaviour. Extinguishing a behaviour, however, is rarely enough on its own. A list needs to be drawn up of alternative, positive behaviours that can replace the negative behaviour once it is gone. Failure to replace negative behaviours with positive ones can lead to a behaviour vacuum in which the student simply finds an alternative negative behaviour to replace the last one. An example may be a student who identifies speaking out of turn as a behaviour she wishes to extinguish. Positive alternatives to this behaviour that she can adopt might include putting up her hand or placing her hand on her head.

Identify reasons

The next stage is to identify the reason for this misbehaviour based on Albert's (2003) goals of misbehaviour discussed earlier. Make the student aware of what these four goals are, and then ask them to identify why they are demonstrating a particular unacceptable behaviour.

Identify solutions

This stage involves brainstorming possible solutions for the problem. You might want to involve parents or other students (with the focus student's consent) in the process. Discuss, negotiate, and select the 'best' solution with the student.

Identify consequences and rewards

The final stage involves you and the student negotiating consequences for continued misbehaviour as well as rewards for improved behaviour. Remember that consequences should be reasonable, respectful, and related (Nelsen, Lott & Glen, 1993).

Violence and touching

It is our view that physical violence in any form should not be tolerated in schools. Notwithstanding our commitment to inclusion, we believe that students who pose an immediate and present physical danger to themselves or to others as a result of their behaviour do not belong at school until that immediate risk has been dealt with adequately. Any removal of a student for reasons of violence should only be for a very short period of time to enable that student to seek the appropriate intervention (perhaps medical or psychological) before returning to the classroom. Safety must always be our first consideration, as teachers, and other students, have a basic right not to become the victims of violent acts.

Teachers often speak of their frustration at no longer being allowed to touch students. This is a frequent misconception and misinterpretation of the 'no touching' rule. The general practice of limiting physical contact between teachers and students has been introduced in order to protect students from physical and sexual harassment and abuse. It is wise not to unduly touch the students you are teaching. This can, however, be taken too far. In situations where students are behaving in such a way as to pose a physical risk to themselves and/or others, a teacher is morally (and often legally) obliged to step in and control that behaviour, even if it means touching the student concerned. Of course, the level of physical intervention needs to be reasonable and appropriate to the situation, and based on the principle of minimum intervention. This means using the least intrusive means necessary to control a given situation.

We strongly advise you to check with your school jurisdiction, and consult and follow its policies and the law on the issue of dealing with instances of classroom violence. Furthermore, there are a variety of different courses available to teachers, such as 'non-violent crisis intervention' courses, that can teach you not only how to diffuse potentially violent situations, but also how to avoid hurting students or yourself if a situation does get physical.

Building a classroom community

To this point, this chapter has focused on addressing the behaviour of individual students who might require some additional support. However, this support can only be effective if it is provided within the context of a classroom community with a shared understanding of the rules of that class, and the obligations each member of the community has to others in terms of giving respect, practising acceptance, and demonstrating kindness. In short, a classroom community must be built within (hopefully) the context of a feeling of a wider school community. A classroom community is not an idea that can be actualised through a teacher declaring that 'we are now a classroom community' in the same way that one might turn on a light switch. Rather, a sense of community is something that must be built, and building a strong, supportive community can take some time. Like all matters of classroom management, taking the time to do this is worth it in the long run. A more harmonious classroom produced through the building of community will likely save time otherwise spent resolving classroom management issues after the fact—time that can be spent productively on instruction. Behar-Horenstein, Isaac, Seabert & Davis (2006) found a loss of allocated instructional time ranging from 14 per cent to 39 per cent across the elementary, middle and high school levels due to both student and teacher factors, and suggested a heightened focus on classroom management as one remedy for this loss. Further, Ryan and Cooper (2007) report that those they labelled as efficient teachers were able to get about 30 minutes per day of extra instructional time compared with the average teacher, and nearly 60 minutes when compared with inefficient teachers. This efficiency—tantamount to effective classroom management—results in 180 more hours of instructional time per year than for students of inefficient teachers. A number of studies have shown that effective classroom management is the most important factor when it comes to influencing student learning (Shinn, Stoner & Walker, 2002; Wang, Haertel & Walberg, 1997).

Canadian educator Dean Caouette asks that his teaching staff dedicate a significant portion of the first month of school to working with students on issues of classroom management, including the development of a classroom community (Loreman, 2009). The idea is to provide the students with a clear understanding of what the rules are, and what appropriate behaviour looks like. Caouette believes that children need to be taught what appropriate behaviour is; too often teachers assume that students learn this through osmosis and experience, when in fact they may not. Indeed, Caouette even formalises the process by asking his teachers to prepare unit and lesson plans for teaching about classroom management. The argument is that many of the ideas of classroom management meet curriculum objectives anyway (such as engagement in productive and positive working relationships), and the time spent engaged in this task in the first month pays off in time saved by not having to correct behaviour down the road.

A community, however, is more than simply a sum of its parts, and simply because a collection of students who know their individual responsibilities exists does not mean that they are necessarily empowered to act as a community. Peterson and Loreman (2005) suggest that, rather than isolating students experiencing difficulties with their behaviour through time-outs and classroom exclusion, a resilient community should be built that can gather around those members of the group who are troubled and support them in making better choices about how to act. In a community, students, staff, and the wider school community positively contribute to the overall school experience and the well-being of the individuals in the school. Indeed, this notion of community is recognised in the majority of texts on classroom management (Bloom, 2009; Emmer & Evertson, 2009; Hardin, 2004; Jones & Jones, 2004; Larrivee, 2005). If the building of a classroom community is recognised as positive, then, what does it look like and how can it be achieved? Box 10.1 provides advice on building a classroom community:

Box 10.1: Tips for building a classroom community

- Provide frequent opportunities each day for students to work together.
- Encourage students to look at issues from another's point of view.
- Network with parents, family members and friends of students.
- Use inclusive rituals and traditions in the classroom.
- As a teacher, demonstrate the value you place on your relationship with students and healthy relationships between students through respect, sincerity, thoughtfulness and emotional honesty.
- Get to know your students.
- Allow democracy in your classroom to flourish by giving students a voice in decisions (consult them!).
- Keep communication channels open.
- Create opportunities for students and staff to demonstrate that they care for one another.
- Reward instances of kindness and forgiveness.
- Create a classroom covenant (a code of conduct) with students.
- Avoid punitive responses to mistakes: treat them as a learning opportunity.

Source: Adapted from Bloom (2009); Deiro (1996); Hardin (2004); Kohn (1996, 1997); Larrivee (2005).

One further—and in our view critical—element of building classroom community is to allow students to experience democracy at first hand, and to make decisions that impact their community. This can be done most effectively through class meetings.

Class meetings

Regular class meetings are an excellent way of building a sense of community, promoting positive behaviour in your classroom, and helping students to think about their behaviour and take responsibility for it. Class meetings should be scheduled on at least a weekly basis, and possibly more frequently if required. Class meetings are viewed by some as taking too much time out of an already overloaded schedule. While this is a legitimate concern, in most instances class meetings contribute to the promotion of good behaviour in the classroom, which then enables the teacher to concentrate on teaching the curriculum. Generally, the time investment required for class meetings is more than compensated for by the time that is freed up through improved behaviour, and we have known this to be the case since the mid-1980s (Rightmyer, 2003; Sorsdahl & Sanche, 1985). Students of all ages, including those in high school and very young children, can successfully participate in class meetings, although the terminology and process may need to be simplified for younger children.

Class meetings can be adapted to suit your own classroom context, but there are some features that other teachers have found helpful in running their own class meetings that you might wish to adopt (see Box 10.2).

Box 10.2: Eight building blocks of successful class meetings

1. Forming a circle
2. Practising giving compliments and appreciation
3. Creating an agenda
4. Developing communication skills
5. Learning about separate realities
6. Solving problems through role-playing and brainstorming
7. Recognising the four reasons why people do what they do
8. Applying logical consequences and other non-punitive solutions.

Source: Nelsen et al. (1993).

Students need to be specifically taught what the eight building blocks mean in order to be successful participants in class meetings. This can be done while holding your initial meetings.

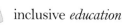

Forming a circle

Wherever possible, class meetings should be conducted with everyone seated in a circle. This feels more democratic and egalitarian. All students and the teacher need to be included in the circle.

Practising giving compliments and appreciation

Complimenting others in the class on things they have done well is an essential part of keeping your class meetings positive in nature and boosting the self-esteem of your students. Giving compliments does take practice for some students, however, so modelling how to give sincere compliments is important. It is also important for all students to receive compliments—not necessarily at every class meeting, but on a regular and frequent basis.

Creating an agenda

It is important that the students have the opportunity to place items for discussion on the agenda at class meetings. In fact, it should primarily be students who place items on the agenda, rather than the teacher—who has the opportunity to discuss discipline issues on other occasions. When students form the agenda, it helps them to 'buy in' to the process and take some responsibility for, as well as assume ownership of, the class meetings. An agenda notebook or noticeboard should be placed somewhere in the room where students can access it at specific times designated by you to contribute items. They may remove items they have put on, but not the items of others, and there needs to be a clear rule that the issues placed on the agenda are not to be discussed outside the times allocated for class meetings. This will help to avoid arguments. The list of agenda items should be reviewed by the teacher or, if possible, the lead student at each meeting. The student who contributed the item should be asked whether it still needs to be discussed (often problems are resolved prior to the class meeting).

Developing communication skills

An ineffective class meeting involves a class sitting in a circle, all talking at once and not listening to anything. Students need to learn and develop communication skills that are appropriate for class meetings. This means that they need to be able to express their concerns as well as listen to the concerns of others. A good way to ensure that this happens is to use a small bean bag or 'talking stick'. Only the person with the bean bag or stick is allowed to talk, and everyone else may listen. If someone wants to respond to a comment or contribute to the discussion, they must raise their hand and the teacher will indicate that the bean bag or stick be given to them. Those who choose not to follow this rule can be given one warning before being asked to leave the meeting, or sit in a 'penalty box'-type situation where they can observe but not participate for a set period of time. Students should be reminded frequently that the purpose of the meeting is not to blame others, but rather to find solutions to problems in a mature way.

Learning about separate realities

Through class meetings, students will learn that not everybody sees things in the same way. They need to be prepared to accept that different people will have different perspectives and views, and develop the skills to negotiate an outcome that benefits everyone.

Solving problems through role-playing and brainstorming

The purpose of class meetings is to solve problems. The best way for students to do this is to either act out the scenario and its possible other solutions, or to brainstorm possible solutions. These solutions should be discussed without judgement. The student who put the item on the agenda can then pick the best solution from the list devised by the class. In instances where that student is unable to select a solution, the entire list of possible solutions can be put to a vote by the entire class. The selected solution should be tried for a week and then discussed again if it has not worked. It is then important for reasons of preserving healthy self-esteem that the concept of appreciations and giving compliments is briefly revisited, particularly for those involved in placing the item on the agenda and the student who made the mistake.

Recognising the four reasons why people do what they do

Before consequences and solutions are applied, it is important for students to reflect on the reasons for misbehaviour as identified by Albert (2003). This should help to develop some empathy and enable them to come up with more sensitive and appropriate consequences.

Applying logical consequences and other non-punitive solutions

All problems require solutions, and all instances of misbehaviour should be met with appropriate consequences. The final 'building block' students need to develop in order to participate in effective class meetings is how to apply these solutions and consequences. In devising consequences, they need to be reminded that the consequence must meet three criteria. Any consequence must be related to the misbehaviour. For example, if a student has damaged another student's property, then a related consequence may be to spend time at recess repairing the damage. A consequence must also meet the criterion of being respectful. A student should not be demeaned as a result of the consequence. Third, a consequence needs to be reasonable. Being asked to write a 20-page paper over two full weeks of recess may not be a reasonable consequence for a student who litters, but spending two recesses cleaning up in the school may. All consequences devised by students need to be compared against each criterion before being applied.

Box 10.3 provides a simple format for a class meeting.

Box 10.3: Class meeting format

1. Compliments and appreciations
2. Follow-up on past solutions
3. Agenda items:
    (a) Share feelings while others listen
    (b) Discuss without fixing
    (c) Ask for problem-solving help
4. Future plans (field trips, parties, etc.)

Source: Nelsen et al. (1993, p. 90).

Sometimes, despite our best efforts as teachers, our classroom management does not have the impact we desire. At this point, it is a good idea to reflect and take stock of the situation. Is there something missing? The following questions can be used to help you guide self-evaluation and critical reflection of your approach to classroom management:

- How much teacher talk was there compared with student talk? Which students talked? Who listened? When did they talk?
- Who was off task? On task?
- Were the instructions presented so that all the students could understand?
- Was the task too easy? Too difficult?
- Was there enough time for students to complete the activity?
- Were distractions and disruptions minimised?
- Were some students provided with alternatives?
- Were students who did not have the prerequisite skills given scaffolds to support their participation and learning?

This chapter has covered classroom management from two angles. The first angle has been understanding and addressing misbehaviour with individual students. The second focus has been on strategies for promoting positive behaviour that can be used with the whole class, such as building a classroom community and class meetings. We now conclude with a list of general tips for effective classroom management (Box 10.4) based on our own experience as teachers and researchers. These coincide with strategies found to be successful in the literature (Albert, 2003; Bloom, 2009; Deppeler, 1998; Jones & Jones, 2004).

Box 10.4: Classroom management tips that work

1. Get to know your *students as individuals* and develop a personal relationship with them. Friends and common interests can provide a focus for conversation.
2. *Be positive!* Make constant attempts to build on each student's success—encourage, reward, and praise their appropriate actions. Help them see how good they are at what they do.
3. *Model* the standards for behaviour that you expect. At all times, be polite and courteous and expect the same of your students.
4. Regularly *observe* the behaviour of the classroom. Try to be aware of a number of behaviours that are occurring simultaneously. *Record* incidents of ongoing 'problem' behaviour.
5. Make all *classroom rules explicit* and list three important, reasonable class rules clearly on the wall. Communicate your expectations clearly. Involve students in establishing the rules for classroom behaviours.
6. Implement strong, predictable *routines*.
7. Plan to *minimise disruption* and maximise students' interest. Seating layout, student grouping, pacing and humour are all vital to minimising opportunities for disruption. Avoid down time and boredom—this can lead to trouble. Expect your students to be on task.
8. Some students do not work well together, so take care with seating and grouping. Do not seat easily distracted students near windows, doors or high-traffic areas.
9. *Pace* your lessons appropriately. If they are too fast, students may get left behind and give up; too long and they may become bored.
10. Be careful, cautious and consistent in using *reprimands*—choose private over public reprimands. Be fair and firm, never sarcastic.

Never make empty threats—ensure your reprimand is appropriate and you can carry it out. Choose your battles: some small details are not worth fighting for. Know when to ignore and when to step in. Avoid reprimanding or punishing a class or group.

11. *Use non-verbal gestures.* Maintain a high rate of *eye contact.* Use a signal that all students know means 'Quiet, please'. Give 'the eye' and use silence and facial expressions to keep some misbehaviour in check. Smile and nod positively. Use 'proximity control'. Move near to students acting disruptively.

12. *Don't yell.* Students can become 'teacher deaf' after a while. Speaking softly can help keep the classroom calm.

13. Give students special responsibilities around the classroom or school.

14. Require students to say three nice things ('put ups') for each time they 'name call' or 'put down' another student.

15. Display student work samples to promote self-esteem and confidence.

16. Be a *physical presence* during times of transition between activities. The absence of structure at these times can sometimes create problems.

17. Monitor and critically reflect on your classroom management and identify areas for improvement. Monitor your handling of the beginning, transition and end of a lesson as well as responses to an unexpected event or a classroom crisis.

Key terms

Challenging behaviour. When a student responds to his or her educational environment in ways that differ significantly from age-appropriate expectations and interfere with the student's own learning or that of others.

Minimum intervention. The least intrusive means necessary to control a given situation.

For discussion and reflection

10.1 Behaviour which is viewed as thoroughly unacceptable in some contexts (such as poor language) is regarded as barely worthy of note in other contexts. Is there a universal standard for what is and what is not poor behaviour?

10.2 How might one be able to tell the difference between attention-seeking and avoidance of failure behaviour? What about revenge and power behaviour? Why does this matter?

10.3 Are there other ways of building classroom community not listed in Box 10.1?

Further reading

Albert, L. (2003). *A teacher's guide to cooperative discipline* (2nd ed.). Minnesota, MI: AGS Publishing.

Bloom, L.A. (2009). *Classroom management: Creating positive outcomes for all students*. Upper Saddle River, NJ: Pearson.

Hieneman, M., Dunlap, G. & Kincaid, D. (2005). Positive support strategies for students with behavioural disorders in general education settings. *Psychology in the Schools*, 42(8), 779–94.

Jones, V. & Jones, L. (2004). *Comprehensive classroom management: Creating communities of support and solving problems*. Boston: Allyn & Bacon.

11
Social and emotional learning

Key ideas in this chapter
- Defining social and emotional learning
- Developing social and emotional competencies
- Effective social and emotional learning programs
- Teacher social and emotional competence

Throughout this book, we have emphasised the idea that creating inclusive schools requires the collaboration and commitment of the whole school community. Our vision is schools where families, schools and communities work together to promote the healthy development and success in schooling of all students. Preparing students to participate constructively in a democratic society requires a broad, balanced education that both ensures their mastery of basic academic skills and also prepares them to become responsible adults (Association for Supervision and Curriculum Development, 2007). This chapter outlines ways in which schools can create socially and emotionally sound learning environments that develop social and emotional competence and promote the positive social interaction of all members of the school community. The goal is to create places where students and adults are engaged as learners, are caring and connected to others, interact in socially skilled and respectful ways, practise positive, safe and healthy behaviours, and are responsible for their decisions and actions as engaged citizens. If we are to have social cohesion and increase social capital, it is critical that schools develop the social and emotional learning of the members of their communities.

What is social and emotional learning?

Various terms have been used to describe social and emotional learning (SEL), including personal and social development, social and emotional and behavioural skills, and social and emotional competence (Department for Education and Skills UK, 2005). Social and emotional learning has been defined as a process by which students 'enhance their ability to integrate thinking, feeling and behaving to achieve important life tasks' (Zins, Bloodworth, Weissberg & Walberg, 2004, p. 6). We use the broadly accepted definition of social and emotional learning developed by the Collaborative for Academic, Social and Emotional Learning (CASEL, 2007, p. 1):

> *SEL is a process for helping children and even adults develop the fundamental skills for life effectiveness. SEL teaches the skills we all need to handle ourselves, our relationships and our work, effectively and ethically.*

SEL is an approach that supports students to build knowledge and understanding of their identity, to develop relationships, and to understand the impact of their actions and decision-making in various social contexts (see Box 11.1). Through social and emotional learning, students learn to recognise, regulate and successfully manage the social and emotional aspects of their lives in constructive and ethical ways.

Box 11.1: Social and emotional learning

Social and emotional learning is the process through which children and adults acquire the knowledge, attitudes, and skills to:
- recognise and manage their emotions
- set and achieve positive goals
- demonstrate caring and concern for others
- establish and maintain positive relationships
- make responsible decisions
- handle interpersonal situations effectively.

Source: Dymnicki, Taylor, Schellinger & Pachan; Payton, Weissberg, Durlak, Dymnicki, Taylor, Schellinger & Pachan, 2008.

Although different cultures and contexts value a variety of social and emotional competencies, there is some general consensus across most societies as to what is acceptable and valued in positive social interaction. Social and emotional competencies allow students to 'calm themselves when angry, make friends, resolve conflicts respectfully, and make ethical and safe choices . . . and be good communicators and problem solvers' (CASEL, 2007, p. 1). Social and emotional learning develops in five core areas of competence: self-awareness, self-management, social awareness, relationship skills and responsible decision-making (Collaborative for Academic, Social and Emotional Learning, 2005; Devaney, O'Brien, Keister, Resnik & Weissberg, 2006; Zins, Bloodworth, Weissberg & Walberg, 2004) (see Box 11.2).

Box 11.2: Core social and emotional competencies

1. **Self-awareness:** accurately assessing one's feelings, interests, values and strengths; maintaining a well-grounded sense of self-confidence.
2. **Self-management:** regulating one's emotions to handle stress, controlling impulses and persevering in addressing challenges; expressing emotions appropriately; setting and monitoring progress towards personal and academic goals.
3. **Social awareness:** being able to take the perspective of and empathise with others; recognising and appreciating individual and group similarities and differences; recognising and making the best use of family, school and community resources.
4. **Relationship skills:** establishing and maintaining healthy and rewarding relationships based on cooperation; resisting inappropriate social pressure; preventing, managing and resolving interpersonal conflict; seeking help when needed.
5. **Responsible decision-making:** making decisions based on a consideration of ethical standards, safety concerns, appropriate social norms, respect for others and likely consequences of various actions; applying decision-making skills to academic and social situations; contributing to the well-being of one's school and community.

Benefits of social and emotional learning

It is now well established in the research literature that social and emotional competencies are integral to academic learning and success in schools (CASEL, 2007). Recent research developments regarding students' social and emotional competence have had an important impact on how we understand students' pro-social behaviour and positive social and academic functioning (Spinrad & Eisenberg, 2009). Although there is increasing research evidence indicating the complexity of the relationships between emotional competence and academic and behavioural outcomes, it is also clear that students who are able to manage their feelings (particularly strong negative feelings) do much better socially, behaviourally and academically (Buckley & Saarni, 2009). Further, students who are pro-social, showing empathy and sympathy for others, are likely to cooperate in class and be engaged in their schooling (Eisenberg, Fabes & Spinrad, 2006; Spinrad & Eisenberg, 2009).

A recent meta-analysis of 207 research studies conducted by CASEL (Durlak et al., 2007) determined that effective social and emotional learning (SEL) programs had an impact in schools—relative to their peers who did not receive the program, students showed significant improvement in:

- their standard of achievement
- their social-emotional skills
- attitudes about themselves and others
- the quality of their social interactions, and
- levels of emotional distress and depression, as well as disruptive and challenging behaviours—all of which were reduced.

The research review also provided strong evidence that school programs which specifically promote social and emotional learning are effective:

- across the K–8 grade range
- for racially and ethnically diverse students from urban, rural and suburban settings
- for improving social-emotional skills, and attitudes about self and others
- for improving engagement in schooling
- for improving pro-social behaviour and academic performance
- in reducing students' conduct problems and emotional distress, and
- in being easily integrated into routine practice by teachers, students and other members of the school community (Payton et al., 2008).

Comparing these findings to reviews of other research interventions focused on social and emotional competencies, it is clear that schools are a highly effective context for SEL programs. Many of the programs that teach social and emotional competencies have now been evaluated rigorously. In particular, the Collaborative for Academic, Social and Emotional Learning (CASEL) is at the forefront of applying this research in schools. The CASEL website (<www.casel.org>) identifies a range of SEL programs that provide systematic evidence-based classroom teaching and resources. These programs are designed with a focus on *student competencies* to:

- recognise and manage their emotions
- appreciate the perspectives of others
- develop pro-social goals
- use a range of interpersonal skills to solve social challenges.

SEL programs also focus on creating supportive climates in the classroom and throughout the school:

- promoting and developing positive relationships between students and adults, and
- developing practices that build trust and rapport among and between students and adults.

What supports social and emotional learning?

The same principles of effective teaching and learning apply to social and emotional learning as to any other learning area. Teaching and learning content and activities need to:

- be relevant to students so they see the benefits
- respond to individual understandings and competencies
- connect past experiences and knowledge with current understandings and skills
- ensure learners are challenged and successful
- make explicit success criteria for the social and emotional competencies
- model the social and emotional competencies for students
- create a positive context that is emotionally, socially and physically supportive
- provide sufficient practice
- be connected to everyday life.

When learning social and emotional skills, the same assessment principles apply and the use of AFL approaches (Chapter 4) is a necessary part of learning and teaching.

Social and emotional learning and the school curriculum

Inclusive schools that engage students in their learning will have a range of guiding principles that underpin their teaching and frame the learning environment. Teaching and learning is relational practice, and 'creating trusting and respectful relationships in schools and classrooms is the indispensable

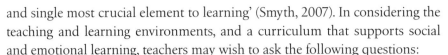

and single most crucial element to learning' (Smyth, 2007). In considering the teaching and learning environments, and a curriculum that supports social and emotional learning, teachers may wish to ask the following questions:

- How does teaching connect with and respect the prior experiences, interests, cultures and expectations of students?
- How does teaching expand and build cultural understanding for the students who are marginalised or at risk for being excluded?
- How does the school recognise and celebrate students' learning success?
- How does this school make students feel comfortable and safe?
- How does this school encourage students to have a strong voice?
- How does this school create a context for students to take responsibility for the consequences of their actions on their learning?
- How are partnerships with families and other members of the community developed to support and foster caring relationships?
- How is teaching and learning an enjoyable, challenging and rewarding experience?
- How does this school promote a sense of belonging and connectedness?

Social and emotional learning programs

There are numerous social and emotional learning (SEL) programs that are promoted to schools in Australia, Canada, the United States and the United Kingdom. Individual schools may also have designed programs to involve teachers and other members of the school community in the teaching and as a way of building common understandings about social and emotional learning. There are substantive challenges in developing and/or selecting an effective social and emotional learning program from the wide range of resources that are currently available. Box 11.3 outlines ten features that are considered to be key to successful social and emotional learning programs. These are based on UNESCO (2003) principles for academic and social learning and the characteristics for *effective* programs (CASEL, 2002). Many of the activities and processes are consistent with principles and practices that have been advocated throughout this book—in particular, practices that emphasise community, collaboration and the systematic use of evidence and school-wide efforts to create positive environments that promote healthy adaptive and pro-social behaviour for *all* students. Box 11.4 provides a tool to assist in selecting or developing an effective social and emotional learning program. This tool draws upon guidelines described in *Safe and sound: An educational leader's guide to evidence-based social and emotional learning (SEL) programs* (CASEL, 2005).

Box 11.3: Features of effective SEL programs

1. **Community of care.** Builds caring relationships and connection to schooling through positive, challenging, supportive and safe learning environments that connect families, students and teachers with the wider school community. Schools are places where all members of the school community feel welcomed and valued, and are viewed as partners.

2. **Informed by research.** Programs are evidence-based and grounded in theory and research about student learning and development.

3. **Home–school collaboration.** Involves families and the school community as partners in applying the espoused SEL values and behaviours of the SEL program at home, at school and in the wider community.

4. **Coherent and unified.** Policies and programs provide a unified approach to promote social and emotional learning with clear and coherent messages about values, behaviour, citizenship and health.

5. **Integrated learning.** Social and emotional dimensions of learning with key academic areas using teaching practices that engage learners actively, including problem-solving and collaborative learning arrangements.

6. **Explicit teaching.** Systematic and explicit teaching of social and emotional competencies, applied to everyday situations and contexts, enhances students' recognition and management of their emotions, builds an understanding of the perspectives of others, and develops the interpersonal skills and values necessary to make responsible and respectful decisions.

7. **Responsive pedagogies.** Pedagogy is responsive to the diverse learners in the school, including varied approaches and levels that are respectful of and responsive to difference.

8. **Professional learning.** High-quality and ongoing professional support for teachers is integrated and an ongoing part of the social and emotional learning program in schools. It includes modelling of teaching and feedback from colleagues in a supportive context.

9. **Evidence-informed.** Includes regular auditing and evaluation of practices informed by a range of data to assess effectiveness, align practices and inform change. Evidence from all members of the school community—including teachers, students and families—is key to the process.

10. **Organisational support.** Builds social and emotional programs systematically and over the long term, establishing resources and structures to foster success and sustain the process.

Box 11.4: Guidelines for selecting/developing an effective social and emotional learning program

In considering a social and emotional learning program, the school should provide:
- opportunities for students to develop and practise positive social competencies
- opportunities for students to develop understandings of identity and social contexts
- sequenced learning experiences that connect past with present learning
- learning of the five core social and emotional competencies
- evidence-informed teaching practices
- a means to make quality judgements about student learning.

Finally, and most importantly, the social and emotional learning program should be delivered in the context of the curriculum relevant to the school. Teachers will need to make explicit the links between the program and the school curriculum. Research findings point to the need to value and explicitly include social and emotional learning as an integral component of the curriculum.

Whole-school approaches to the implementation of SEL programs will ensure consistent messages across the various teaching areas, and reinforce the social and emotional learning. Collaboration has been emphasised as an important feature of inclusive classrooms and schools. The use of collaborative learning arrangements (Chapter 8) has been found to promote the acceptance of others and pro-social behaviour (Johnson & Johnson, 1989, 2002). In general, creating a positive climate in classrooms and schools that includes a focus on others' feelings can enhance students' social and academic outcomes. The CASEL *Safe and Sound* program (CASEL, 2005) provides a comprehensive program that can be integrated with school curricula to replace one-off or short-term interventions. The CASEL research clearly demonstrates that SEL can be developed along with academic learning within the school.

Several commercially available programs are available to educators that may support whole-school approaches and connect SEL with the school curriculum. In considering commercially available programs, the guidelines in Box 11.4, along with the key features of effective programs in Box 11.3, can be used to inform decisions about selecting programs and determining their suitability. Social and emotional learning programs that are specifically targeted to address the five core social emotional competencies outlined in Box 11.2, and which have been evaluated by research demonstrating their effectiveness, are listed in Box 11.5. All of these programs have features consistent with what is advocated for effective social and emotional programs in Box 11.3. Additional information on effective SEL programs can be found on the websites of your relevant education authority or on the CASEL website.

Box 11.5: Effective SEL Programs

Bounce Back: Classroom Resiliency Program—McGrath & Noble (2003)

K–Year 9. A collection of practical classroom strategies to help students cope with the complexity of their everyday lives and learn to 'bounce back' when they experience sadness, difficulties, frustrations and hard times. The program teaches the personal skills of resilience through key learning areas: literacy; science and technology; and social studies. The parent program shows parents how to reinforce the teaching of the same skills at home.

Caring School Community—Developmental Studies Centre (2004)

K–Year 6. Four principles are at the heart of this research-based program: respectful, supportive relationships; opportunities for collaboration; autonomy and influence; and common purposes and ideals. Aims to build a classroom and school-wide community with a focus on strengthening students' connectedness to school.

FisT: Feeling is Thinking—Pavlidis & Bunston (2004)

Year 3–Year 6. Aims to assist students to understand and explore the origins of their feelings, to problem-solve and to express their feelings. The program provides feedback, information and strategies, and actively engages the family and school in supporting and extending the positive skills and strategies developed through students' participation.

Friendly Kids, Friendly Classrooms—McGrath & Francey (1991)

K–Year 6. Used by teachers and counsellors to teach students social skills that will help them to get along well with their classmates. The book incorporates diagnostic tools and practical steps on how to teach 21 important classroom and playground skills. Games and activities are designed to create a positive and fun-filled classroom, and to help students who are shy or awkward. Teachers are encouraged to follow the suggested program or create their own, based around the four areas of the book.

Friendly Schools and Families Program—Cross & Erceg (2005)

K–Year 7. This program aims to prevent bullying in its social context—for students, families and/or the wider school community. The program assists with the design, development, implementation, and evaluation of a whole-school social and emotional learning and anti-bullying program. The program provides strategies and practical tools for a building ethos, creating policy, practices, and physical, social and learning environments, and for engaging families, along with case studies to demonstrate how other schools have tailored and used these strategies.

I Can Problem Solve (ICPS)—Sure (1993)

P–Year 6. Based on 25 years of research, ICPS has proven to be extremely effective in helping young children learn how to generate solutions to everyday interpersonal problems, consider others' views and understand possible consequences in order to develop pro-social behaviour.

Lions Quest Programs—Lions Clubs International Foundation (2006)

K–Year 12. Three Lions Quest programs—*Skills for Growing* (K–Year 5), *Skills for Adolescence* (Years 6–8) and *Skills for Action* (Years 9–12)— aim to develop positive attitudes and important life skills that promote health and safety, and prevent violence and other high-risk behaviours. The program emphasises five components: classroom curriculum; parent and family participation through shared homework assignments, a parent book and direct involvement in school activities; a positive school climate; community involvement; and professional development. To implement the program, it is necessary to attend an introductory two- to three-day workshop.

PATHS Curriculum—Kusche & Greenberg (1994)

K–Year 5. This program teaches primary school children how to change behaviours and attitudes that contribute to violence and bullying; how to express and control their emotions; and how to develop effective conflict-resolution strategies. The preschool PATHS program aims to improve children's knowledge about emotions as well as their social and emotional competence. PATHS covers five conceptual domains: self-control; emotional understanding; positive self-esteem; relationships; and interpersonal problem-solving skills.

Safe and Sound: Educational Leaders' Guide to Social and Emotional Learning—CASEL (2005)

P–Year 12. Based on a three-year study funded by the Office of Safe and Drug-Free Schools (OSDFS) in the US Department of Education, *Safe and Sound* is a comprehensive and inclusive guide to SEL for school leaders. This guide provides a map for schools to set up and add social, emotional and academic learning programs within an integrated framework. The guide also reviews 80 multi-year, sequenced SEL programs designed for use in general education classrooms.

Second Step—Committee for Children (2002)

K–Year 9. This violence-prevention program integrates academic and SEL elements. It is designed to develop social and emotional skills such as empathy, emotion-management, problem-solving and cooperation while teaching students to change behaviours and attitudes that contribute to violence. The program focuses on teaching empathy, anger management and impulse control, and provides broad, multi-year coverage of violence prevention. The research-based program has been shown to reduce discipline referrals, improve school climate by building feelings of inclusiveness and respect, and increase the sense of confidence and responsibility in students. The program includes teacher-friendly lessons, training for educators and parent-education tools.

Social Decision-Making and Social Problem-Solving—Elias & Butler (2005)

Year 2–Year 8. Aims to support students in learning social and decision-making skills and in developing their ability to effectively use those skills in real life. The program has three developmental phases: self-control and social awareness; social decision-making; and application of social decision-making. The overall aim is to prevent violence, substance abuse and related problem behaviour. It is a primary prevention program conceptually grounded in research from public health, child development, clinical psychology, the cognitive sciences, and organisational and community psychology.

Stop Think Do Social Skills Curriculum—Petersen (2006)

K–Year 7. The program is designed to promote social skills, conflict-resolution, academic achievement and a positive school climate. It aims to develop self-control, perceptual and communication skills, and cognitive problem-solving skills, particularly for students who have challenging behavioural or social challenges and are 'stuck' at one of the Stop, Think or Do steps. The program aims to train all children to move through all steps with positive feedback and support from adults and peers.

Learning for Life—Learning for Life Corporation (<www.learning-for-life.org>)

K–Year 12. Offers seven programs designed to support schools and community-based organisations to teach students to handle the challenges of today's society successfully, and at the same time enhance their self-confidence, motivation and self-esteem. Programs are delivered on site and online.

Tribes Learning Communities—<www.tribes.com>

P–Year 12. Used in schools throughout the United States, Canada and Australia and in other countries. Aims to promote learning and human development by creating a positive school and classroom learning community. The program is designed to help students feel included, respected for their differences and actively involved in their learning, and teaches them to have positive expectations about their ability to succeed.

You Can Do It Education (YCDI)—Bernard (2006)

K–Year 12. The purpose of this program is to support communities, schools and homes in a collaborative effort to optimise the social, emotional and academic outcomes of all students. Structured to explicitly support students' development of twelve positive Habits of the Mind (e.g. self-acceptance, high frustration tolerance, acceptance of others) and eliminate negative Habits of the Mind (e.g. self-deprecation, low frustration tolerance, lack of other acceptance). It also teaches students how they can influence their emotions and behaviours by changing their thinking.

Service learning

Service-learning is a general approach that integrates community service into the classroom curriculum. The goal is to support students to further develop social awareness, tolerance and respect for others while applying academic and real-world problem-solving skills; they do this while performing a needed service in the community. Service learning is taking place in a wide variety of settings throughout the world, including schools, universities, and community-based and faith-based organisations. Students can reflect on and learn from their experiences while providing real practical benefits to the community. Service learning is built on partnerships within the school or between the school and a wide range of community service organisations (e.g. those that support the aged, homeless, various disabilities, and youth or environmental and social service groups). In collaboration with teachers, students are actively involved in directly working in school or community service. It is expected that, as students actively engage and reflect on their participation in service learning activities, they will further develop their self- and social-awareness, self-management, responsible decision-making and relationship skills, and will be more effective in their service roles.

Teachers and social and emotional competence

There is growing recognition that teachers make a vital contribution to the social and emotional learning of their students (Hamre & Pianta, 2006; Murray & Greenberg, 2000; Osher, Cartledge, Oswald, Sutherland, Artiles

& Coutinho, 2007). Of all the school relationships that students form, teacher–student relationships have the most influence on students' success in schooling (Doll et al., 2009). Students develop stronger bonds with effective teachers who are warm, helpful, honest, even-tempered and encourage students to be independent (Doll et al., 2009). Classrooms support a diversity of students with varied cultural backgrounds, abilities and interest in learning. Teachers shape the learning context for these students. When teachers foster a sense of community in their classrooms, students show more pro-social behaviours such as cooperation, helpfulness and concern for others, and exhibit fewer disruptive behaviours (Battistich, Solomon, Watson & Schaps, 1997). Recently, Jennings and Greenberg (2009) proposed a model that highlights the importance of teachers' social and emotional competencies in the development of a pro-social classroom and the successful implementation of SEL programs. Teachers who are socially competent (high in the five core social and emotional competencies) implement SEL programs 'more effectively because they are outstanding role models of desired social and emotional behaviour' (2009, p. 493).

Socially competent teachers:
- recognise their own emotional patterns and know how to use positive emotions to generate and motivate learning for themselves and their students (self-awareness)
- regulate their emotional expressions, and are able to handle stress and challenging situations in respectful ways (self-management).
- know how they appear to others and can understand and empathise with the perspectives of students, parents and colleagues (social awareness)
- establish and build strong relationships with students, colleagues and families based on mutual understandings, sharing of school and community resources and collaboration (relationship skills)
- make responsible and ethical decisions based on pro-social values, and on how their decisions are likely to affect their well-being and other members of the school community, and take responsibility for their decisions (responsible decision-making).

Teacher social competence has implications for schools. As outlined in Chapter 5, a school community is built on trust and collaboration, and these are essential when it comes to improving schools. Like their students, teachers learn when they are happy, respected, supported and feel connected to those in their school community. Effective SEL programs must be delivered as a whole-school community approach—connecting and developing the social and emotional competencies of teachers, students and their families. This SEL approach will necessarily include teacher professional development as an integral and critical component.

Students' social and emotional competence and well-being depend upon the strength of their relationships with their families, school and community. While many students are actively engaged in schooling, others become more disengaged from school as they progress from primary to secondary levels (Klem & Connell, 2004). This chapter has described a framework for effective social and emotional learning in schools that is grounded in research and is currently advocated by many educational systems internationally. Establishing positive learning environments and teaching SEL competencies to meet the diverse social and emotional needs of students can help students succeed in school and life, and prevent disengagement.

Key terms

Social and emotional learning (SEL). A process for helping children and even adults develop the fundamental skills for life effectiveness. SEL teaches the skills we all need to handle ourselves, our relationships and our work, effectively and ethically.

Social and emotional competence. Social and emotional learning develops in five core areas of competence: self-awareness, self-management, social awareness, relationship skills and responsible decision-making.

Service learning. A general approach that integrates community service into the classroom curriculum.

For discussion and reflection

11.1 Why is social and emotional learning important to the process of inclusion? Why should teachers have to address it?

11.2 What can teachers do to facilitate the building of close social and emotional bonds between students?

11.3 Should teachers develop emotional bonds with their students? Are there limits to this?

Further reading

Many resources are available on the edna website that are suitable for the teaching of social and emotional learning. See <www.edna.edu.au/edna/go/schooled/school theme pages/emotion>.

There are also resources and briefs on social and emotional learning on the CASEL website—the following are examples:

Payton, J., Weissberg, R.P., Durlak, J. A., Dymnicki, A., Taylor, R.D., Schellinger, K.B. & Pachan, M. (2008). *The positive impact of social and emotional learning for kindergarten to eighth-grade students: Executive Summary*. CASEL. Available from <www.casel.org/pub/index.php>.

Zins, J.E. & Elias, M.E. (2006). Social and emotional learning. In G.G. Bear & K.M. Minke (Eds.), *Children's needs III* (pp. 1–13). Bethesda, MD: National Association of School Psychologists.

12
Reflection: The key to lasting change

Key ideas in this chapter

- Mentally coping with diversity
- Reflecting on practice
- Tools for teacher reflection
- The effects of reflective teaching

Chapter 3 ended with the assertion that, when it comes to making classrooms work, the two attitudes that matter most are the belief that all children can learn, and that it is the teachers who believe they can make a difference who do. In a sense, those two statements sum up the purpose and function of this book: that inclusive classrooms can work and the teachers who believe they can make them work will. But of course, intention is not enough. Let's decide we want to be star golfers—after all, we can say we meet the two criteria above: we have no impediments to doing what golfers do (i.e. we can learn to play golf); and we believe we can actually go out there and do what golfers do (i.e. we believe in our abilities or capacities to succeed). But obviously these attributes are not enough. Together with the right attitudes, we also need other things. In the case of learning to play golf, we need to find out how to hold a club and know which club to use and when, and we need to learn the rules of the game.

The same principles apply to becoming the best teachers we can be. In Chapter 1 we said there were four things that were needed to be a successful inclusive teacher. The fourth, 'support from colleagues and the school', is something we may not be able to control, but that is no excuse for missing out on the first three. They are:

1. attitude,
2. skills as a teacher, and
3. ability to solve problems.

Attitude was discussed in Chapter 3. Teacher skills are referred to throughout the book. With regard to being able to solve problems, coming up with creative solutions to problems in teaching situations involves:

- solid pedagogical practices,
- shared values, and
- positive leadership.

This book has attempted to provide you with hints and ideas that will make it easier for you to plan and implement procedures or organisational strategies that will allow you to meet your objectives as a teacher who matters.

To become successful inclusive teachers, we need two main things: we need to understand how complexities are dealt with; and we need to find working strategies that will allow us to capitalise on those insights to make us better teachers.

Mentally coping with diversity

There is no doubt that teachers today face far more complex problems than were experienced by teachers in times gone by. Tyler (1995), an international figure in the field of the study of individual differences, notes:

> *Human diversity constitutes [a] greater challenge in the complex societies of our time than it did in simpler societies of the past. Our society could not function without the unique contributions of unique individuals. Its members cannot be considered to be identical, interchangeable parts. They do not just compete with one another; they complement one another. Just.*
> *(p. 12)*

The advent of the inclusive classroom is a continuation of that trend from simpler societies to more complex ones, but along with the challenges of the complexities come the possibilities of greater and more extensive successes.

How we can make life less complex, or how we can deal with these undoubted complexities, is very important. One thing is certain: we cannot make the world simpler—rather, we need to understand something about the processes by which it has become more complicated. Our lives have become more complicated because of the increase in knowledge and travel, and the breakdown of simple geographical and cultural boundaries. Those are givens—now let's look at what we can do about them.

One of the ways in which we understand our world is by categorising everything and being able to distinguish one set of phenomena from another by means of a defining characteristic or set of characteristics. If we could not do this, everything would be a blur and everything would be the same. Hence almost all language and all understanding of the world is based on the capacity to group ideas into concepts.

These concepts are abstract and mental; they are real but not observable, and they begin at the most basic levels. Light and dark, hard and soft, tangible and abstract, and so on through all the things we know—everything fits into one category or another, and with increasing sophistication and experience our concepts reflect our individual experiences. For example, the words most people have for snow are fairly limited but it is reported that the Inuit, in the snowy regions of the Arctic, have many words to describe it. Concepts are many-faceted and hierarchical in their order. Being able to work through these orders is often taken as an indication of intellectual ability. The Wechsler Intelligence Scales include a sub-test that asks the examinee to say how numerous pairs of ideas or objects are alike, even though in normal life we think of them as being completely different from one another. This sub-test asks for an explanation of the way in which item 'a' is similar to item 'b'—items that can be as close as two colours or as distant as an animal and a plant. The task involves the examinee 'stepping back' from the two items and working through their orders of concepts until they can find a link. The more facility people have for doing this task, the more intellectually able they are considered to be.

We use individual names to differentiate and identify individuals. As teachers, we also use personal characteristics or physical characteristics to do something similar. But it is not only to identify individuals that we make use of information about these individual characteristics or physical states. We also use these characteristics to determine what we should teach and how we should go about our teaching. How we use them determines whether we can claim to be teaching all our students or just some of them; how we use them displays our attitudes to our profession and our responsibilities as teachers of all students.

We cannot live without categorising and giving descriptive terms to things, but at the same time this phenomenon can be taken too far. If it is true that without categorisation everything would be a blur, it is also true that at some point we must join things together to form homogeneous or like-minded groups. Our minds cannot cope with everything being different. Individual characteristics can separate, but they can also be used to collect or join things together. Age and gender are common categories with which we are all familiar. Common categories also apply in almost all aspects of teaching. But groupings become much more sophisticated when learning needs of identified age groups are concerned. An important task facing all teachers is to know when it is appropriate to put all students into one group and when to separate out individual students.

Separation of students will normally be based on learning needs or accomplishments, but discussions of difference and the identification of those with needs that differ from the rest lead us again into the problems associated with labelling. In Chapter 2 we looked at some of the negative outcomes of categorising—especially the concept of labelling, which is an unfortunate outcome of misusing our needs for grouping into an excuse for not attending to the needs of certain outlying groups. The way teachers use labels or 'diagnostic tags' is often a clear indicator of their attitudes towards their profession. Is a label used as a reason for not doing something or is it used as an insight into where the educational plans must be focused?

On the positive side, labels can be used to find out what is known about the learning needs of special groups where there are some common characteristics. When learning groups of words, most of us will automatically reorder the words into similar groups. If our task is to learn and recall a list of ten words—cat, rose, cream, crocodile, bread, lily, horse, tulip, parrot and cake—we would group the animals together, and the flowers, and the foods through a memory process known as chunking. In that way we would be able to cope with the range of items more easily. As an example of how some students differ from others, some students with intellectual disabilities may not group things together in this way automatically, but they can be taught this strategy. In discussion, the three different kinds of objects can be highlighted and then grouped together so that only three categories of items effectively need to be recalled. Knowing this about some students with particular intellectual disabilities is an example of a label being used to the child's advantage. On the other hand, failure on the part of the student with the intellectual disability to pick up on the strategy automatically could lead to the teacher explaining (read 'excusing') the failure to complete the task satisfactorily on the grounds that the student has 'an intellectual disability'.

Diagnostic categories are useful when they alert teachers to learner characteristics associated with a category, but they do not tell all about either an individual or the category into which the person might fit. The *Diagnostic and Statistical Manual of Mental Disorders* (*DSM*), an official publication of the American Psychiatric Association (APA), first appeared in 1952 and is now in an updated, text-revised fourth edition (American Psychiatric Association, 2000), with a fifth edition due out in 2012. It contains many indicators of a range of disorders, including intellectual disability and learning disorders, but it is neither complete nor fully informed in all its categories. What is noticeable about many of the entries is the range of indicators that can be used to diagnose a condition, of which only a few are required in order to complete the diagnosis. The authors of the *DSM* are also keen to point out that there is no assumption that individuals sharing a diagnosis are alike in all important ways, and encourage professionals to view disorders in terms of information that exceeds the mere lists of behaviours given in their text. Its publishers continue to view the manual as being in need of constant revision, and more versions can be expected as information and further data accumulate.

The process of differentiating mental conditions is complex, and although the *DSM* is an invaluable asset to the medical and psychological professions, it reminds teachers that categories of disability give us only very general definitions and only broadly indicate where instructional needs might lie. A category or diagnosis will give us hints, but only by understanding the individual student can we hope to understand where our teaching efforts should be placed.

Where knowledge of specific conditions may be helpful is in reflecting on our teaching goals and linking these in with the curriculum standards that guide our classroom work. Even where adaptations are required, they are unlikely to apply only to one student in the class, and even then only in very specific areas. What is more likely to happen is that, in considering the needs of a particular student, our habits of grouping things and people together will come to our aid and we will begin to see how commonly within a certain group particular learning gaps or particular strengths are to be found. Once we do that sort of grouping, we can really be aware that we are inclusive teachers, looking to enhance each student's advantage, not using excuses for failing to achieve our goals.

There is nothing new about the attitudes and approaches we advocate. Research has consistently highlighted the fact that teachers at all levels have significant effects on their students. Teachers, say this research, are not simply implementers of administrative policies but are active agents, thinking professionals, who have important effects on student learning (e.g. see Good & Brophy, 1990; Feiman-Nemser & Floden, 1986).

Brophy and Everston (1976) investigated the differences between relatively effective and relatively ineffective teachers, judged in terms of learning outcomes for students. Successful teachers saw teaching as an interesting and worthwhile challenge that they approached by assuming personal responsibility for the learning of their students. They believed that problems could be overcome by searching for solutions and were courageous enough to test their solutions in the classroom. Less successful teachers saw teaching as merely a dull job, discussed problems as if they were too serious to be solved and behaved in ways that ensured they were not solved. Those in this group did not believe they could make a difference, and therefore did not. Good attitudes need to be backed up by professional knowledge, but professional knowledge without commitment is of little use. This research was conducted in the 1970s but there has been nothing since to show that a teacher's role has changed from what Brophy and Everston found.

The importance of practice

A lecturer in architecture, a friend of one of the authors, used to bemoan the difficulties inherent in inducting budding architects into the mysteries and challenges of professional practice. He claimed that his first task when faced with a class of keen young architects was to convince them that being a good and creative architect was not a matter of sitting in a comfortable chair with a warm moist cloth placed across the forehead and dreaming dreams of new buildings or fantastic new ways of designing structures. There are always times for standing back and looking and thinking and dreaming, but mostly it is a case of working at designs, modifying them to meet new needs, and constantly evaluating the concepts and their implementation. In other words, they had to get out and start practising their profession, not just dream about it.

So it is with classrooms. An important key to successful implementation of good teaching ideas is to practise the skills in the classroom and to follow them up with reflection on their outcomes in what has been termed reflective practice. We argue that reflective practice is an important behaviour for teachers who want to become successful, inclusive professionals.

Deliberate practice

Practice is an interesting concept that can be applied to many of our endeavours, with music and sport two that quickly come to mind. 'Have you done your piano practice today?' or 'I have to go to cricket practice after school' are common enough statements. The word can be used as a synonym for the verb '*do*', as in 'we put into practice', or as a synonym for the verb '*rehearse*', as in 'prepare' or 'exercise' or 'repeat', or as a synonym for the noun '*rehearsal*', as in 'exercise' or 'training'. It is a given in most people's thinking that if we are to become good at anything we need to practise, and all three meanings of the word have some relevance to our purposes in this book. But we are not talking about *practice* for its own sake—after all, there are many instances where what we think of as practice for a favourite sport, for example, may be doing our skills no good at all. Golf is one of those sports where practice is thought to be essential, but if our practice is consolidating an error in a swing then all it is doing is making sure that our play will be worse next time we are out on the course. Colvin (2008) has suggested that the key to being very good at anything is to adopt the concept of *deliberate practice*. Deliberate practice is activity designed specifically to improve performance. It may require the help of someone else more experienced, it can be repeated a lot, and it is highly demanding mentally. It is a concept we advocate for teachers who want to be successful inclusive practitioners. Colvin (2008) says that 'deliberate practice requires that one identify certain elements of performance that need to be improved and then work intently on them' (p. 68).

Reflecting on practice

PAVOT is the acronym for an international approach aimed at encouraging teachers to take a researcher's view of their own teaching. Standing for 'Perspective and Voice of the Teacher', it arose out of another teacher-based research orientation to teaching, PEEL—or 'Project for the Enhancement of Effective Learning'—that has active groups in Canada, Australia, New Zealand, Sweden and Denmark, and is still growing into other countries.

Whether one wants to join any particular group is not important, but the lessons learned by the many teachers at all school levels and of all types who are involved in either PEEL or PAVOT can be put into practice in any school or formal learning situation. The teachers who started the group were initially interested in why some students did not learn; the analysis of poor learning tendencies led to the identification of good learning behaviours. The teachers identified six major behaviours that indicated good learning (Baird & Northfield, 1992). A student:

- seeks assistance—tells the teacher what they do not understand
- checks progress—refers to earlier work before asking for help
- plans work—anticipates and predicts possible outcomes
- reflects on work—makes links between activities and ideas
- links ideas and experiences—offers relevant and personal examples
- develops a view—justifies opinions.

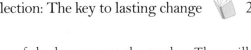

Note that these are behaviours of the learner, not the teacher. They will be shown by any learner, although how each person displays them will vary according to the developmental age of the student concerned. Very young learners will go through all these phases as they move on from one experience to another, even if they cannot explain what is happening. Some older students may be able to articulate what is happening; however, for most the processes will not be at the level of overt awareness. Indeed, in the research, it was only through discussing, observing and analysing that the teachers were able to make up their lists of what constitutes good learning.

Teachers want all their students to learn everything they have been taught. That seems very natural. If teachers did not want the children to learn, then they wouldn't bother teaching in the first place. But not all children learn at the same pace or in the same quantities. That is a truism about teaching that has always been the case, but with homogeneous groupings of children it can sometimes be overlooked. The policies of inclusion mean teachers have to think more carefully about this as it is a very important concept. The more a teacher comes to realise what it means to be a successful inclusive teacher, the more obvious this will become.

Amanda Berry (Berry & Milroy, 2002), teaching a regular science class of 15-year-olds, found that she could no longer teach as if the tacit assumption that everyone in the class was learning at the same pace were in any sense true. She termed that assumption the 'big comfortable lie'. She wrote:

> *The biggest shift [in thinking about student learning] for me has been in scrapping any assumptions I had about the whole group moving en masse. It's a big lie. It's important to 'pick on' individuals (in the nicest possible way) to understand where they're at. I understand concepts in much greater depth than before because we're going slowly and coming at them again and again. If it is so for me then surely it must be the same for my students.* (p. 199)

If the PAVOT and PEEL experiences teach us anything, it is that just thinking some time should be spent reflecting on one's teaching is not enough. To do this successfully, it is necessary to approach the task in a systematic and continuous way. That is, of course, the secret behind Colvin's (2008) deliberate practice concept. Identify the elements of significance and work intently and specifically on them. An integral part of teacher training is to spend time in schools observing teachers at work. Most practicum programs expect student teachers to keep some sort of a diary and to record their impressions and ideas about teaching on a daily basis. Those techniques need not be restricted to pre-service training, but can be used as the basis of your own continued professional development. An example of how a reflective diary may be used is presented below.

Tools for teacher reflection

In addressing the topic of collaborating with colleagues Chapter 5 suggested working closely with others not only to plan and run an inclusive classroom, but also to improve practice. Indeed, many strategies for improving reflective practice were already addressed in some detail in that chapter. Some specific strategies and tools for teacher reflection are discussed below, with some of these ideas building on those already presented in Chapter 5.

Help from colleagues

One effective strategy for reflection on teaching at any level is to solicit the help of a trusted colleague to fulfil the role of 'critical friend'. A critical friend can help you to examine aspects of your teaching that you may not be able to see objectively or adequately by yourself. There are, however, some criteria and mutual understandings that should be considered prior to embarking on a collegial relationship to review teaching. These are as follows:

- The critical friend should be someone you trust, so you need to choose the person rather than having someone assigned to you. As you delve into your teaching, you want to be honest with your colleague, and in order to do that you need to be sure your colleague is someone who will neither judge you, nor breach the confidentiality implicit in the relationship.
- The critical friend should be readily available, and should be willing to spend time with you. Being a critical friend might entail conversations, classroom observations, and reviews of your plans and student work and assessments.
- At times, the critical friend might make suggestions; however, the main role of the friend is to ask questions or act as a mirror to your thoughts, enabling you to think through and solve issues yourself.
- The critical friend should have adequate expertise in a teaching area to enable them to provide informed feedback.
- The critical friend should not be in a supervisory role over you. You want to be honest, and such a relationship might not allow for that. You need to be equals.

Reflective diaries

A reflective diary should contain ideas, questions and reflections that arise as a result of your everyday experience. We suggest that a 'reflection' should be written up on each occasion when you notice or do something 'critical'. How you define the critical moments of your teaching or student learning is up to you, but clearly completing any more than one reflection sheet per day, or a few per week, will quickly become onerous and unrealistic given time constraints. Simply record the events that really matter in your view. Your reflections should include questions that arise out of your practice as well as steps you will take to answer those questions. Two examples of reflective diary entries are given below.

Example: Diary entries

Entry 1

Date: 21 August

Setting: Art session, my school

Reflections

I have been watching a class that included a student with a severe language disorder participate in an art session.

Students who have difficulties expressing themselves using verbal language may find an outlet for their inner thoughts and feelings through art. There are a number of different forms of art. A trained art therapist may be able to help a student with differing needs find the art form that best suits his or her interests, abilities, and needs.

Creating visual art such as drawing, painting or making objects allows the artist to express themselves in visual ways, which are often a release for strong emotions that they can't put into words. Students may also choose music as an outlet for their feelings. Music has a universal quality that links people together and helps the students overcome their feelings of isolation.

Questions arising

Some students with severe physical disabilities may not be able to manipulate art tools or musical instruments. Can they still express themselves through the arts? Do they need to find other alternatives?

Next steps

Observe music and another art class.

Entry 2

Date: 25 August
Setting: Local business trip

Reflections

The class went on a school trip that included a visit to some local businesses. I noticed that some of the people we met were uncomfortable talking to one of the students who has Down Syndrome.

The views of business people towards the presence of persons with disabilities as customers were investigated by Parsons, Elkins & Sigafoos (2000) in Queensland, Australia.

They investigated 89 individuals representing a range of convenience stores, video rental shops, fast-food restaurants, pharmacies, hairdressers, newsagents and a variety of other businesses. Eighty-five per cent of the interviewees expressed positive responses about people with intellectual disabilities coming to their stores, such as, 'Love it', 'Good customers' and 'Good to see them getting out'. There were a few other responses—for example, one respondent said he felt 'impatient if it is busy', and one expressed his concern that other customers may 'prefer not to shop with them'.

Very little is known about the community's reaction to people with disabilities using local amenities and resources. The above research was conducted to provide additional supporting data to the research by Saxby, Thomas, Felce & De Kock (1986), who found that attitudes towards persons with intellectual disabilities as customers in shops, pubs and cafes in the United Kingdom were favourable.

As a teacher in my town, I think I need to consider whether I will take a class that includes a student or two with a disability into town shops. I want to treat everyone in my class as important and accepted and I will take them anywhere as a group but I think I need to be aware that I don't put any of them in situations where they might be embarrassed by the reactions of people in shops or anywhere else.

Questions arising

How can I ensure I treat all my students as equals but not allow myself to over-compensate for the one or two who may be different? How can I work out ways to ensure that everyone in my class thinks everyone else in the group is just as important as them?

Next steps

Talk this over with other colleagues and the principal.

Video

Video of your teaching is an excellent means of promoting self-reflection on practice. Video evidence of a teaching session tells us much not only about instructional practices, but also about our mannerisms and how we might be perceived by our students. Although it is sometimes uncomfortable to watch ourselves on video it can be extremely enlightening. We have two recommendations for the use of video evidence in reflective teaching. The first is that you review video evidence of your teaching with a trusted colleague. Acting as a critical friend, this colleague can help point out aspects of your teaching that might otherwise escape your attention. Further, watching a video with a critical friend will force you to be more focused on areas that might need improvement. The second recommendation is that you analyse the video in a structured way. McGhie-Richmond, Underwood, and Jordan (2007) developed the Classroom Observation Scale (COS) which, after a period of familiarisation, is a helpful tool for analysing classroom practice. The COS contains many of the behaviours of effective teachers and presents them in such a way that it is possible to evaluate classroom practice lesson by lesson. This introduces some structure and purpose to classroom observations, and might produce an excellent basis for discussion with colleagues and personal reflections.

Feedback from students and parents

Ignoring feedback from students and parents would be a mistake. They are the 'end users' of the educational process, and in the case of students they are the people you are trying to reach. While students and parents may not have the background to be able to comment on the content of your teaching, they probably do have the background to comment on the effectiveness of delivery. Reflective teachers can invite feedback from students in written or verbal form, either informally or through a more formal process. The same can be done with parents. It is helpful in these situations to guide and structure what is being asked for. First, you should decide exactly what it is you want feedback on, then design questions that will elicit that information. Sometimes focus groups are helpful. A few students and/or parents who volunteer to sit down with a teacher together and have a conversation can sometimes yield invaluable information for improving teaching, although once again the conversation should be guided by questions relating to a specific purpose.

Observing others

Inter-visitations to other classrooms are helpful for reflection. If you are a Grade 2 teacher, it might be helpful to visit a few other local Grade 2 classrooms and engage in dialogue with those teachers. In return, other teachers can visit your room. In visiting other classrooms, you might notice strategies that would work for you, and when others visit your room their questions about your practice might point you in the direction of improvement, or provide affirmation of your good practices.

The effects of reflective practice on teaching

What will be the outcome for you, the teacher, if you embark on the practices we have been advocating in this book? We believe you will find that there are four things that will happen—which match Mitchell's (2002) effects on teachers who develop a reflective, thinking, research-oriented approach to their work.

1. *You will be willing to take risks.* Often there is comfort in just doing the same old things, day after day. This is not a crime, because we know that stability and security are based on being able to predict outcomes, but stability and security for their own sakes also blight progress. Sometimes there is a need to try new ways of doing things, for it is only in this way that we will progress.

   Courage is needed to take these steps. Courage is not the same as just doing something different for the sake of it. That could well be credulity, or foolhardiness. The courage to try something new in the present context is based on the need for change that becomes apparent as you reflect on present practice and see where gaps are obvious. Continual evaluation of teaching outcomes will provide the knowledge we need in order to find out what works and what doesn't. Spending time working out what will enhance the learning of students with different needs will also benefit those who do not have obvious differences in learning. That is one of the real gains of the movement from special schools to inclusive schools.

2. *You will learn to generalise from the particular to the larger group and be able to articulate your practice.* A success of the inclusive schools movement has been the necessity to take accepted patterns of work that appear to have worked with homogeneous groups of average students and reflect on how they need to be changed in order to meet the needs of all students. These needs include not only those recognised as gifted and talented but also those with intellectual or physical disabilities, or different cultural backgrounds.

The wider range of needs means new frames of reference are required in order to grasp the magnitude of the task. These can only come about through paying attention to the special needs groups, identifying common factors that apply to them initially but may also apply to the rest of the class, and being able to say what is required and how the new ways of thinking can be implemented.

Consider the reflective diary entries earlier in the chapter. Here we see how the questions arose from regular school activities; there was some delving into known research on the issue(s), there was reflection on the individual teacher's response and there were questions to ask about how action was to take place in the future. It is important to note that they are written out, not just thought about. They are observable, permanent, and able to be modified.

Throughout this book, we have reiterated that writing down ideas, thoughts, reflections, lessons, etc., is a key to successful and thoughtful implementation of good teaching. Language is our means of communicating and written language is our means of ensuring ideas are not lost, that others can contribute to their further development, and that they can be implemented when appropriate. Writing is a skill—one that improves with practice. Writing helps us to define our terms, our ideas and our hopes. The more we can write, the more easily and efficiently we can articulate our ideas and share our insights.

3. *Your perceptions of your role will change.* Writing down what you believe, what you do and why you think you are teaching will change your self-image as a teacher. Being thoughtful and reflective about your work may initially make you wonder why you do the job you do, because inevitably you will begin to notice gaps in your practice that might otherwise have escaped your attention.

   As you get more confidence in being self-critical and using the information to seek improvements in your practice and planning, the sense that your opinions are valuable will increase. This increase in confidence will be evidence based—that is, your own journals will map out the development of your thinking and the manner in which your practice has changed. The experience of systematic data collection about your own practice is to increase self-confidence and the enhancement of learning outcomes in your class.

4. *Your journey will be irreversible.* Mitchell (2002) makes the point that the PAVOT teachers who continued on with the tasks of becoming teacher-researchers found that their classroom practices changed in ways that

were permanent and important, and notes: 'Even though teaching in some ways becomes more demanding, with higher standards for a "good" lesson, there is no going back.' (p. 254)

The satisfaction and pride generated by doing a good job, the joy of seeing progress in one's students and the knowledge that these students— some of whom may well have been overlooked for years—are learning and growing are the reasons for us doing what we do—for *all* our students.

Key terms

Deliberate practice. A concept that believes practice on its own is not enough but that practice should be designed specifically to improve performance after careful analysis of where improvement is required and how it can be achieved.

PAVOT (Perspective and Voice of the Teacher). An international approach that encourages teachers to take a researcher's view of their own teaching.

PEEL (Project for the Enhancement of Effective Learning). An international approach that encourages teachers to take a researcher's view of their own teaching. It has active groups in Canada, Australia, New Zealand, Sweden and Denmark, and is still growing into other countries.

For discussion and reflection

12.1 What are some concrete steps you can take towards ensuring your teaching practice and attitudes remain current and thoughtful?

12.2 In what ways has the role of the teacher changed with respect to catering to diversity since you were a student?

Further reading

Colvin, G. (2008). *Talent is overrated*. New York, NY: Portfolio/Penguin.

Erickson, G., Minnes-Brandes, G., Mitchell, I. & Mitchell, J. (2005). Collaborative teacher learning: Findings from two professional development projects. *Teaching and Teacher Education: An International Journal of Research and Studies, 21*(7), 787–98.

Loughran, J., Mitchell, I. & Mitchell, J. (Eds.) (2002). *Learning from teacher research*. Sydney: Allen & Unwin.

McGhie-Richmond, D., Underwood, K. & Jordan, A. (2007). Developing effective instructional strategies for teaching in inclusive classrooms. *Exceptionality Education Canada 17*(1), 27–51.

Useful forms

These blank forms are designed for you to photocopy and complete for your inclusive school activities. You may wish to modify them for your own specific requirements. You can also download PDFs of these forms from the website: www.allenandunwin.com/InclusiveEducation.asp

Form 1

Interview analysis sheet

For _____ Date _____

Question	Parent response	Child response	Staff response	Summary of all responses

Form 2

Therapy implementation permission form

I, _____ , give permission for staff at _____ school

to implement the therapy listed below to my child _____

Therapy type _____

Description _____

_____

_____

_____

_____

_____

_____

_____

_____

_____

_____

_____

_____

Supervising therapist name _____ Phone contact _____

Staff member implementing therapy _____

The supervising therapist has outlined the assessment and treatment to me. I am aware that the staff member implementing the therapy has been shown the correct procedure by the therapist.
The therapist will review the program and the progress of my child on a regular basis and will inform me of the results. I will notify the school, in writing, if there are any changes to the conditions listed above.

Signed _____ (Parent/Guardian) Date _____

Form 3

Daily therapy plan

For _____ Date _____

Daily classroom activity	Therapy opportunity?	Person to implement therapy	Brief description of therapy

Form 4

Daily plan schedule

Teacher _____ Class _____ Date _____

Time	Lesson	What teacher does	What paraprofessional does

Form 5

Single lesson plan

Subject area/grade _____ Date and time _____

Lesson topic

Lesson goal:
Materials:
Procedure:
Homework task:
Teacher does:
Paraprofessional does:
Assessment:

Form 6

Learning at home planning sheet

For _____

Objective	What happens at school	What can happen at home

Form 7

Agenda for meeting of Program Support Group

Child: _____   Date of meeting: _____

Place: _____   Time: _____

PSG members:

Purpose: _____

Status _____

Time	Activity	Program Support Group members responsible

Form 8

Medical advice form

Any specific medical considerations?   Yes   No
Description/action required: _____

_____

Level and type of extra supports to be provided
(e.g. Therapy, teachers aide, personal care,accommodations in exams etc.):

Review dates:

Program support group signatures: Date: _____

_____ _____ _____ _____

Form 9

Individual program plan

Child name:		Age:	Grade/Year
Coordinating Teacher		Date:	

Vision Statement:

Assessment Results summary:

Assessment Type	Description of Results

Form 10

Long-term goals

Individual list   Group list   (please circle whichever applies)

Child name:	Date:

Learning Priorities
(in order of most important to least important)

1)	
2)	
3)	
4)	
5)	
6)	
7)	
8)	
9)	
10)	
11)	
12)	
13)	
14)	
15)	

Form 11

Indicators of achievement

Long-term goal:

Behavioural objective 1:	Inclusive teaching strategies for this objective:	Indicators of achievement:	Date achieved:
Behavioural objective 2:	Inclusive teaching strategies for this objective:	Indicators of achievement:	Date achieved:
Behavioural objective 3:	Inclusive teaching strategies for this objective:	Indicators of achievement:	Date achieved:
Behavioural objective 4:	Inclusive teaching strategies for this objective:	Indicators of achievement:	Date achieved:

Modified materials required for this goal—summary:

Form 12

Unit planner

Dates:	Class:

Subject area:

Central issues/problems

Opening grabber/motivator:

Summary of series of linked lessons:

Culminating projects:

Ongoing assessments (additional to culminating projects):

When?	What content/skills?	What form will it take?	How did student/s demonstrate learning?

Form 13

Unit planner—Infusing individual targets

Dates:	Child:	Class:

Subject area:

Central issues/problems	Relevant goals:

Summary of series of linked lessons:	Relevant linked individual objectives:

Suggested culminating project:

Form 14

Individual lesson planning form

Subject area/grade _____   Date and time _____

Lesson topic

Lesson goal:	
Central problem:	
Materials:	
Procedure:	
Diverse learner objectives for this lesson:	
Inclusive materials and procedures:	
Alternative assessment:	
Teacher does:	
Paraprofessional does:	
Assessment:	

Form 15

Medication administration permission form

I, _____ , give permission for staff at _____ school

to administer the medication listed below to my child _____ .

This medication has been prescribed to my child by the family doctor listed below. I have disclosed, in writing, all relevant information pertaining to this medication, such as possible side-effects and negative reactions, to school staff.

Medication name _____

Dosage _____

Date authorised administration begins _____

Days of the week medication is to be administered _____

Administration time _____

Special conditions under which the medication should be administered

_____

_____

Name of family doctor _____ Phone number_____

Emergency contact _____ Phone _____

I agree that I will provide the medication to the school staff in person and not permit my child to be in possession of the medication at any time, including to and from school. I will also notify the school, in writing, if there are any changes to the conditions of medication administration listed above.

Signed _____ (Parent/Guardian) Date _____

Form 16

Medication administration form

Child name _____

Medication _____

Dosage _____

Administration times & days _____

Special Conditions/information_____

_____

Written permission for administration on file from: ❏ family doctor?   ❏ parent?

Medication name	Dosage	Time	Date	Administerd by (print name)	Initials	Checked by (print name)	Initials

Form 17

External school trip medication form

Child name _____ Grade/Year _____

Teacher _____

Date _____

Medication name _____

Dosage _____

Time to be given _____

Person giving medication _____

Date and time medication actually given _____
                                                                  (signature)

Please return this paper to school office on return. Ensure that child medication administration records are updated.

(Adapted from Briggs et al. 1998, p. 42)

Form 18

Medication incident report

Child _____   D.O.B _____

School _____

Date of incident _____

Medication(s) _____

Dosage _____   Time administersed _____

Incident description (e.g. missed medication). Please provide detailed account.

_____

_____

_____

_____

_____

_____

Action taken _____

_____

_____

(Adapted from Briggs et al. 1998, p. 72)

Form 19

Positive behaviour action plan

Student _____ Teacher _____ Date _____

The behaviour that needs changing is:

I would like to change that behaviour and do the following instead:

The reason for that behaviour is:

The best solution to this problem is:

What the student will do:	What the teacher will do:

The consequences for continued misbehaviour are:

The rewards/benefits of improved behaviour are:

Form 20

Social skill behaviour rating scale

The following areas are suggested as a focus for your observations.

Self control	Never	Sometimes	Often	Always
1 Can cope with criticism or direction from adults	☐	☐	☐	☐
2 Can wait for needs to be met	☐	☐	☐	☐
3 Responds appropriately when peers push or hit	☐	☐	☐	☐
4 Controls temper in problem situations	☐	☐	☐	☐

Peer interaction	Never	Sometimes	Often	Always
5 Initiates conversations or interactions with peers	☐	☐	☐	☐
6 Can compromise when others wish to change an activity	☐	☐	☐	☐
7 Invites others to join in activities	☐	☐	☐	☐
8 Makes friends easily	☐	☐	☐	☐
9 Can respond to good-natured teasing from peers	☐	☐	☐	☐
10 Gets along with others who are different	☐	☐	☐	☐
11 Can give compliments appropriately	☐	☐	☐	☐
12 Volunteers to help peers when necessary	☐	☐	☐	☐
13 Cooperates with peers on class activities without direction	☐	☐	☐	☐
14 Seeks company from peers	☐	☐	☐	☐
15 Can stick up for him/herself with peers	☐	☐	☐	☐

Work habits	Never	Sometimes	Often	Always
16 Can use free time appropriately	☐	☐	☐	☐
17 Finishes school work in reasonable time	☐	☐	☐	☐
18 Takes pride in school work	☐	☐	☐	☐
19 Looks after own belongings	☐	☐	☐	☐
20 Can change from one activity to the next without upset	☐	☐	☐	☐
21 Follows instructions carefully	☐	☐	☐	☐
22 Ignores distractions from peers when doing class work	☐	☐	☐	☐
23 Copes with moments of embarrassment	☐	☐	☐	☐
24 Acts as if self-esteem is high	☐	☐	☐	☐
25 Is invited to join in group activities	☐	☐	☐	☐

Identify areas for further observation and for specific social skills instruction.

	Never	Sometimes	Often	Always
26 _____	☐	☐	☐	☐
27 _____	☐	☐	☐	☐
28 _____	☐	☐	☐	☐
29 _____	☐	☐	☐	☐
30 _____	☐	☐	☐	☐

Bibliography

Ainscow, M., & Kaplan, I. (2005). Using evidence to encourage inclusive school development: Possibilities and challenges. *Australasian Journal of Special Education, 29*(2), 106–16.

Ainscow, M., Muijs, D., & West, M. (2006). *Using collaboration as a strategy for improving schools in complex and challenging circumstances: What makes the difference?* London: National College of School Leadership.

Ainscow, M., & Sebba, J. (1996). International developments in inclusive schooling: Mapping the issues. *Cambridge Journal of Education, 26*(1), 5–18.

Albert, L. (2003). *A teacher's guide to cooperative discipline* (2nd ed.). Minneapolis, MN: AGS Publishing.

Alberta Education. (1984). *Program of studies: Art*. Edmonton, AB: Alberta Education.

Alexander, R.J., Rose, J., & Woodhead, C. (1992). *Curriculum organization and classroom practice in primary schools: A discussion paper*. London: Department of Education and Science.

Allport, G.W. (1954). *The nature of prejudice*. Cambridge, MA: Addison-Wesley.

Alper, S., & Ryndak, D. L. (1992). Educating students with severe handicaps in regular classes. *Elementary School Journal, 92*(3), 373–87.

American Psychiatric Association (2000). *Diagnostic and statistical manual of mental disorders* (4th ed.), *Text Revision*. Washington, DC: American Psychiatric Association.

Americans With Disabilities Act. (1990). 42 USCA. Retrieved 28 January 2010 from <www.usdoj.gov/crt/ada/adahom1.htm>.

Ames, C., & Ames, R.I.C. (1989). Perspectives on motivation. In C. Ames & R. Ames (Eds.), *Research on motivation in education, Volume 3: Goals and cognitions* (pp. 1–10). San Diego: Academic Press.

Anderson, C., Klassen, R., & Georgiou, G. (2007). What teachers say they need and what school psychologists can offer. *School Psychology International, 28*(2), 131–47.

Anderson, V., & Finney, M. (2008). 'I'm a TA not a PA!': Teaching assistants working with teachers. In G. Richards & F. Armstrong (Eds.), *Key issues for teaching assistants: Working in diverse and inclusive classrooms* (pp. 73–83). London, UK: Routledge.

Ashman, A., & Elkins, J. (Eds.). (1998). *Educating children with special needs*. Sydney: Prentice Hall.

Association for Supervision and Curriculum Development. (2007). *The learning compact redefined: A call to action—a report of the commission on the whole child*. Alexandria, VA: Author.

Atweh, B. (2003). On par with young people: Learnings from the SAURA project. *Educational Action Research, 11*(1), 23–40.

Australian Government Department of Education, Employment, and Workplace Relations. (2008). *Disability Discrimination Act Education Standards.* Retrieved 17 February 2009, from <www.ddaedustandards.info/glossary.php>.

Avramidis, E., & Norwich, B. (2002). Teachers' attitudes towards integration/inclusion: A review of the literature. *European Journal of Special Needs Education, 17*(2), 129–47.

Baird, J.R., & Northfield, J.R. (Eds.). (1992). *Learning from the PEEL experience.* Melbourne: Monash University.

Barber, N., & Turner, M. (2007). Even while they teach, newly qualified teachers learn. *British Journal of Special Education, 34*(1), 33–9.

Barron, B. (2003). When smart groups fail. *The Journal of the Learning Sciences, 12,* 307–59.

Barth, R. (1990). A special vision of a good school. *Phi Delta Kappa, 71*, 514–15.

Battistich, V., Solomon, D., Watson, M.S., & Schaps, E. (1997). Caring school communities. *Educational Psychologist, 32,* 137–51.

Behar-Horenstein, L., Isaac, C., Seabert, D., & Davis, C. (2006). Classroom instruction and the loss of instructional time: A case study. *Education & Society, 24*(3), 83–99.

Bellanca, J., Chapman, C., & Swartz, E. (1994). *Multiple assessments for multiple intelligences.* Palatine, IL: IRI/Skylight Publishing.

Benard, B. (1993). Fostering resiliency in kids. *Educational Leadership, 51*(3), 44–9.

Bernard, M.E. (2006). *You can do it education* (YCDI). Retrieved from <http://www.youcandoiteducation.com/pdf/Brochure-US-3-08.pdf> and at <http://www.youcandoiteducation.com/whatis.html>.

Bernell, S.L. (2003). Theoretical and applied issues in defining disability in labor market research. *Journal of Disability Policy Studies, 14*(1), 36.

Berry, A., & Milroy, P. (2002). Changes that matter. In J. Loughran, I. Mitchell, & J. Mitchell (Eds.), *Learning from Teacher Research* (pp. 196–221). Sydney: Allen & Unwin.

Biggs, A., Long, P., Perreault, C., Ritchen, B., & Hertel, V. (Eds.). (1998). *Guidelines for school medication administration.* Denver, CO: Colorado State Board of Nursing.

Bjorklund, D.F., & Harnishfeger, K.K. (1990). The resources construct in cognitive development: Diverse sources of evidence and a theory of inefficient inhibition. *Development Review, 10,* 48–71.

Bjorklund, D.F., & Schneider, W. (1996). The interaction of knowledge, aptitude, and strategies in children's memory performance. *Advances in child development and behaviour, 26,* 58–89.

Black, P., Harrison, C., Lee, C., Marshall, B., & William, D. (2003) *Assessment for learning: Putting it into practice.* Berkshire, UK: Open University Press.

Black, P., McCormick, J.M., & Pedder, D. (2006). Learning how to learn and assessment for learning: A theoretical inquiry. *Research Papers in Education, 21*(2), 119–32.

Black, P., & William, D. (1998). *Inside the black box: Raising standards through classroom assessment.* London: School of Education, King's College.

Bland, D., & Atweh, W. (2004). A critical approach to collaborating with students as researchers. In E. McWilliam, S. Danby, & J. Knight (Eds.), *Performing educational research: Theories, methods and practices* (pp. 331–44). Flaxton, Qld: Post Pressed.

Bloom, L.A. (2009). *Classroom management: Creating positive outcomes for all students.* Upper Saddle River, NJ: Pearson.

Bodenheimer, A.R. (1974). *Doris: The story of a disfigured deaf child.* Detroit: Wayne State University Press.

Borkowski, J.G. (1992). Metacognitive theory: A framework for teaching literacy, writing and math skills. *Journal of Learning Disabilities, 25*(4), 253–7.

Boswell, S., & Gray, D. (1998). *Applying structured teaching principles to toilet training.* Retrieved 18 January 2010 from <www.teach.com/toilet.htm>.

Boulware-Gooden, R., Carreker, S., Thornhill, A., & Joshi, R. (2007). Instruction of metacognitive strategies enhances reading comprehension and vocabulary achievement of third-grade students. *The Reading Teacher, 61*(1), 70–7.

Bounds, J. (2001). The modeled reading program used with students identified as having a specific learning disability and cross-age peer tutors: A study of its effects on reading ability and an exploration of its effects on motivation in terms of self-efficacy and attitude, a research paper for Master of Education (Special Education) thesis. Melbourne: Monash University.

Broderick, A., Mehta-Parekh, H., & Reid, D. (2005). Differentiating instruction for disabled students in inclusive classrooms. *Theory into Practice, 44*(3), 194–202.

Brophy, J., & Everston, C. (1976). *Learning from teaching: A developmental perspective.* Boston: Allyn & Bacon.

Brown, A.L., Bransford, J.D., Ferrara, R.A., & Campione, J.C. (1983). Learning, remembering, and understanding. In P.H. Mussen (Ed.), *Handbook of child psychology: Cognitive development Vol. III* (pp. 77–166). New York: Wiley.

Brownlee, J-A., & Carrington, S. (2000). Opportunities for authentic experience and reflection: A teaching program designed to change attitudes towards disability for pre-service teachers. *Support for Learning, 15*(3), 99–105.

Buckley, M., & Saarni, C. (2009). Emotion regulation: Implications for positive youth development. In R. Gilman & M.J. Furlong (Eds.), *Handbook of positive psychology in schools* (pp. 107–17). New York: Taylor & Francis.

Burns, T. (2008). Learning and teaching, schools and communities. *Journal of Educational Change, 9*, 305–9.

Calgary Board of Health. (2008). *Healthy diverse populations.* Retrieved 13 February 2009 from <www.calgaryhealthregion.ca/programs/diversity/diversity_resources/definitions/definitions_main.htm>.

Canada Council on Learning (CCL). (2009, September). Effective literacy strategies for immigrant students, Canada Council On Learning. Retrieved 26 October 2009 from <www.ccl.ca>.

Carrington, S., Allen, K., & Osmolowski, D. (2007). Visual narrative: A technique to enhance secondary students' contribution to the development of inclusive, socially just school environments—lessons from a box of crayons. *Journal of Research in Special Education Needs, 7*(1), 8–15.

Carrington, S., & Holm, K. (2005). Student direct inclusive school development in an Australian secondary school: An example of student empowerment. *The Australasian Journal of Special Education, 29*(2), 155–71.

Carrington, S., & Robinson, S. (2004). A case study of inclusive school development: A journey of learning. *International Journal of Inclusive Education, 8*(2), 141–53.

Carrington, S., & Saggers, B. (2008) Service-learning informing the development of an inclusive ethical framework for beginning teachers. *Teaching and Teacher Education, 24*, 795–806.

Carter, E.W., & Kennedy, C.H. (2006). Promoting access to the general curriculum using peer support strategies. *Research & Practice for Persons with Severe Disabilities, 31*(4), 284–92.

Cattell, R.B. (1963). Theory of fluid and crystalized intelligence: A critical experiment. *Journal of Educational Psychology, 54*(1), 1–22.

Ceci, S.J. (1990). *On Intelligence . . . more or less: A bio-ecological treatise on intellectual development*. Century Series in Psychology. Englewood Cliffs, NJ: Prentice-Hall.

Center for Applied Special Technology. (2009). *What is universal design for learning?* Retrieved 20 January 2009 from <www.cast.org/research/udl>.

Chi, M.T., & Ceci, S.J. (1987). Content knowledge: Its restructuring with memory development. In H. Reese & L. Lipsett (Eds.), *Advances in Child Development and Behavior, 20*, 91–146.

Choi, S.H. (2007). Peer training methods for children and adolescents with autism: A review. *International Journal of Pedagogies and Learning, 3*(3), 92–100.

Clarke, S. (2005). *Formative assessment in the secondary classroom*. London: Hodder & Stoughton.

Clay, D., Farris, K., McCarthy, A., Kelly, M., & Howarth, R. (2008). Family perceptions of medication administration at school: Errors, risk factors, and consequences. *Journal of School Nursing, 24*(2), 95–102.

Clough, P. (1988). Bridging 'mainstream' and 'special' education: A curriculum problem. *Journal of Curriculum Studies, 20*(4), 327–338.

Coenen, M. (2002). Using gifted students as peer tutors: An effective and beneficial approach. *Gifted Child Today, 25*(1), 48–56.

Cohen, E.G., & Lotan, R.A. (1995). Producing equal-status interaction in the heterogeneous classroom. *American Educational Research Journal, 32*(1), 99–120.

Cole, C.M., Waldron, N., & Majd, M. (2004). Academic progress of students across inclusive and traditional settings. *Mental Retardation, 42*(2), 136–44.

Collaborative for Academic, Social, and Emotional Learning (CASEL). (2002). *Guidelines for social and emotional Learning*. Chicago, IL: Author.

Collaborative for Academic, Social, and Emotional Learning (CASEL). (2005). *Safe and sound: An educational leader's guide to evidence-based social and emotional learning (SEL) programs*. Chicago, IL: CASEL.

Collaborative for Academic, Social, and Emotional Learning (CASEL). (2007, December). *CASEL briefs: Background on social and emotional learning (SEL)*. Chicago, IL: Author.

Collet-Klingenberg, L., & Chadsey-Rusch, J. (1991). Using a cognitive-process approach to teach social skills. *Education and Training in Mental Retardation, 26,* 258–270.

Colvin, G. (2008). *Talent is overrated.* New York: Portfolio/Penguin.

Committee for Children. (2002). *Second step: A violence prevention curriculum.* Retrieved from <www.cfchildren.org>

Commonwealth of Australia. (1986). *Human Rights and Equal Opportunity Commission Act.* (1986). Retrieved 16 November 2009 from <www.austlii.edu.au/au/legis/cth/consol_act/hraeoca1986512>.

Connor, D. J., & Ferri, B.A. (2007). The conflict within: Resistance to inclusion and other paradoxes in special education. *Disability & Society, 22*(1), 63–77.

Cook, L., & Friend, M. (1995). Co-teaching guidelines for effective practice. *Focus on Exceptional Children, 28*(2), 1–12.

Cook-Sather, A. (2001). Translating themselves: Becoming a teacher through text and talk. In C.M. Clark (Ed.), *Talking shop: Authentic conversation and teacher learning.* New York: Teachers College Press.

Cook-Sather, A. (2006). Sound, presence, and power: Exploring 'student voice' in educational research and reform. *Curriculum Inquiry, 36*(4), 359–90.

Corbett, J. (1993). Postmodernism and the 'special needs' metaphors. *Oxford Review of Education, 19*(4), 547–53.

Cosden, M.A., Iannaccone, C.J., & Wienke, W.D. (1990). Social skills instruction in secondary education: Are we prepared for integration of difficult-to-teach students? *Teacher Education & Special Education, 13*(3–4), 154–9.

Cross, D., & Erceg, E. (2005). *Friendly schools and families: An evidence-based bullying reduction program.* Retrieved from <www.friendlyschools.com.au>.

Cruddas, L. (2001). Rehearsing for reality: Young women's voices and agendas for change. *Forum, 43*(2), 62–6.

Cruddas, L. (2007). Engaged voices: Dialogic interaction and the construction of shared social meanings. *Educational Action Research, 15*(3), 479–88.

Cruddas, L., & Haddock, L. (2003). *Girls' voices: Supporting girls' learning and emotional development.* London: Trentham.

Cushing, L.S., Clark, N.M., Carter, E.W., & Kennedy, C.H. (2005). Access to the general education curriculum for students with severe disabilities: What it means and how to accomplish it. *Teaching Exceptional Children, 38*(2), 6–13.

Danforth, S. (1997). On what basis hope? Modern progress and postmodern possibilities. *Mental Retardation, 35*(2), 93–106.

Davern, L., & Schnorr, R. (1991). Public schools welcome students with disabilities as full members. *Children Today, 20*(2), 21–5.

Davidson, G.R., & Freebody, P.R. (1986). Children and adults or novices and experts? A dilemma for cross-cultural developmental research. Special issue: Contributions to cross-cultural psychology. *Australian Journal of Psychology, 38,* 215–29.

Davidson, G.R., & Freebody, P.R. (1988). Cross-cultural perspectives on the development of metacognitive thinking. *Hiroshima Forum for Psychology, 13,* 21–31.

Davidson, N. (1994). Cooperative and collaborative learning: An integrative perspective. In J.S. Thousand, R.A. Villa, & A.I. Nevin (Eds.), *Creativity and collaborative learning: A practical guide to empowering students and teachers* (pp. 13–30). Baltimore: Brooks.

Deiro, J.A. (2006). *Teaching with heart: Making healthy connections with students.* Thousand Oaks, CA: Corwin Press.

Delaney, E.A., & Hopkins, T.F. (1987). *The Stanford–Binet Intelligence Scale: Fourth edition. Examiner's handbook.* Itasca, IL: Riverside.

Delquadri, J., Greenwood, C.R., Whorton, D., Carta, J.J., & Hall, R.V. (1986). Classwide peer tutoring. *Exceptional Children, 52,* 535–42.

Dembo, T., Leviton, G.L., & Wright, B.A. (1956). Adjustment to misfortune: A problem of social psychological rehabilitation. *Artificial Limbs, 3,* 4–62.

Demeris, H., Childs, R.A., & Jordan, A. (2008). The influence of students with special needs included in Grade 3 classrooms on the large-scale achievement scores of students with special needs. *Canadian Journal of Education, 30*(3), 609–27.

Denzin, N.K. (1978). *The research act: A theoretical introduction to sociological methods.* New York: McGraw-Hill.

Department for Education and Skills (UK). (2005). *The National Strategies: Social and Emotional Aspects of Learning (SEAL).* Retrieved 21 November 2009 from <http:// nationalstrategies.standards.dcsf.gov.uk/inclusion/behaviourattendanceandseal>.

Deppeler, J. (1994). Characteristics of empirically derived subgroups of gifted children based on cognitive processing patterns. Unpublished doctoral thesis, Monash University, Melbourne.

Deppeler, J. (1998). *Professional development workshops: Supporting people with disabilities.* Melbourne: Impact.

Deppeler, J. (2003, July). Improving inclusive practice through collaborative inquiry: A university and school-system professional development project. Paper presented at the ICET Teachers as Leaders: Teachers Education for a Global Profession conference, Melbourne.

Deppeler, J. (2006). Improving inclusive practices in Australian schools: Creating conditions for university–school collaboration in inquiry. *European Journal of Psychology of Education, 21*(3), 347–60.

Deppeler, J. (2007). Collaborative inquiry for professional learning. In A. Berry, A. Clemens, & A. Kostogriz (Eds.), *Dimensions of professional learning* (pp. 73–87). Rotterdam: Sense.

Deppeler, J. (in press). Professional learning as collaborative inquiry: Working together for impact. In C. Forlin (Ed.), *Teacher education for inclusion: Changing paradigms and innovative approaches.* Abbingdon, UK: Routledge.

Deppeler, J., & Gurry, P. (1994). *Helping you and your partner: Modelled reading resource kit.* Melbourne: Education: Curriculum & Resources.

Deppeler, J., Moss, J., & Agbenyega, J. (2008). The ethical dilemmas of working the visual and digital across space. In J. Moss (Ed.), *Researching education: Visually— Digitally—Spatially* (pp. 209–27). Rotterdam: Sense.

Dettmer, P., Dyck, N., & Thurston, L.P. (1999). *Consultation, collaboration, and teamwork for students with special needs.* Needham Heights, MA: Allyn & Bacon.

Devaney, E., O'Brien, M.U., Resnik, H., Keister, S., & Weissberg, R.P. (2006). *Sustainable school-wide social and emotional learning: Implementation guide and toolkit*. Chicago, IL: Collaborative for Academic, Social, and Emotional Learning.

Developmental Studies Centre. (2004). *Caring school community*. Retrieved May 17, 2010 from <http://www.devstu.org>.

Dickson, E. (2005). Disability discrimination in education: *Purvis v New South Wales (Department of Education and Training)*, amendment of the education provisions of the *Disability Discrimination Act* 1992 and the formulation of Disability Standards for Education. *University of Queensland Law Journal*, 24(1), 213–22.

Dinsmore, C., Daugherty, S., & Zeitz, H. (2001). Student responses to the gross anatomy laboratory in medical curriculum. *Clinical Anatomy*, 14, 231–6.

Disabilities Discrimination Act. (1992). Commonwealth of Australia. Retrieved 29 November 2009 from <www.austlii.edu.au/au/legis/cth/consol_act/dda1992264>.

Doll, B., Kurien, S., LeClair, C., Spies, R., Champion, S., & Osborn, A. (2009). The class maps survey: A framework for promoting positive classroom environments. In R. Gilman, & M.J. Furlong (Eds.), *Handbook of Positive Psychology in Schools* (pp. 213–27). New York: Taylor & Francis.

Downing, J., & Peckham-Hardin, K. (2007). Inclusive education: What makes it a good education for students with moderate to severe disabilities? *Research & Practice for Persons with Severe Disabilities*, 32(1), 16–30.

Doyle, M.B., & Lee, P.A. (1997). Creating partnerships with paraprofessionals. In M.F. Giangreco (Ed.), *Quick guides to inclusion: Ideas for educating students with disabilities* (pp. 57–84). Baltimore, MD: Paul H. Brookes.

Duffy, H. (2007). *Meeting the needs of significantly struggling learners in high school: A look at approaches to tiered intervention*. Washington, DC: National High School Centre.

Dufour, R., Dufour, R., & Eaker, R. (2008). *Revisiting professional learning communities at work: New insights for improving schools*. Bloomington, IN: Solution Tree.

Dunn, R. (1983). Learning style and its relation to exceptionality at both ends of the spectrum. *Exceptional Children*, 49, 496–506.

Dunn, R. (1989). Individualizing instruction for mainstreamed gifted children. In R. Milgram (Ed.), *Teaching gifted and talented learners in classrooms* (pp. 63–111). Springfield, IL: Charles C. Thomas.

Dunn, R., & Price, G.E. (1980). Identifying the learning style characteristics of gifted children. *Gifted Child Quarterly*, 24, 33–6.

Durlak, J.A., Taylor, R.D., Kawashima, K., Pachan, M.K., Du Pre, E.P., Celio, C., & Weissberg, R.P. (2007). Effects of positive youth development programs on school, family, and community systems. *American Journal of Community Psychology*, 39(3–4), 269–86.

Dymond, S., Renzaglia, A., Gilson, C., & Slagor, M. (2007). Defining access to the general curriculum for high school students with significant cognitive disabilities. *Research & Practice for Persons with Severe Disabilities*, 32(1), 1–15.

Earl, L. (2004). Collecting the evidence. *Network of Performance Based Schools*, 2(2), 41–3.

Earl, L., Watson, N., Levin, B., Leithwood, K., & Fullan, M. (2003). *Watching and Learning 3: The final report of the OISE/UT External evaluation of the national literacy and numeracy strategies.* London: Department for Education and Employment.

Educational Response Centre. (1992). *Behavior challenges: A shared approach.* Edmonton, AL: Alberta Education.

Eisenberg, N., Fabes, R.A., & Spinrad, T.L. (2006). Prosocial development. In N. Eisenberg (Ed.), *Handbook of child psychology, Volume 3: Social, emotional, and personality development* (pp. 646–718). New York: Wiley.

Elias, M.J., & Butler, L.B. (2005). *Social decision making/social problem solving: A curriculum for academic, social, and emotional learning.* USA: Research Publications.

Emmer, E.T., & Evertson, C.M. (2009). *Classroom management for middle and high school teachers* (8th ed.), Upper Saddle River, NJ: Pearson.

Erickson, G., Minnes-Brandes, G., Mitchell, I., & Mitchell, J. (2005). Collaborative teacher learning: Findings from two professional development projects. *Teaching and Teacher Education: An International Journal of Research and Studies, 21*(7), 787–98.

Erwin, E.J., & Soodak, L.C. (1995). I never knew I could stand up to the system: Families' perspectives on pursuing inclusive education. *Journal of the Association for Persons with Severe Handicaps, 20*(2), 136–46.

Evans, J., & Vincent, C. (1997). Parental choice and special education. In R. Glatter, P.A. Woods, & C. Bagley (Eds.), *Choice and diversity in schooling: Perspectives and prospects* (pp. 102–15). London: Routledge.

Farmer, S. (1996). Finding Amy's voice: A case for inclusion. *Voices from the Middle, 3*(4), 27–31.

Feiman-Nemser, S., & Floden, R. (1986). The cultures of teaching. In M. Witrock (Ed.), *Handbook of research on teaching* (3rd ed.). New York: Macmillan.

Feldhusen, J.F., Proctor, T.B., & Black, K.N. (1986). Guidelines for grade advancement of precocious children. *Roeper Review, 9*, 25–7.

Field, S., Kuzcera, M., & Pont, B. (2007). *No more failures: Ten steps to equity in education.* Paris: OECD.

Fielding, M. (2007). Jean Rudduck (1937–2007) carving a new order of experience: A preliminary appreciation of the work of Jean Rudduck in the field of student voice. *Educational Action Research, 15*(3), 323–36.

Fisher, D. (2001). Cross-age tutoring: Alternatives to the reading resource room for struggling adolescent readers. *Journal of Instructional Psychology, 28*(4), 234–41.

Fisher, D., Roach, V., & Frey, N. (2002). Examining the general programmatic benefits of inclusive schools. *International Journal of Inclusive Education, 6*(1), 63–78.

Fitch, E.F., & Hulgin, K.M. (2008). Achieving inclusion through CLAD: Collaborative Learning Assessment through Dialogue. *International Journal of Inclusive Education, 12*(4), 423–39.

Fletcher, A. (2005). Meaningful student involvement: Guide to students as partners. *Created for SoundOut.org in partnership with Human Links Foundation.* Retrieved 29 November 2009 from <www.soundout.org/MSIGuide.pdf>.

Flutter, J., & Rudduck, J. (2004). *Consulting pupils: What's in it for schools?* London: Routledge Falmer.

Ford, A., Pugach, M.C., & Otis-Wilborn, A. (2001). Preparing general educators to work with students who have disabilities: What's reasonable at the pre-service level? *Learning Disability Quarterly, 24*(4), 275–86.

Foreman, P.J. (2007). *Inclusion in action* (3rd ed.). Sydney: Thompson Learning.

Forlin, C. (2003). Pre-service teacher education: Involvement of students with intellectual disabilities. *International Journal of Learning, 10,* 183–200.

Fox, N.E., & Ysseldyke, J.E. (1997). Implementing inclusion at the middle school level: Lessons from a negative example. *Exceptional Children, 64*(1), 81–98.

Fox, S., Farrell, P., & Davis, P. (2004). Factors associated with the effective inclusion of primary-aged pupils with Down's syndrome. *British Journal of Special Education, 31*(4), 184–90.

Frederickson, N., Dunsmuir, S., Lang, J., & Monsen, J. (2004). Mainstream-special school inclusion partnerships: Pupil, parent and teacher perspectives. *International Journal of Inclusive Education, 8*(1), 37–57.

French, N. (2001). Supervising paraprofessionals: A survey of teacher practices. *Journal of Special Education, 35*(1), 41–53.

Frey, N. (2001). Tying it together: Personal supports that lead to membership and belonging. In C.H. Kennedy & D. Fisher (Eds.), *Inclusive middle schools*. Baltimore, MD: Paul H. Brookes.

Friend, M., & Bursuck, W.D. (2008). *Including students with special needs: A practical guide for classroom teachers* (5th ed.). Upper Saddle River, NJ: Allyn & Bacon.

Friend, M., & Cook, L. (1996). *Interactions: Collaboration skills for school professionals*. White Plains, NY: Longman.

Frith, G.H., & Edwards, R. (1981). Misconceptions of regular classroom teachers about physically handicapped students. *Exceptional Children, 48*(2), 182–4.

Fuchs, D., Fuchs L.S., Thompson, A., Svenson, E., Yen, L., Al Otalba, S., & Saenz, L. (2001). Peer-assisted learning strategies in reading: Extensions for kindergarten, first grade, high school. *Remedial and Special Education, 22*(1), 15–21.

Gabriele, A.J. (2007). The influence of achievement goals on the constructive activity of low achievers during collaborative problem solving. *British Journal of Educational Psychology, 77,* 121–41.

Gadow, K.D., & Kane, K.M. (1983). Administration of medication by school personnel. *Journal of School Health, 53*(3), 178–183.

Gallagher, P.A., & Lambert, R.G. (2006). Classroom quality, concentration of children with special needs, and child outcomes in Head Start. *Exceptional Children, 73,* 31–52.

Gardner, H. (1983). *Frames of mind: The theory of multiple intelligences*. New York: HarperCollins.

Gardner, H. (1999). *Intelligence reframed: Multiple intelligences for the 21st Century*. New York: Basic Books.

Gardner, H., & Boix-Mansilla, V. (1994). Teaching for understanding in the disciplines and beyond. *Teachers College Record, 96*(2), 198–218.

Gartin, B.C., & Murdick, N.L. (2005). IDEA 2004: The IEP. *Remedial and Special Education, 26*(6), 327–31.

Gartner, A., & Lipsky, D.K. (1990). Students as instructional agents. In W. Stainback & S. Stainback (Eds.), *Support networks for inclusive schooling: Independent integrated education.* Grand Rapids, MI: Paul H. Brookes.

Gersten, R. (2001). Sort out the roles of research in the improvement of practice. *Learning Disabilities: Research and Practice, 16*(1), 45–50.

Gettinger, M. (2003). Promoting social competence in an era of school reform: A commentary on Gifford Smith and Brownell. *Journal of School Psychology, 41*(4), 299–304.

Giangreco, M. (2007). Extending inclusive opportunities. *Educational Leadership, 64*(5), 34–7.

Giangreco, M., Broer, S.M., & Edelman, S. (1999). The tip of the iceberg: Determining whether paraprofessional support is needed for students with disabilities in general education settings. *Journal of the Association for Persons with Severe Handicaps, 24*(4), 281–91.

Giangreco, M., Cloninger, P., Mueller, S., & Ashworth, S. (1991). Perspectives of parents whose children have dual sensory impairments. *Journal of the Association for Persons with Severe Handicaps, 16*(1), 14–24.

Giangreco, M.F., Dennis, R., Cloninger, C., Edelman, S., & Schattman, R. (1993). 'I've counted Jon': Transformational experiences of teachers educating students with disabilities. *Exceptional Children, 59*(4), 359–72.

Giangreco, M., Edelman, S., & Broer, S.M. (2001). Respect, appreciation, and acknowledgment of paraprofessionals who support students with disabilities. *Exceptional Children, 67*(4), 485–98.

Giangreco, M.F., Edelman, S.W., Evans Luiselli, T., & MacFarland, S.Z.C. (1997). Helping or hovering? Effects of instructional assistant proximity on students with disabilities. *Exceptional Children, 64*(1), 7–18.

Gilliam, J.E. (2001). *Gilliam Asperger Disorder Scale.* Austin, TX: PRO-ED.

Gillies, R.M. (2007). *Cooperative learning: Integrating theory and practice.* Thousand Oaks, CA: Sage.

Gilman, R., & Furlong, M.J. (2009) *Handbook of positive psychology in schools.* New York: Taylor & Francis.

Goddard, A. (2005). Special educational needs: Critical reflections regarding the role of behavioural objectives in planning the curriculum. *Education, 33*(1), 32–9.

Goessling, D.P. (1998). The invisible elves of the inclusive school—paraprofessionals. In *Annual Meeting of the American Educational Research Association.* San Diego, CA: AERA.

Good, T.E., & Brophy, J.L. (1990). *Educational psychology: A realistic approach.* New York: Longman.

Goodman, J.F., & Bond, L. (1993). The individualized educational program: A retrospective critique. *Journal of Special Education, 26*(4), 408–22.

Gow, L., Ward, J., Balla, J., & Snow, D. (1988). Directions for integration in Australia:

Overview of a report to the Commonwealth Schools Commission Part II. *Exceptional Child*, 35(1), 5–22.

Greenway, A.P., & Harvey, D.H.P. (1980). Reaction to handicap. In R.S. Laura (Ed.), *Problems of handicap* (pp. 27–32). Melbourne: Macmillan.

Greenwood, C.R. (1997). Classwide peer tutoring. *Behaviour and Social Issues*, 7(1), 53–7.

Greenwood, C.R., Arreaga-Mayer, C.A., Utley, C., Gavin, K.M., & Terry, B.J. (2001). Class wide peer tutoring programs: A learning management system. *Technology, Curriculum, and Professional Development, 4*, 61–86.

Greenwood, C.R., Delquadri, J.C., & Carta, J.J. (1999). *Class wide peer tutoring (CWPT) for teachers*. Longmont, CO: Sopris West.

Greenwood, C.R., Delquadri, J.C., & Hall, R.V. (1989). Longitudinal effects of classwide peer tutoring. *Journal of Educational Psychology*, 81(3), 371–83.

Grenot-Scheyer, M., Fisher, M., & Staub, D. (2001). *At the end of the day: Lessons learned in inclusive education*. Baltimore, MD: Paul H. Brookes.

Gresham, F., & MacMillan, L. (1997). Social competence and affective characteristics of students with mild disabilities. *Review of Educational Research*, 67(4), 377–420.

Griffin, J. (1989). *Well-being*. Oxford: Oxford University Press.

Griggs, S.A. (1991). Counselling gifted children with different learning-style preferences. In R.M. Milgram (Ed.), *Counseling gifted and talented children: A guide for teachers, counselors and parents* (pp. 53–74). Norwood, NJ: Ablex.

Gronlund, N.E., & Waugh, C.K. (2009). *Assessment of student achievement* (9th ed.). Upper Saddle River, NJ: Pearson.

Groundwater-Smith, S., & Dadds, M. (2004). Critical practitioner inquiry: Towards responsible professional communities of practice. In C. Day & J. Sachs (Eds.), *International handbook on the continuing professional development of teachers* (pp. 238–63). Berkshire: Open University Press.

Haager, D., & Vaughn, S. (1995). Parent, teacher, peer, and self-reports of the social competence of students with learning disabilities. *Journal of Learning Disabilities, 28*, 205.

Hacker, D., & Tenent, A. (2002). Implementing reciprocal teaching in the classroom: Overcoming obstacles and making modifications. *Journal of Educational Psychology, 94*(4), 699–718.

Hadadian, A., & Yssel, N. (1998). Changing roles of paraeducators in early childhood special education. *Infant-toddler Intervention: The Transdisciplinary Journal*, 8(1), 1–9.

Hahn, H. (1985). Towards a politics of disability: Definitions, disciplines, and policies. *Social Science Journal, 22*, 87–105.

Hall, L., & McGregor, J. (2000). A follow-up study of the peer relationships of children with disabilities in an inclusive school. *Journal of Special Education, 34*(3), 114.

Hallam, S. (2002). Mixed up? The pros and cons of ability grouping. *Education Journal, 64*, 24–6.

Halvorsen, A.T., Neary, T., Hunt, P., & Cesca, P. (1996). A cost benefit comparison of inclusive and integrated classes in one California district. In *California Peers outreach project: Application and replication of inclusive models at the local level Final report* (ERIC Document EC304 691).

Hamre, B., & Pianta, R.C. (2006) Student–teacher relationships. In G. Bear & K.M. Minke (Eds.), *Children's needs III: Development, prevention and intervention* (pp. 59–72). Bethesda, MD: NASP.

Hardin, C.J. (2004). *Effective classroom management: Models and strategies for today's classrooms.* Upper Saddle River, NJ: Pearson Merrill Prentice Hall.

Hargreaves, A. (1997). Introduction. In A. Hargreaves (Ed.), *1997 ASCD Yearbook. Rethinking educational change with heart and mind* (pp. vii–xv). Alexandria, VA: Association of Supervision and Curriculum Development.

Hayes, A. (1998). Families and disabilities: Another facet of inclusion. In A. Ashman & J. Elkins (Eds.), *Educating children with special needs* (pp. 39–66). Sydney: Prentice-Hall.

Hehir, T. (2007). Confronting ableism. *Educational Leadership, 64*(5), 8–14.

Higgins, M. (1985). Beginning reading. In G. Winch & V. Hoogstad (Eds.), *Teaching reading: A language experience* (pp. 68–82). Melbourne: Macmillan.

Hill, C.A., & Whiteley, J.H. (1985). Social interactions and on-task behavior of severely multihandicapped and nonhandicapped children in mainstream classrooms. *Canadian Journal for Exceptional Children, 1*(4), 136–40.

Hilton, Z. (2006). Disaffection and school exclusion: Why are inclusion policies still not working in Scotland? *Research Papers in Education, 21*(3), 295–314.

Hines, R.A. (2001). *Inclusion in middle schools.* Champaign, IL: ERIC Clearinghouse on Elementary and Early Childhood Education.

Holdsworth, R. (2008). Student action teams: Challenging limited ideas of student leadership. *Learning Matters, 13*(2), 45–7.

Hollinger, C.L., & Koesek, S. (1986). Beyond the use of full scale IQ scores. *Gifted Child Quarterly, 34*, 21–6.

Hollowood, T.M., Salisbury, C.L., Rainforth, B., & Palombaro, M.M. (1995). Use of instructional time in classrooms serving students with and without severe disabilities. *Exceptional Children, 61*(3), 242–53.

Idol, L. (1997). Key questions related to building collaborative and inclusive schools. *Journal of Learning Disabilities, 30*(4), 384–94.

Jaffe, M.B. (1989). Feeding at-risk infants and toddlers. *Topics in Language Disorders, 10*(1), 13–25.

Jenkins, J., Antil, L., Wayne, S., & Vadasy, P. (2003). How cooperative learning works for special education and remedial students. *Exceptional Children, 69*, 279–92.

Jennings, P., & Greenberg, M.T. (2009). The prosocial classroom: Teacher social and emotional competence in relation to student and classroom outcomes. *Review of Educational Research, 79*(1), 491–525.

Jeon, Y., & Haider-Markel, D.P. (2001). Tracing issue definition and policy change: An analysis of disability issue images and policy response. *Policy Studies Journal, 29*(2), 215.

Johnson, D.W., & Johnson, F.P. (1994). *Joining together.* Boston: Allyn & Bacon.

Johnson, D.W., & Johnson, R.T. (1989). *Cooperation and competition: Theory and research.* Edina, MN: Interaction.

Johnson, D.W., & Johnson, R.T. (2002). Learning together and alone: Overview and meta-analysis. *Asia Pacific Journal of Education, 22*, 95–100.

Johnson, D.W., & Johnson, R.T. (2009). An educational psychology success story: Social interdependence theory and cooperative learning. *Educational Researcher, 38*(5), 365–79.

Jones, V. (2007). 'I felt like I did something good': The impact on mainstream pupils of a peer tutoring programme for children with autism. *British Journal of Special Education, 34*(1), 3–9.

Jones, V., & Jones, L. (2004). *Comprehensive classroom management: Creating communities of support and solving problems.* Boston: Allyn & Bacon.

Jorgensen, C.M. (Ed.). (1998). *Restructuring high schools for all students: Taking inclusion to the next level.* Baltimore, MD: Paul H. Brookes.

Jung, L. (2007). Writing smart objectives and strategies that fit the routine. *Teaching Exceptional Children, 39*(4), 54–8.

Kagan, S. (1992). *Cooperative learning* (7th ed.). San Juan Capistrano, CA: Resources for Teachers.

Kalambouka, A., Farrell, P., Dyson, A., & Kaplan, I. (2007). The impact of placing pupils with special educational needs in mainstream schools on the achievement of their peers. *Educational Research, 49*(4), 365–82.

Karcher, M.J. (2008). The cross-age mentoring program: A developmental intervention for promoting students' connectedness across grade levels. *Professional School Counselling, 12*(2), 137–43.

Kauffman, J.M., & Hallahan, D.P. (1995a). From mainstreaming to collaborative consultation. In J.M. Kauffman & D.P. Halloran (Eds.), *The illusion of full inclusion: A comprehensive critique of a current special education bandwagon* (pp. 5–17). Austin, TX: Pro-Ed.

Kauffman, J.M., & Hallahan, D.P. (Eds.). (1995b). *The illusion of full inclusion: A comprehensive critique of a current special education bandwagon.* Austin, TX: Pro-Ed.

Kauffman, J., & Hallahan, D. (2005). *Special education: What it is and why we need it.* Auckland: Pearson Education.

Kavale, K., & Forness, S. (1996). Learning disability grows up: Rehabilitation issues for individuals with learning disabilities. *The Journal of Rehabilitation, 62*(1), 34–42.

Kennedy, C.H., & Fisher, D. (2001). *Inclusive middle schools.* Baltimore, MD: Paul H. Brookes.

Klem, A.M., & Connell, J.P. (2004). Relationships matter: Linking teacher support to student engagement and achievement. *Journal of School Health, 74*, 262–73.

Koegel, R., & Kern Koegel, L. (1996). *Teaching children with autism: Strategies for initiating positive interactions and improving learning opportunities.* Baltimore, MD: Paul H. Brookes.

Kohn, A. (1996). *Beyond discipline: From compliance to community.* Alexandria, VA: Association for Supervision & Curriculum Development.

Kohn, A. (1997). How not to teach values? *Education Digest, 62*, 12–17.

Kournea, L., & Musti-Rao, S. (2007). Improving the reading skills of urban elementary students through total class peer tutoring. *Remedial and Special Education, 28*(2), 95–107.

Krongold Centre. (1995). *Gifted and talented: Blessing or curse? Parenting strategy*. Melbourne: Monash University, Krongold Centre.

Kubany, E.S., & Sloggett, B.B. (1973). Coding procedure for teachers. *Journal of Applied Behaviour Analysis, 6*, 339–44.

Kucan, L., Palincsar, A.S., Khasnabis, D., & Chang, C.I. (2008). The video viewing task: A source of information for assessing and addressing teacher understanding of text-based discussion. *Teaching and Teacher Education, 25*(3), 415–23.

Kusche, C. A., & Greenberg, M. T. (1994). *The PATHS curriculum*. Seattle: Developmental Research and Programs, INC.

Lamont, I.L., & Hill, J.L. (1991). Roles and responsibilities of paraprofessionals in the regular elementary classroom. *B.C. Journal of Special Education, 15*(1), 1–24.

Lane, K., Wehby, J., Little, M., & Cooley, C. (2005). Students educated in self-contained classrooms and self-contained schools: Part II—How do they progress over time? *Behavioral Disorders, 30*(4), 363–74.

Langhout, R. (2005). Acts of resistance: Student (in)visibility. *Culture & Psychology, 11*(2), 123–58.

Larrivee, B. (2005). *Authentic classroom management: Creating a learning community and building reflective practice* (2nd ed.). Boston: Pearson.

Lederer, J. (2000). Reciprocal teaching of social studies in inclusive elementary classrooms. *Journal of Learning Disabilities, 33*(1), 91.

Lewis, A., & Norwich, B. (Eds.). (2005). *Special teaching for special children? Pedagogies for inclusion*. Maidenhead: Open University Press.

Lewis, M. (1992). *Parent involvement in the special education process: A synopsis of exemplary models*. Bloomington, IN: Indiana University Press.

Lincoln, Y.S., & Guba, E.G. (1985). *Naturalistic inquiry*. Beverley Hills, CA: Sage.

Lindsay, G. (2007). Educational psychology and the effectiveness of inclusive education/mainstreaming. *British Journal of Educational Psychology, 77*(1), 1–24.

Lions Clubs International Foundation. (2006) *Lions Quest website*. Retrieved from <http://www.lionsclubs.org/EN/lci-foundation/our-programs/lions-quest/index.php>.

Lipsky, D.K. (1989). The roles of parents. In D.K. Lipsky & A. Gartner (Eds.), *Beyond separate education: Quality education for all* (pp. 159–79). Baltimore. MD: Paul A. Brookes.

Lipsky, D.K., & Gartner, A. (1994). Inclusion: What it is, what it's not and why it matters. *Exceptional Parent, 26*, 36–8.

Lloyd, A. (1987). *Payment by results: Kew Cottages: First 100 years 1887–1987*. Melbourne: Kew Cottages & St Nicholas Parents' Association.

Lloyd, C. (2008). Removing barriers to achievement: A strategy for inclusion or exclusion? *International Journal of Inclusive Education, 12*(2), 221–36.

Lloyd, C., Wilton, K., & Townsend, M. (1996). Children at high risk for mild intellectual disability in regular classrooms: Six New Zealand case studies. *Proceedings of 10th*

World Congress of the International Association for Scientific Study of Intellectual Disability (p. 16). Helsinki: ERIC Clearinghouse.

Lodge, C. (2005). From hearing voices to engaging in dialogue: Problematising student participation in school improvement. *Journal of Educational Change*, 6(2), 125–46.

Loreman, T. (1999). Integration: Coming from the outside. *Interaction*, 13(1), 21–3.

Loreman, T. (2000). School inclusion in Victoria, Australia: The results of six case studies. In M. Ainscow & P. Mittler (Eds.), *International Special Education Congress 2000*. Manchester: Inclusive Technology and the University of Manchester.

Loreman, T.J. (2001). *Secondary school inclusion for students with moderate to severe disabilities in Victoria, Australia*. Melbourne: Faculty of Education, Monash University.

Loreman, T. (2009). *Respecting childhood*. London: Continuum.

Loreman, T. (in press). Essential inclusive education-related outcomes for Alberta preservice teachers. *Alberta Journal of Educational Research*.

Loreman, T., & Deppeler, J.M. (2001). Working towards full inclusion in education. *Access: The National Issues Journal for People with a Disability*, 3(6), 5–8.

Loughran, J., Mitchell, I., & Mitchell, J. (Eds.). (2002). *Learning from teacher research*. Sydney: Allen & Unwin.

MacMullin, C., & Flinders University of South Australia, Institute for the Study of Learning Difficulties. (1992), *The Sheidow Park Social Problem Solving Program*. Adelaide: Flinders University.

MacPherson-Court, L., McDonald, L., & Sobsey, D. (2003). Inclusive education survey: Meeting the educational needs of preservice teachers. *Developmental Disabilities Bulletin*, 31(1), 57–85.

Maheady, L., Harper, G.F., & Mallette, B. (1991). Peer-mediated instruction: A review of potential applications for special education. *Reading, Writing, and Learning Disabilities International*, 7, 75–103.

Maheady, L., Harper, G.F., & Mallette, B. (2001). Peer-mediated instruction and interventions and students with mild disabilities. *Remedial and Special Education*, 22(1), 4–15.

Maheady, L., Harper, G.F., Sacca, K.C., & Mallette, B. (1991). *Classwide student tutoring teams (CSTT): Instructor's manual and video package*. Fredonia, NY: SUNY-Fredonia, School of Education.

Mastropieri, M.A., & Scruggs, T.E. (2007). *The inclusive classroom: Strategies for effective instruction* (3rd ed.). Upper Saddle River, NJ: Prentice Hall.

McCarthy, A.M., Kelly, M.W., & Reed, D. (2000). Medication administration practices of school nurses. *Journal of School Health*, 70(9), 371–6.

McCoy, S., & Major, B. (2007). Priming meritocracy and the psychological justification of inequality. *Journal of Experimental Social Psychology*, 43(3), 341–51.

McDonnell, J., Thorson, N., Disher, S., Mathot-Buckner, C., Mendel, J., & Ray, L. (2003). The achievement of students with developmental disabilities and their peers without disabilities in inclusive settings: An exploratory study. *Education and Treatment of Children*, 26(3), 224–36.

McGhie-Richmond, D., Barber, J., Lupart, J., & Loreman, T. (2008). Teacher perspectives on inclusive education in rural Alberta, Canada. Manuscript submitted for publication.

McGhie-Richmond, D., Underwood, K., & Jordan, A. (2007). Developing effective instructional strategies for teaching in inclusive classrooms. *Exceptionality Education Canada*, 17(1), 27–51.

McGrath, H., & Francey, S. (1991). *Friendly kids, friendly classrooms*. New York: Pearson Education. Retrieved from <http://www.kidsmatter.edu.au/programs-guide/friendly-kids-friendly-classrooms/>.

McGrath, T., & Noble, H. (2003). *Bounce back: Classroom resiliency program*. Retrieved May 17, 2010 from <http://www.bounceback.com.au>.

McGregor, G., & Vogelsberg, R.T. (1998). *Inclusive schooling practices: Pedagogical and research foundations*. Baltimore, MD: Paul H. Brookes.

McGuire, W.J. (1989). The structure of individual attitudes and attitude systems. In A.R. Pratkanis, S.J. Breckler, & A.G. Greenwald (Eds.), *Attitude, structure and function* (pp. 37–69). Hillsdale, NJ: Lawrence Erlbaum.

McInerney, D.M., & McInerney, V. (2002). *Educational psychology: Constructing learning*. Sydney: Prentice-Hall.

McLaughlin, M.J., & Warren, S. H. (1994). The costs of inclusion. *School Administrator*, 51(10), 8–12.

McNamara, D.R., & Waugh, D.G. (1993). Classroom organization: A discussion of grouping strategies in the light of the 'Three Wise Men' report. *School Organization*, 13(1), 41–50.

McTighe, J., Seif, E., & Wiggins, G. (2004). You can teach for meaning. *Educational Leadership*, 62(1), 26–30.

Meadan, H. (2008). Collaboration to promote social competence for students with mild disabilities in the general classroom: A structure for providing social support. *Intervention in School and Clinic*, 43(3), 158–67.

Meisels, S.J., Atkins-Burnett, S., Xue, Y., Nicholson, J., Bickel, D.D., & Son, S. (2003). Creating a system of accountability: The impact of instructional assessment on elementary children's achievement test scores. *Educational Policy Analysis Archives*, 11(9) 1–18.

Mertler, C.A. (2001). Designing scoring rubrics for your classroom. *Practical Assessment, Research & Evaluation*, 7(25), 1–10.

Microsoft Corporation. (2008). Types of assistive technology products. Retrieved 2 February 2009 from <www.microsoft.com/enable/at/types.aspx>.

Mishna, F. (2003). Learning disabilities and bullying: Double jeopardy. *Journal of Learning Disabilities*, 36(4), 336–48.

Mitchell, I. (2002). Learning from teacher research for teacher research. In J. Loughran, I. Mitchell, & J. Mitchell (Eds.), *Learning from teacher research*, Sydney: Allen & Unwin.

Mock, D., & Kauffman, J. (2005). The delusion of full inclusion. Controversial therapies for developmental disabilities: Fad, fashion and science in professional practice (pp. 113–28). Mahwah, NJ: Lawrence Erlbaum.

Mohr, L.L. (1995). Teaching diverse learners in inclusive settings: Steps for adapting instruction. *Annual International Convention of the Council for Exceptional Children*. Indianapolis, IN: Council for Exceptional Children.

Morse, J.S., Colatarci, S., Nehring, W., Roth, S.P., & Barks, L.S. (1997). Administration of medication by unlicensed assistive personnel to persons with mental retardation and developmental disabilities. *Mental Retardation, 35*(4), 310–11.

Moss, J. (2003). Inclusive schooling policy: An educational detective story. *Australian Educational Researcher, 30*(1), 63–81.

Moss, J., Hay, T., Deppeler, J., Astley, L., & Pattison, K. (2007). Student researchers in the middle: Using visual images to make sense of inclusive education. *Journal of Research in Special Education Needs, 7*(1), 46–54.

Mulford, B. (2008). *The leadership challenge: Improving learning in schools*. Melbourne: Australian Council for Educational Research.

Murray, C., & Greenberg, M.T. (2000). Children's relationship with teachers and bonds with school: An investigation of patterns and correlates in middle childhood. *Journal of School Psychology, 38*, 423–45.

Naraian, S. (2008). I didn't think I was going to like working with him, but now I really do! Examining peer narratives of significant disability. *Intellectual & Developmental Disabilities, 46*(2), 106–19.

Natasi, B., & Clements, D.H. (1991). Research on cooperative learning: Implications for practice. *School Psychology Review, 20*, 110–31.

National Board of Employment Education and Training. (1992), *Curriculum Initiatives: Commissioned Report No. 12*. Canberra: AGPS.

National College for School Leadership (NCSL). (2006). What does a critical friend do? In *Network leadership in action: Network leadership roles*. Nottingham: NCSL.

Nelsen, J., Lott, L., & Glen, S.H. (1993). *Positive discipline in the classroom*. Rocklyn, CA: Prima.

New South Wales Board of Education (2008). *All NSW Syllabuses*. Retrieved 3 February 2009 from <www.boardofstudies.nsw.edu.au/syllabus_sc>.

Newman, L., & Institute of Education Sciences. (2006). *General education participation and academic performance of students with learning disabilities. Facts from NLTS2. NCSER 2006-3001*. Washington, DC: National Center for Special Education Research.

Nowicki, E.A., & Sandieson, R. (2002). A meta-analysis of school-age children's attitudes towards persons with physical or intellectual disabilities. *International Journal of Disability, Development and Education, 49*(3), 243–65.

O'Brien, J., & Pearpoint, J. (2002). *Person-centered planning with MAPS and PATH: A workbook for facilitators*. Toronto: Inclusion Press.

Odom, S.L., McConnell, S.R., & McEvoy M.A. (1992). *Social competence of young children with disabilities: Issues and strategies for intervention*. Baltimore, MA: Paul H. Brookes.

OECD. (1994a). *The curriculum redefined: Schooling for the 21st century*, Paris: OECD.

OECD. (1994b). *The integration of disabled children into mainstream education: Ambitions, theories and practices*. Paris: OECD.

OECD. (1999). *Inclusive education at work: Students with disabilities in mainstream schools*, Paris: OECD.

OECD. (2005a). *Education at a glance 2005: OECD Indicators 2005*. Paris: OECD.

OECD. (2005b). *Formative assessment: Improving learning in secondary classrooms.* Paris: OECD.

Onosko, J.J., & Jorgensen, C.M. (1998). Unit and lesson planning in the inclusive classroom: Maximising learning opportunities for all students. In C.M. Jorgensen (Ed.), *Restructuring high schools for all students: Taking inclusion to the next level* (p. 273). Baltimore, MD: Paul H. Brookes.

O'Shea, D.J., & O'Shea, L.J. (1998). Learning to include: Lessons learned from a high school without special education services. *Teaching Exceptional Children, 31*(1), 40–8.

Osher, D., Cartledge, G., Oswald, D., Sutherland, K.S., Artiles, A.J., & Coutinho, M. (2007). A comprehensive approach to promoting social, emotional, and academic growth in contemporary schools. In A. Thomas & J. Grimes (Eds.), *Best practices in school psychology, Vol. 5* (5th ed., pp. 1263–78). Bethesda, MD: National Association of School Psychologists.

O'Toole, T.J., & Switlick, D.M. (1997). Integrated therapies. In D.F. Bradley, M.E. King-Sears, & D.M. Tessier-Switlick (Eds.), *Teaching students in inclusive settings: From theory to practice*. Needham Heights, MA: Allyn & Bacon.

Pallincsar, A.S., & Brown, A.L. (1984). The reciprocal teaching of comprehension-fostering and comprehension-monitoring activities. *Cognition and Instruction, 1*, 117–75.

Pallincsar, A.S., David, Y.M., & Brown. A.L. (1989). Using reciprocal teaching in the classroom: A guide for teachers. Unpublished manual.

Pallincsar, A.S., & Herrenkohl, R. (2002). Designing collaborative learning contexts. *Theory into Practice, 41*(1), 26–33.

Pallincsar, A.S., & Klenk, L. (1992). Fostering literacy learning in supportive contexts. *Journal of Learning Disabilities, 25*, 221–5.

Pallincsar, A.S., Spiro, R., Kucan, L., & Magnusson, S. (2007) Designing a hypermedia environment to support comprehension instruction. In D.S. McNamara (Ed.), *Reading comprehension strategies: Theories, interventions and technologies* (pp. 441–62). London: Routledge.

Parsons, G., Elkins, J., & Sigafoos, J. (2000). Are people with intellectual disabilities just another customer? Interviews with business owners and staff. *Mental Retardation, 38*, 244–52.

Pavlidis, T., & Bunston, W. (2004). *Feeling is Thinking (FIST)*. Retrieved from <http://www.kidsmatter.edu.au/programs-guide/fist/>.

Payton, J., Weissberg, R.P., Durlak, J.A., Dymnicki, A., Taylor, R.D., Schellinger, K.B., & Pachan, M. (2008). *The positive impact of social and emotional learning for kindergarten to eighth-grade students: Findings from three scientific reviews*. Chicago, IL: Collaborative for Academic, Social, and Emotional Learning (CASEL). Retrieved 28 October 2009 from <www.casel.org/pub/index.php>.

Pendarvis, E.D., Howley, A.A., & Howley, C.B. (1990). *The abilities of gifted children*. Englewood Cliffs, NJ: Prentice-Hall.

Petersen, L. (2006). *Stop. Think. Do. Social skills curriculum*. Retrieved May 17, 2010 from <http://www.stopthinkdo.com>.

Peterson, L., & Gannon, A. (1992). *The Stop, Think, Do teachers' manual for training social skills while managing student behaviour*. Melbourne: ACER.

Peterson, M., & Loreman, T. (2005, April). Walking and talking the road to trusting community: Relationship-based schoolwide positive behavioural supports. Paper presented at the Whole Schooling conference, Edmonton, Alberta.

Phinney, M.Y. (1988). *Reading with the troubled reader*. Toronto: Scholastic.

Pickett, A.L., Vasa, S.F., & Steckelberg, A.L. (1993). *Using paraeducators in the classroom: Fastback 358*. Bloomington, IN: Phi Delta Kappa.

Pourdavood, R., Svec, L., & Cowen, L. (2005). Social constructivism in practice: Case study of an elementary school's mathematics program. *Focus on Learning Problems in Mathematics, 27*(1/2), 15–37.

Pressley, M. (1998). Comprehension strategies instruction. In J. Osborn & F. Lehr (Eds.), *Literacy for all: Issues in teaching and learning* (pp. 113–33). New York: Guilford.

Pressley, M. (2002). Reading instruction that works: The case for balanced teaching. *Solving problems in the teaching of literacy*. New York: Guilford.

Pressley, M., Borkowski, J.G., & Schneider, W. (1987). Cognitive strategies: Good strategy users coordinate metacognition and knowledge. In R. Vasta & G. Whitehurst (Eds.), *Annals of Child Development, Vol. 4* (pp. 89–129). Greenwich, CT: JAI Press.

Pugach, M. (1982). Regular classroom teacher involvement in the development and utilization of IEPs. *Exceptional Children, 48*(4), 371–4.

Putnam, J.M. (2009). Inclusive and effective schools: Challenges and tensions. In P. Hick, R. Kerschner, & P. Farrell (Eds.), *A psychology for inclusive education: New directions in theory and practice*. London: Routledge.

Redding, R.E. (1990). Learning preferences and skill patterns among underachieving gifted adolescents. *Gifted Child Quarterly, 34*, 72–5.

Richards, G., & Armstrong, F. (2008) *Key issues for teaching assistants: Working in diverse and inclusive classrooms*. London: Routledge.

Richardson, K. (1999). *The making of intelligence*. London: Weidenfeld & Nicolson.

Riddell, S., Kane, J., Banks, P., Wilson, A., Baynes, A., Dyson, A., & Millward, A. (2002). Individualised educational programmes. Part 2: Raising the attainment of pupils with special educational needs. *Journal of Research in Special Educational Needs, 2*(3), 1–11.

Rightmyer, E. (2003). Children creating solutions. *Young Children, 58*(4), 38–45.

Roahrig, P. L. (1993). *Special Education Inclusion. Fiscal Analysis of Clark County Schools Inclusion Site Grant*. Terre Haute, Indiana: Indiana State University Blumberg Center for Interdisciplinary Studies in Special Education.

Robinson, D.R., Schofield, J.W., & Steers-Wentzell, K.L. (2005). Peer and cross-age tutoring in math: Outcomes and their design implications. *Educational Psychology Review, 17*(4), 327–62.

Robinson, R. (1964). *An atheist's value*. Oxford: Blackwell.

Rodriguez, M.C. (2004). The role of classroom assessment in student performance on TIMSS. *Applied Measurement in Education. 17*(1), 1–24.

Rogan, J., LaJeunesse, C., McCann, P., McFarland, G., & Miller, C. (1995). Facilitating inclusion: The role of learning strategies to support secondary students with special needs. *Preventing School Failure*, *39*(3), 35–9.

Rohrbeck, C.A., Ginsburg-Block, M.D., Fantuzzo, J.W., & Miller, T.R. (2003). Peer-assisted learning interventions with elementary school students: A meta-analytic review. *Journal of Educational Psychology*, *95*, 240–57.

Rojewski, J.W., & Schell, J.W. (1994). Cognitive apprenticeship for learners with special needs: An alternate framework for teaching and learning. *Remedial and Special Education*, *15*(4), 234–43.

Rose, R., & Howley, M. (2007). *The practical guide to special educational needs in inclusive primary classrooms (primary guides)*. London: Paul Chapman.

Rosenshine, B., & Meister, C. (1994). Reciprocal teaching: A review of the research. *Review of Educational Research*, *64*, 479–530.

Roseth, C.J., Johnson, D.W., & Johnson, R.T. (2008, March). Promoting early adolescents' achievement and peer relationships: The effects of cooperative, competitive, and individualistic goal structures. *Psychological Bulletin*, *134*(2), 223–46.

Rowe, H.A. (1985). *Australian Council for Educational Research: Problem solving and intelligence*. Hillsdale, NJ: Lawrence Erlbaum.

Rudduck, J., & Flutter, J. (2000). Pupil participation and pupil perspective: 'Carving a new order of experience'. *Cambridge Journal of Education*, *30*(1), 75–89.

Ryan, K., & Cooper, J. (2007). *Those who can teach*. New York: Houghton Mifflin.

Ryndak, D., & Alper, S. (1996). *Curriculum content for students with moderate and severe disabilities in inclusive settings*. Needham Heights, MA: Allyn & Bacon.

Sailor, W., & Skrtic, T.M. (1995). American education in the postmodern era. In L. Paul, D. Evans, & H. Rosselli (Eds.), *Integrating school restructuring and special education reform, Vol. 1* (pp. 214–36). Orlando, FL: Brace Coll.

Salisbury, C., & Chambers, A. (1994). Instructional costs of inclusive schooling. *Journal of the Association for Persons with Severe Handicaps*, *19*(3), 215–22.

Salvia, J., & Hughes, C. (1990). *Curriculum based assessment: Testing what is right*. New York: Macmillan.

Saxby, H., Thomas, M., Felce, D., & De Kock, U. (1986). The use of shops, cafes and public houses by severely and profoundly mentally handicapped adults. *British Journal of Mental Subnormality*, *32*, 69–81.

Schneider, W., & Weinert, F.E. (Eds.). (1990). *Interactions among aptitude, strategies, and knowledge in cognitive performance*. New York: Springer-Verlag.

Searle, Y., & Streng, I. (1996). *The social skills game*. London: Taylor & Francis.

Seigel, C. (2005). Implementing a research-based model of cooperative learning. The Journal of Educational Research, *98*(6), 339–51.

Sharma, U., & Desai, I. (2002). Measuring concerns about integrated education in India. *Asia & Pacific Journal on Disability*, *5*(1), 2–14.

Sharpe, M.N., York, J.L., & Knight, J. (1994). Effects of inclusion on academic performance of classmates without disabilities: A preliminary study. *Remedial and Special Education*, *15*(5), 281–7.

Shinn, M.R., Stoner, G., & Walker, H.M. (Eds.). (2002). *Interventions for academic and behavior problems: Preventive and remedial approaches.* Bethesda, MD: National Association of School Psychologists.

Shultz, W. (1988). The interpersonal world. In R.B. Adler & G. Rodman (Eds.), *Understanding human communication* (3rd ed.). London: Holt Rinehart & Winston.

Skårbrevik, K.J. (2005). The quality of special education for students with special needs in ordinary classes. *European Journal of Special Needs Education, 20*(4), 387–401.

Slater, W., & Horstman, F. (2002). Teaching reading and writing to struggling middle school and high school students: The case for reciprocal teaching. *Preventing School Failure, 46*(4), 163.

Slavin, R.E. (1990). *Cooperative learning: Theory, research, and practice.* Englewood Cliffs, NJ: Prentice Hall.

Slavin, R.E. (1996). Research on cooperative learning and achievement: What we know, what we need to know. *Contemporary Educational Psychology, 21*(1), 43–69.

Slavin, R.E., Cheung, A., Groff, C., & Blake, C. (2008). Effective reading programs for middle and high schools: A best-evidence synthesis. *Reading Research Quarterly, 43*(3), 290–322.

Slavin, R.E., & Lake, C. (2008). Effective programs in elementary mathematics: A best-evidence synthesis. *Review of Educational Research, 78.*

Slee, R. (1996). Bullying in the playground: The impact of inter-personal violence on Australian children's perceptions of their play environment. *Children's Environments, 12,* 320–7.

Slee, R. (2008). Beyond special and regular schooling? An inclusive education reform agenda. *International Studies in Sociology of Education, 18*(2), 99–116.

Slee, R., & Cook, S. (1994). Creating cultures of disability to control young people in Australian schools. *Urban Review, 26*(1), 15–23.

Smyth, J. (2007). *Teacher development against the policy reform grain: An argument for recapturing relationships in teaching and learning.* Teacher Development, *11*(2), 221–36.

Sommerstein, L.C., & Wessels, M.R. (1996). Gaining and utilising family and community support for inclusive schooling. In S. Stainback & W. Stainback (Eds.), *Inclusion: A guide for educators* (pp. 367–82). Sydney: Paul H. Brookes.

Sorsdahl, S., & Sanche, R. (1985). The effects of classroom meetings on self-concept and behavior. *Elementary School Guidance & Counseling, 20*(1), 49–56.

Soukup, J., Wehmeyer, M., Bashinski, S., & Bovaird, J. (2007). Classroom variables and access to the general curriculum for students with disabilities. *Exceptional Children, 74*(1), 101–20.

Spinelli, C.G. (2002). *Classroom assessment for students with special needs in inclusive settings.* Englewood Cliffs, NJ: Merrill Prentice Hall.

Spinrad, T. L., & Eisenberg, N. (2009). *Empathy, prosocial behavior, and positive development in the schools: Handbook of positive psychology in schools.* Abingdon, UK: Routledge/Taylor & Francis Group.

Spörer, N., Brunstein, J.C., & Kieschke, U. (2009). Improving students' reading comprehension skills: Effects of strategy instruction and reciprocal teaching. *Learning and Instruction*, 19(3), 272–86.

Stainback, S., & Stainback, W. (1996). *Inclusion: A guide for educators*. Sydney: Paul H. Brookes.

Stenhoff, D.M., & Lignugaris, B. (2007). A review of the effects of peer tutoring on students with mild disabilities in secondary settings. *Exceptional Children*, 74(1), 8–30.

Sternberg, R.J. (1986). A triarchic theory of intellectual giftedness. In R.J. Sternberg & J.E. Davidson (Eds.), *Conceptions of giftedness* (pp. 223–43). New York: Cambridge University Press.

Sternberg, R.J., & Davidson, J.E. (Eds.). (1986). *Conceptions of giftedness*. New York: Cambridge University Press.

Stiggins, R.J. (2008). *An introduction to student-involved assessment for learning* (5th ed.). Upper Saddle River, NJ: Pearson/Merrill Prentice Hall.

Stoll, L., Bolam, R., McMahon, A., Thomas, S., Wallace, M., Greenwood, A., & Hawkey, K. (2006). *What is a professional learning community?* London: National College of School Leadership.

Stoll, L., & Louis, K.S. (Eds.). (2007). *Professional learning communities: Divergence, depth and dilemmas*. London/New York: Open University Press/McGraw Hill.

Strickland, B., & Turnbull, A. (1990). *Developing and implementing individualized education programs*. Columbus, OH: Merrill.

Sure, M. B. (1993). *I Can Problem Solve (ICPS)*. Retrieved May 17, 2010 from <http://www.thinkingpreteen.com/researchsummary.htm>.

Suter, E., Arndt, J., Arthur, N., Parboosingh, J., Taylor, E., & Deutschlander, S. (2009). Role understanding and effective communication as core competencies for collaborative practice. *Journal of Interprofessional Care*, 23(1), 41–51.

Sutherland, K.S., Wehby, J.H., & Gunter, P.L. (2000). The effectiveness of cooperative learning with students with emotional and behavioral disorders: A literature review. *Behavioral Disorders*, 25, 225–38.

Takala, M. (2006). The effects of reciprocal teaching on reading comprehension in mainstream and especial (SLI) education. *Scandinavian Journal of Educational Research*, 50(5), 559–76.

Tannenbaum, A.J. (1986). Giftedness: A psychosocial approach. In R.J. Sternberg & J.E. Davidson (Eds.), *Conceptions of giftedness* (pp. 21–52). New York: Cambridge University Press.

Taylor, R.L. (2000). *Assessment of exceptional students: Educational and psychological procedures* (5th ed.). Needham Heights, MA: Allyn & Bacon.

Tennant, G. (2007). IEPs in mainstream secondary schools: An agenda for research. *Support for Learning*, 22(4), 204–8.

Tetlow, P. (1990). *Health care: Infection control, medication administration, and seizure management*. Miami, FL: Dade County Public Schools.

Timperley, H., & Robinson, V. (2001). Achieving school improvement through challenging and changing teachers' schema. *Journal of Educational Change*, 2, 281–300.

Timperley, H., & Alton-Lee, A. (2008). Reframing teacher professional learning: An alternative policy approach to strengthening valued outcomes for diverse learners. *Review of Research in Education, 32*, 328–69.

Tomlinson, C.A. (2001). *How to differentiate instruction in mixed-ability classrooms* (2nd ed.). Alexandria, VA: Association for Supervision and Curriculum Development.

Tomlinson, C.A., & McTighe, J. (2006). *Integrating differentiated instruction and understanding by design: Connecting content and kids.* Alexandria, VA: Association for Supervision and Curriculum Development.

Tomlinson, C.A., Moon, T.R., & Callahan, C.M. (1997). Use of cooperative learning at the middle level: Insights from a national survey. *Research in Middle Level Education Quarterly, 20*, 37–55.

Tonn, N. (2002). Reading change during and following modeled reading using cross-age peer tutors. Unpublished research thesis. Monash University, Melbourne.

Topping, K.J. (2005). Trends in peer learning. *Educational Psychology, 25*(6), 631–45.

Topping, K.J., & Bryce, A. (2004). Cross-age peer tutoring of reading and thinking: Influence on thinking skills. *Educational Psychology, 24*, 595–621.

Topping, K., & Ehly, S. (1998). Introduction to peer-assisted learning. In K. Topping & S. Ehly (Eds.), *Peer-assisted learning* (pp. 1–23). Mahwah, NJ: Lawrence Erlbaum.

Topping, K.J., Peter, C., Stephen, P., & Whale, M. (2004). Cross-age peer tutoring of science in the primary school: Influence on scientific language and thinking. *Educational Psychology, 24*, 57–75.

Turnbull, A.P., & Turnbull, H.R. (1982). Parent involvement in the education of handicapped children: A critique. *Mental Retardation, 20*(3), 115–22.

Tyler, L. (1995). The challenge of diversity. In D. Lubinski & R.V. Dawis (Eds.), *Assessing individual differences in human behavior* (pp. 1–14). Paolo Alto, CA: Davies-Black.

Uditsky, B. (1993). From integration to inclusion: The Canadian experience. In R. Slee (Ed.), *Is there a desk with my name on it? The politics of integration* (pp. 79–92). Washington, DC: Falmer Press.

UNESCO. (1994). *The Salamanca statement and framework for action on special needs education.* Paris: UNESCO.

UNESCO. (2000). *Education for all: meeting our collective commitments.* Paris: UNESCO.

UNESCO. (2003). *Academic and social emotional learning,* Geneva: International Bureau of Education.

Van Kraayenoord, C. (2007). School and classroom practices in inclusive education in Australia. *Childhood Education, 83*(6), 390–4.

Vaughan, G.M., & Hogg, M.A. (2002). *Introduction to social psychology.* Sydney: Pearson Education.

Vaughn, S., Klingner, J.K., & Bryant, D.P. (2001). Collaborative strategic reading as a means to enhance peer-mediated instruction for reading comprehension and content-area learning. *Remedial and Special Education. 22*(2), 66–75.

Vaughn, S., & Schumm, J.S. (1995). Responsible inclusion for students with learning disabilities. *Journal of Learning Disabilities, 28*(5), 264–70.

Vislie, L., & Langfeldt, G. (1996). Finance, policy making and the organization of special education. *Cambridge Journal of Education*, 26(1), 59–70.

Vygotsky, L.S. (1978). *Mind in society: The development of higher psychological processes*. Cambridge, MA: Harvard University Press.

Wade, A., Abrami, P., Poulsen, C., & Chambers, B. (1995). *Current resources in cooperative learning*. Lanham, MD: University Press of America.

Walker, H., Todis, B., Holmes, D., & Horton, G. (1988). *The walker social skills curriculum*. Austin, TX: Pro-Ed.

Wallace, T., Shin, J., Bartholomay, T., & Stahl, B. (2001). Knowledge and skills for teachers supervising the work of paraprofessionals. *Exceptional Children*, 67(4), 520–33.

Wang, M.C., Haertel, G.D., & Walberg, H.J. (1997). Fostering resilience: What do we know? *Principal*, 77(2), 18.

Warren, B. (1980). Some thoughts towards a philosophy of physical handicap. In R. Laura (Ed.), *Problems of Handicap* (pp. 76–85). Melbourne: Macmillan.

Weinberger, A., Stegmann, K., & Fischer, F. (2007). Knowledge convergence in collaborative learning: Concepts and assessment. *Learning & Instruction*, 17(4), 416–426.

Weisenfeld, R.B. (1987). Functionality in the IEPs of children with Down Syndrome. *Mental Retardation*, 25(5), 281–6.

Wells, T., Byron, M., McMullen, S., & Birchall, M. (2002). Disability teaching for medical students: Disabled people contribute to curriculum development. *British Journal of Medical Education*, 36, 788–92.

Welsh, M., Parke, R.D., Widaman, K., & O'Neil, R. (2001). Linkages between children's social and academic competence: A longitudinal analysis. *Journal of School Psychology*, 39(6), 463.

West, M., Ainscow, M., & Stanford, J. (2005). Sustaining improvement in schools in challenging circumstances: A study of successful practice. *School Leadership and Management*, 25(1), 77–93.

Westwood, P. (1997). Moving towards inclusion: Proceed with caution. *Australian Journal of Learning Disabilities*, 2(3), 18–20.

White, J., & Weiner, J.S. (2004). Influence of least restrictive environment and community based training on integrated employment outcomes for transitioning students with severe disabilities. *Journal of Vocational Rehabilitation*, 21(3), 149–56.

Whitmore, J.R. (1980). *Giftedness, conflict, and underachievement*. Boston: Allyn & Bacon.

Wiggins, G., & McTighe, J. (2005). *Understanding by design* (2nd ed.). Alexandria, VA: ASCD.

Wilczynski, S., Menousek, K., Hunter, M., & Mudgal, D. (2007). Individualized education programs for youth with Autism Spectrum Disorders. *Psychology in the Schools*, 44(7), 653–66.

Woolfolk, A. (2001). *Educational psychology*. Needham Heights. MA: Allyn & Bacon.

Wright, B.A. (1983). *Physical disability: A psychosocial approach* (2nd ed.). New York: Harper and Row.

Wu, C., & Komesaroff, L. (2007). An emperor with no clothes? Inclusive education in Victoria. *Australasian Journal of Special Education*, 31(2), 129–37.

Yasutake, D., & Lerner, J. (1997). Parents' perceptions of inclusion: A survey of parents of special education and non-special education students. *Learning Disabilities: A Multidisciplinary Journal, 8*(2), 117–20.

Yong, F.L., & McIntyre, J.D. (1992). A comparative study of the learning style preferences of students with learning disabilities and students who are gifted. *Journal of Learning Disabilities, 25,* 124–32.

Zeff, R. (2007). Universal design across the curriculum. *New Directions for Higher Education, 137,* 27–44.

Zepke, N. (2005). Diversity, adult education and the future: A tentative exploration. *International Journal of Lifelong Education, 24*(2), 165–78.

Zins, J.E., Bloodworth, M.R., Weissberg, R.P., & Walberg, H.J. (2004). The scientific base linking social and emotional learning to school success. In J. Zins, R. Weissberg, M. Wang, & H.J. Walberg (Eds.), *Building academic success on social and emotional learning: What does the research say?* (pp. 3–22). New York: Teachers College Press.

Zins, J.E, & Elias, M.E. (2004) Social and emotional learning. In G.G. Bear & K.M. Minke (Eds.), *Children's Needs III* (pp. 1–13). Bethesda, MO: National Association of School Psychologists.

Index

Active listening
  five-point scale, 174–5
  rules for, 173
Assessment
  and learning goals, 66
  classroom-based, 63–85
  curriculum-based, 71–7
  data collection for, 74
  data triangulation, 74
  for individual program plans, 121–5, 132–3
  for learning, 64–85
  guidelines for effectiveness, 64, 65
  interviews, 82–5
  multiple intelligences, 79–80
  observation wheel, 168–9
  of learning, 64
  peer assessment, 69–70
  portfolios, 77–9
  purpose of, 48–51
  provision of feedback of, 68–9
  psychological, 51–63
  Rubric design, 66–7
  self assessment, 70
  strategic questioning for, 67–8
  summative tests, 70–1
Attitudes
  definition of, 39–40
  historical background to, 37–8
  importance of, 39, 240–41
Case study (secondary school), 14–19
Challenging behaviour
  attention seeking, 208–9
  avoidance of failure, 209–10
  definition of, 207
  individual action plans, 212–13
  power, 210–11
  revenge, 211
Classroom
  ability groups seating plan, 192–3
  community, 214–16
  heterogeneous groups seating plan, 193–4
  individual spaces seating plan, 194–5
  layout, 187
  meetings, 217–22
  traditional seating plan, 190–2
  universal access, 187–190
Collaborative inquiry, 91–5
  steps in, 93–4
Curriculum
  adaptations, and modifications, 139, 152–9
  core, 138–9
  definition of, 138–9
  elaborative, 138–9
  identifying barriers to, 142
Differentiated instruction
  and individualised programs, 9–10
  and knowledge types, 145
  and universal design, 141–2
  considerations for print materials, 144
  instructional strategies, 149–50
  learning outcomes, 150–53
  the materials environment, 143–6
  the resources environment, 146–9
Disability
  reactions to, 45
  discomfort with, 43–5, 241–5
Discrimination, 26
  legislative issues concerning, 27
Diversity
  definition of, 23–26
  functional definitions, 24
  medical definitions, 24, 25
  socio-political definitions, 24, 25–6
Emergency plans, 196–8
Families
  collaboration with, 105–7
Funding, 11, 13
Identification and labelling, 28–34, 241–5

Ideologies, 42–3
Inclusion
  benefits of, 12–14
  definition of, 1–3
  elements of, 3
  reasons for failure of, 4–5
  reasons for success of, 6
Individual programs
  advantages, 116–17
  and poor progress, 135
  assessment results summary, 121–5
  description of, 115–16
  development process, 120
  disadvantages, 117
  indicators of achievement, 132–3
  links to regular curriculum, 153–9
  long-term goals, 125–9
  specific objectives, 129–32
  vision statement, 120–1
Integration
  definition of, 2
Intelligence tests
  cautions about, 52
  development of, 57
  normal (bell) curve, 54–6
  perceptual reasoning subtest, 60
  processing speed, 61
  qualitative assessment, 61–3
  scores from, 55
  types of, 53
  uses of, 51, 52–3
  verbal comprehension subtest, 58–9
  working memory subtest, 60–61
Lesson planning, 155–9
Medication, 202–4
Objectives, development of, 73
Professional learning communities, 88–91
  and collaborative teacher discussion,
    95–7, 99–101
  and teacher moderation, 98–9
  characteristics of, 89–90
  collaboration and the wider school
    community, 101–12
  interdisciplinary collaboration
    challenges, 101–2

Program support group, 118
  meeting agenda, 119
  vision statements, 121
Process approach to inclusive education,
  20, 34
Reflective diaries, 249–51
Social and emotional learning
  and teachers, 236–38
  benefits of, 226–27
  core competencies, 226
  curriculum links, 228–29
  definition of, 225
  programs, 229, 232–6
  program features, 230–31
  supports for, 228
Substitute teacher plans, 198–9
Support staff
  collaboration checklist, 104–5
  roles for, 103–4
Students
  and personal care needs, 199–202
  and positive interdependence, 165–7
  and promotive interaction, 165
  as curriculum negotiators, 108
  as co-researchers, 108–11
  collaborative learning arrangements,
    161–4
  cooperative learning, 164–78
  individual accountability, 167–8
  peer support, 179–83
  peer tutoring, 180–81
  reciprocal teaching, 181–3
  teacher collaboration with, 107–11
Teacher concerns about inclusion
  curriculum, 8–11
  organisational structures, 12
  school resources, 11–12
  training, 7–8
Teacher reflection, 95–98, 246–8, 252–4
  tools for, 248–52
Terminology and appropriate use, 35
Unit planning, 153–15
Universal design for learning, 139–41
Values, 40–2
Violence and touching, 213–14